Carbon Footprints as Cultural–Ecological Metaphors

Through an examination of carbon footprint metaphors, this books demonstrates the ways in which climate change and other ecological issues are culturally and materially constituted through metaphor.

The carbon footprint metaphor has achieved a ubiquitous presence in Anglo-North American public contexts since the turn of the millennium, yet this metaphor remains under-examined as a crucial mediator of political responses to the urgent crisis of climate change. Existing books and articles on the carbon footprint typically treat this metaphor as a quantifying metric, with little attention to the shifting mediations and practices of the carbon footprint as a metaphor. This gap echoes a wider gap in understanding metaphors as key figures in mediating more-than-human relations at a time when such relations profoundly matter. As a timely intervention, this book addresses this gap by using insights from environmental humanities and political ecology to discuss carbon footprint metaphors in popular and public texts.

This book will be of great interest to researchers and students of environmental humanities, political ecology, environmental communication, and metaphor studies.

Anita Girvan is a Visiting Scholar at the Centre for Global Studies and teaches in the School of Environmental Studies at the University of Victoria in Canada.

The *Routledge Environmental Humanities* series is an original and inspiring venture recognising that today's world agricultural and water crises, ocean pollution and resource depletion, global warming from greenhouse gases, urban sprawl, overpopulation, food insecurity and environmental justice are all *crises of culture*.

The reality of understanding and finding adaptive solutions to our present and future environmental challenges has shifted the epicenter of environmental studies away from an exclusively scientific and technological framework to one that depends on the human-focused disciplines and ideas of the humanities and allied social sciences.

We thus welcome book proposals from all humanities and social sciences disciplines for an inclusive and interdisciplinary series. We favour manuscripts aimed at an international readership and written in a lively and accessible style. The readership comprises scholars and students from the humanities and social sciences and thoughtful readers concerned about the human dimensions of environmental change.

Carbon Footprints as Cultural–Ecological Metaphors

Anita Girvan

Routledge
Taylor & Francis Group

LONDON AND NEW YORK

from Routledge

First published 2018
by Routledge

2 Park Square, Milton Park, Abingdon, Oxfordshire OX14 4RN
52 Vanderbilt Avenue, New York, NY 10017

Routledge is an imprint of the Taylor & Francis Group, an informa business

First issued in paperback 2019

British Library Cataloguing-in-Publication Data
A catalogue record for this book is available from the British Library

Library of Congress Cataloging-in-Publication Data
A catalog record for this book has been requested

ISBN: 978-1-138-65806-6 (hbk)
ISBN: 978-0-367-26304-1 (pbk)

Typeset in Times New Roman
by FiSH Books Ltd, Enfield

To my parents, Deanne and Garry Girvan, for the critical support for this project and for your loving support to our family and wider kin. Thank you especially, Mom, Dad and Allison, for my childhood in the forest/farm on Lheidli T'Enneh territory in the central interior of British Columbia. This early formation enabled me to begin to truly connect with what it means to live, struggle and celebrate among larger-than-human relations. My passionate attachment to these earthly relations largely informs the hopes I express in this project.

'Few ecological tropes have achieved as much cultural currency as the carbon footprint. Girvan undertakes to explain why as she traces carbon footprint metaphors through a series of case studies captivatingly posed as "tales". This book does crucial work recalling that footprints are metaphors with profound material and political stakes. As Girvan shows, struggles over the power of metaphor will help determine the ecological futures of humans and non-humans in a time of global climate change.'

Nicole Shukin, author of Animal Capital: Rendering Life in Biopolitical Times *and Associate Professor of English, the University of Victoria, Canada*

'There is an urgent need to review the economy of metaphor in this time of heightened climatic and ecological instability, particularly as we seek to better attune to cultural and material meanings for they consequentially shape nuanced approaches to climate change. The carbon footprint and its affective mediation is innovatively linked to the behaviour of carbon subjects and the geopolitics of energy development in this study's unique contribution to a newly climatic understanding of the materiality of cultural inscription.'

Tom Bristow, Department of English Studies, Durham University, UK

Contents

Acknowledgements

I am extremely grateful for the support for my research from: the Pacific Institute for Climate Solutions (PICS); The Social Sciences and Humanities Research Council (SSHRC) and the Centre for Global Studies (CFGS) at the University of Victoria. The Centre for Global Studies also offered a particularly vibrant intellectual community among too many to name, but including: Miriam Mueller, Hanny Hilmy, J.P. Sapinski, Nicole Bates-Eamer, Jennifer Swift, Laura Brandes, Nathan Bennett, Lewis Williams, Jesse Baltutis, Oliver Schmidtke, Martin Bunton and Rod Dobbell. Jodie Walsh has been an essential and continuing support to this project in intellectual and material ways. Gratitude to Vivian Smith, Janet Sheppard, Arthur Kroker, Kara Shaw, Marilouise Kroker, Eric Higgs, Michael McMahon, Andrew Weaver, Warren Magnusson, and especially, Nicole Shukin for her on-going support. Thanks to Catriona Sandilands for a very helpful read of an earlier draft. For the informative conversations on all things 'environmental humanities', I truly appreciate my former colleagues at Bucknell University including: Amanda Wooden, Peter Wilshusen, Claire Campbell, Carol Kearney High, Maria Antonacci, Janet Jones, Alf Siewers, G.C. Waldrep, and Shauna Barnhart. Especially crucial have been the constant intellectual and personal support of my soul-mates at the University of Victoria, Astrid Pérez Piñán and Bikrum Gill. Thanks to my extended village of powerful women – especially Narda Nelson, Jennifer Sobkin, Laura Sehn and Kate Rosenblood – for the encouragement, inspiration and your generous contributions to the world. Campus View Elementary Green Team and Principal David Hovis: thanks for the privilege of being your 'Coach Anita'. This community and the students that I teach at the University of Victoria have grounded me and kept me believing in the power of making space in the world for past, present and future kin.

Special thanks to my life-partner Rob, and my children, Reina and Kieran who have provided infinite foundational support and inspiration for this project and for the many extra-curricular practices that have always been central to my work and my joys in life.

Finally, I would like to acknowledge the Coast and Straits Salish Nations on whose territory I live. I am only beginning to learn the depth of wisdom and beauty in this place and I humbly submit to understanding my role in further unsettling for transformative futures.

Introduction

How big is yours?

Figure 0.1 An image of a carbon footprint
Source: © Shutterstock

Associated with the carbon footprint and often accompanied by the question 'How Big is Yours?', the image above situates this metaphor within a curious entanglement of narratives in the politics of climate change. On many websites and consumer products for sale, such images feature a similar feminized, green, leafy, and curvaceous footprint, coupled with the phallocentric textual imperative toward bigness.[1] The footprint thus suggestively inserts itself into the imaginary fabric of a (portion of) 'humanity' that is struggling to avert an urgent crisis of its own making, but one that is still hopelessly seduced by its own procreative attributes. Although the carbon footprint has been conventionally understood as a challenge to fossil-fuel intensive life, close attention to its many figurations suggests more nuanced accounts. The question above and the many other instances of carbon footprint metaphors intimate that since its historical emergence, the carbon footprint metaphor has traced a fine line, promising to bring human climate impacts into view so that they may be reduced, but also risking a reification of certain cultural preoccupations with, and legacies of, human 'greatness' that are themselves dependent on (hydro) carbon-intensive systems.

When I began to trace the carbon footprint upon its viral emergence in 2007 to 2009,[2] I was quickly drawn to what seemed to be its easy integration within a liberal individual humanist lifestyle of consumption, as the above question testifies. Yet as this metaphor moved and shifted, as metaphors are wont to, the carbon footprint evaded a one-sided critique of this liberal humanist consumer order. I began to realize that tracing the carbon footprint means not only critically highlighting the ways in which this metaphor reifies problematic fossil fuel-enabled hubristic systems (although this book does its share of this kind of critique); tracing this metaphor also means attending to the myriad forces that animate its shifting metaphorical attachments. As this metaphor has shifted, it has brought into visibility new areas of concern and new possibilities for thinking about and acting upon climate change as a complex socio-ecological matter. These movements of the metaphor feature footprints not simply read as singular marks of consuming individual subjects, but also as: signifiers of unequal global human-to-human relations, and material traces that connect 'us' to the many other larger-than-human relations in a shared increasingly urgent planetary story of carbon.

This untold story, that is at once cultural and material, bears extended elaboration as a potent intervention in climate change politics. Metaphors do crucial work and produce material effects that remain largely un-noticed: this particular metaphor has gained immense traction in various Anglo-American publics, but its effects as a metaphor have yet to be fully explored. The carbon footprint metaphor appeared at the turn of the millennium just as the Intergovernmental Panel on Climate Change added a section in its summary (subsequently removed in follow-up reports) on 'discourse' as a potent site of climate change politics (IPCC 2001). At that time, the semiotic-material element of carbon was beginning to bear the weight as the index of the climate change crisis, and the footprint was emerging to connect this problem to diverse bodies across complex scales. The metaphor went viral in 2007 as the Oxford Dictionary, named it 'word of the year'. (Oxford Dictionary 2017) The carbon footprint continues to carry force in recent years as evidenced by the 'Carbon Footprint Challenge 2017', a global competition sponsored by a number of European Universities with the goal of funding technical innovation projects that reduce emissions from industrial processes (Unitech 2017). What is remarkable about the many iterations of this metaphor is the diversity of scales and interests expressed, ranging from individual consumer, to corporate, to policy-oriented governance to ecological actors; indeed, this diversity reveals that *the* carbon footprint metaphor is not a singular expression of the will to reduce carbon emissions, but rather, a range of expressions, invested with varying interests, affects, and agendas, not all of them biospherical.

The shifts of the carbon footprint suggest that this metaphor be treated not simply as a singular universalizing entity (measure), but rather as a travelling figure with multiple manifestations: a shape-shifter. Its shape-shifting tendencies by no means entirely undermine its universal aspirations: the carbon footprint metaphor might be thought of as what Anna Tsing calls an 'engaged universal'. 'Engaged universals travel across difference and are charged and changed by their travels. Through friction, universals become practically effective. Yet they can never fulfil their promises of universality' (Tsing 2005, 8). Due to the ways in which this travelling figure touches down and is charged and changed by brushing up against different contexts and settings, I sometimes refer to carbon footprints in the plural, especially as I situate the need to examine their pluralities in the case studies that follow. At other times, however, I maintain *the* carbon footprint in the singular as an engaged universal, 'an aspiration, an always unfinished achievement, rather than the confirmation of a pre-formed law' (Tsing 2005, 7). Understanding the carbon footprint's inability to complete an aspirational task – the calculation and definitive management of carbon impacts – potentially tempers the hubris that often accompanies this metaphor. The frivolous-seeming question above and the ambivalent story in which the carbon footprint metaphor is implicated by no means render 'neutral' its effects; on the contrary, its ambivalence and metaphorical shiftiness are at the very heart of its formidable mediating power.

In this book, I trace the promises and risks of the carbon footprint metaphor, suggesting that this metaphor is a powerful, yet underexamined site of the central paradoxes in cultural politics of climate change. The cultural politics of climate change involve 'dynamic and contested spaces ... where formal climate science, policy and politics operating at multiple scales permeate the spaces of the 'everyday'' (Boykoff 2011, 3). Having both a scientific valence – as a quantifying metric that finds itself in policy circles – and a powerful popular cultural valence in its pervasive everyday uses, the carbon footprint metaphor has become what Raymond Williams would call a 'keyword' (key metaphor) of our time (1985). Keywords, in Williams' theorization, are not key simply because they are popular or pervasive at any given time, but because their meanings are contested and these sites of contestation hold special significance and political urgency within a particular historical epoch. Bringing Williams' notion of keywords into urgent matters of the twenty-first century means grasping the particular relationships between key *metaphors* and ecological politics as vital sites of contestation over human attempts of apprehending and responding to a rapidly-shifting more-than-human world. Through a 'collapse of inherited categories, a newly climatic understanding of the materiality of cultural inscriptions is taking place' (Bristow and Ford 2016, 12). If this time of heightened climatic and ecological instability initiates a collapse of inherited categories and creates gaps in ways of knowing and acting, then novel metaphors emerging in such gaps must be taken seriously for their material effects.

As poets who mobilize metaphor and those who study metaphor attest, metaphor is always a stretch or a partial way of knowing that escapes complete human mastery (McKay 2002; Rueckert 2006/1982). To that end, the carbon footprint seems doomed from the start. On the one hand, this trope functions as a conceptual unit that is supposed to represent, and in many cases, quantify impacts in order to reduce these impacts; on the other hand, as a metaphor that shifts, the carbon footprint constantly fails to definitively represent. If this aspect of the carbon footprint constitutes its 'failure', I would like to affirm this failure at definitive representation as one of its' (as well as other metaphor's) most promising features at a time when hubristic attempts at human mastery in the world seem at their most problematic. As we are living through the rapid shifts and transformations indexed through the Sixth Extinction and the highly contested notion of the Anthropocene, we can approach such matters with the Promethean drives that have, in part, created these problems, or we might consider shifting figures such as metaphors as crucial devices with which to think and act *precisely because they fail to index a stable knowable world.* To this end, I situate carbon footprint metaphors as critical sites of struggle over how to apprehend and respond to climate change as a complex matter of concern that is paradoxically at once human-created and yet always larger-than-human. This extended critical journey through instances of the carbon footprint reveals that the power of the carbon footprint turns largely on its *metaphoricity.* The urgency of climate change requires, paradoxically, that we pause and think about the complex effects of these metaphors.

As I describe in what follows, while poststructural sensibilities suggest that all language is metaphorical in its humanly world-*creating* rather than world-*representing* effects, the metaphor as a metaphor itself for 'carry over' (from Greek) holds particular insights into these world-creating effects. Indeed, the 'metaphorical turn' in a range of disciplines from cognitive linguistics (Lakoff and Johnson 1980) to health studies (Sontag 1978; 1989) to environmental sciences (Larson 2011) to geography (Robbins 2013) attests to a growing sensitivity to the privileged mediating role of metaphor in cultural and material relations and their world-creating effects. What is evident, however, even in the most-recent treatments of metaphor and environment is the notion that 'we' human agents might be able to choose the 'right' metaphors 'for sustainability' (Larson 2011) or 'for the Anthropocene' (Robbins 2013, 307).[3] These theorizations are key in centring the timely importance of connecting metaphor and environment/ecology, as I elaborate in Chapter 2, but they too swiftly instrumentalize metaphor and prescribe each different metaphor as having different implications without looking at the internal differences across different instances of what seems to be the same metaphor. By contrast, my extended exploration of what seems to be one metaphor – *the* carbon footprint – yields an understanding of the different worldly effects that emerge from its plural manifestations as it shifts and turns.

The aim of this book is neither to assert the carbon footprint metaphor as right or wrong, but to situate this particular family of footprint metaphors as a uniquely captivating and catalyzing, but tension-ridden, site in the cultural politics of climate change. Although the dominant tendency is to apprehend these footprints quantitatively, their qualitatively divergent paths and their notoriously shifty numbers require recognizing these metaphors not simply as numerical representations of 'impacts' but as constitutive of material worlds. As studies of metaphors suggest, their world-making power lies in their ability to yoke unlikely things together and to bring new (or newly apprehended) entities into popular visibility. Rather than simply *describing* as literary frill or device, metaphors invite certain ways of orienting and acting upon/with the world. My claim is that not all carbon footprint metaphors are built equally, nor do they mediate the same political and ecological practices. By 'charging' carbon footprint metaphors as important sites of struggle, the political and ecological work of metaphor emerges. Shifting the site of contest to metaphor serves not as a distraction from the 'real', critical politics of climate change, but offers an extended exposition of the cultural-material spaces in which climate change is constituted and through which interventions must also take place.

My inquiry begins with two critical questions: 1) What are the promises and risks of carbon footprint metaphors as mediators of political responses to climate change? 2) How can an examination of carbon footprint metaphors generate understandings of the ways in which climate change and other ecological issues are at once culturally and materially constituted?

My approach to answering these questions involves situating carbon footprint metaphors within the context of climate change as a material *and cultural* phenomenon and examining specific instances of this metaphor in-depth. To this end, I begin below by exploring the cultural politics of climate change as a paradox-ridden concern before turning in the next chapter to the cultural imaginaries from which the carbon footprint emerges.

The paradoxes of climate change as physical-cultural phenomenon

This exploration of the effects of carbon footprint metaphors begins by taking seriously Mike Hulme's claim that 'climate change is simultaneously a physical transformation and a cultural object' that requires transformative socio-cultural responses (Hulme 2008, 5). Far from spinning an esoteric tale that detracts from the important scientific work on climate change, I claim that climate change must be understood at its origins to be cultural and political as well as physical or material in the scientific sense. Without the work of climate scientists, there would be no consensus in the world on climate change; however, the expectation that climate science alone can communicate 'the facts' and singularly generate movement and solutions on this urgent topic has led to pitfalls in the politics of climate change. Paradoxically, Western science's own founding principles undermine its ability to generate the kinds of certainty demanded by a still-sceptical portion of the global public. Andrew Weaver, climate scientist, highlights the principle of scientific uncertainty (of, among other things, emissions trajectories and complex climate interactions) that, when taken out of its context, risks enabling climate change deniers to make claims that climate change is unproven (2008, 24, 63–65).

Science conventionally operates with controls and re-producible experiments: the lack of a control planet similar to Earth and the inability to reproduce the 'experiment' of climate change presents deniers with a dubious but endlessly fertile ground for garnering support through confusion, misunderstanding, and manipulation of the very notion of scientific uncertainty. Attempts to establish indisputable facts – connecting particular weather events with climate change or predicting warming accurately, for example – are notoriously problematic. Media analyst, Max Boykoff, also connects this phenomenon of uncertainty to the journalistic norm of 'balanced reporting' – a logic that often amounts to representations of two sides of the climate change story in the media as if there were still a 50–50 split in climate change belief among scientists and the general public, despite the widespread consensus that exists (2011, 108–109). Such impediments forestall the kinds of questions and discussions that catalyze political movement on the subject of climate change. With Bruno Latour, I therefore posit climate change neither as a matter of fact, nor as a matter of values that are singularly socially constructed, but as a 'matter of concern' (Latour 2004, 96) that inextricably entangles facts and values, biophysical processes, and social constructions. One may rightfully claim that climate change is a 'matter of fact', but what it means, for whom, and what should be done about it immediately brings one into the messy realm of values, culture, and politics.

This book thus pitches its intervention at the cultural politics of climate change, where shifting and contested 'everyday' public cultural spaces like those surrounding the carbon footprint, profoundly bear upon political responses. I acknowledge that these politics are both caught up in discourses that are socially constructed *and* situated within a world that is larger than these human constructions. Climate change itself – and responses to it, including the carbon footprint metaphor – are fully entangled in what Donna Haraway calls 'naturecultures', that is, bundled collections of histories, ecologies, and imaginaries (2004, 1–2). While putting nature and culture together in one word might not resolve an existing problematic binary, this assemblage at least permits two terms – from which there seem to be no easy exits in Euro-Western epistemology despite on-going valiant efforts – to be thought together, if in paradoxical ways. Climate change and specifically, my analysis of carbon footprint metaphors, requires engaging with this central paradox, and other attendant paradoxes, that are evident throughout the book.

A related paradox in terms of locating climate change and determining appropriate responses pertains to the notion that '[c]limate change seems to be everywhere and nowhere' (Bristow and Ford 2016, 6). This paradox leads to either an impasse in terms of responses, or to a strange and problematic commitment to singular solutions as *the* way to address the problem. That is to say that some proposed solutions insist that transition to a less carbon-intensive life will emerge 'because of individual behavior change, or through radical technological innovation, or because [of] … successful governance …' (Luke 2016, 196). It is precisely in this 'dimension of singularity' that such approaches fail … since there is 'no single source or site of change'; rather, transitions are 'simultaneously cultural, political, technological and economic. They occur at many spatial scales and they reconstruct those scales in the process' (Luke 2016, 196). Although the carbon footprint's plurality and shiftiness can support myriad problematic practices, as suggested at the outset, its ability to shift across scales and sites – including individual, national, global, larger-than-human, policy, economic, and cultural – enables crucial insights into climate change politics.

In terms of issues of scale, humans (and culture) are undeniably a part of what is signalled by 'nature', but as the contested notion/metaphor of the 'Anthropocene' paradoxically attests, there is something about a *human species force* that is conceptually and politically important to recognize, even as postcolonial sensibilities remind of the violence that takes place through the work of universalizing the human species despite its inherent differences (Chakrabarty 2009; Rickards 2015). Anthropogenic climate change and the associated metaphor of the Anthropocene signal the contemporary epoch as one in which certain dominant human systems and logics have achieved planetary forms of disruptive agency; thus, such phenomena centrally figure 'human' effects and responsibilities. However, such human-induced phenomena also simultaneously and paradoxically displace the logic of the centrality of humans as master agents since the effects of this disruptive agency escape the ability to foresee or definitively manage. Such a logic of mastery has, as many commentators attest, not only in part generated the urgent problem of climate change, but it might also further exacerbate socio-ecological issues through proposed solutions that also suffer from delusions of mastery, as do some climate engineering schemes (Bulkeley et al. 2016; Hulme 2014). Anthropogenic climate change thus might suggest that we read effects not simply as linear outcomes or 'symptoms' of the impacts of a singular human-species agent, but rather in a more complex entanglement, where certain humans might indeed be seen as exerting the strongest force as a species at this moment, but they do so not as singular intentional agents acting in isolation. This is not to absolve (especially certain) humans of their responsibility for climate change effects, but to locate human forces within a larger-than-human set of relations that must be kept in close proximity in 'our' ways of knowing about and responding to climate change. The Anthropocene is, without a doubt, another metaphor that requires treatment beyond the confines of this book (Robbins 2013; Rickards 2015); however, as a contested figure that might orient 'a way of being in the world that recognizes ... simultaneous power and vulnerability' (Mikaluk 2013), its paradoxes underlie the cultural politics of climate change in which the carbon footprint metaphor is embroiled. Part of the aim of this book, then, is to explore under what circumstances the carbon footprint metaphor might act as a figure that enables the recognition of the *simultaneous power and vulnerability of (internally differentiated) humans and other companion species* through the participation of both human and non-human actors.

Relatedly, even as climate change denotes a planetary concern that requires thinking in terms of planetary scales of humanity and larger-than-human collectives, such scales can also be problematically universalizing in their failure to address key differences in terms of unequal power relations, responsibilities, and felt impacts of climate change. This linguistic and conceptual conundrum appears in my provisional use of the subject position 'we'. I occasionally use 'we' in this text to refer to a global collective that is affecting and affected by climate change even as I unpack the hidden asymmetries buried within this term. As Cary Wolfe enigmatically suggests with regard to climate change 'there is no "we" yet there is nothing but "we"' (Wolfe 2011, personal communication). For a posthumanities/animal studies scholar to make such a statement reveals a certain need to keep the universal/global *and* the particular/local in play, as mutually troubling categories. Treating the carbon footprint metaphor as an engaged universal, helps to attend to these mutually troubling categories and fosters what Ursula Heise calls a 'sense of place and a sense of planet' as an intersecting set of concerns (2008).

While many of the paradoxes mentioned above are more explicitly cited by a number of scholars thinking along such naturalcultural axes (Borgmann 1995; Bristow and Ford 2016; Cronon 1996; Haraway 1988; 2004; Morton 2013), perhaps the one that is the most contentious in terms of ecological politics, one on which my book pivotally turns, is the paradox of metaphor. Metaphor might be considered a unit of 'discourse' which is, on the one hand, socially (humanly) constructed. A key poststructuralist contribution to science studies and political ecology has been its insistence that the scientific ways in which 'we' come to know and talk about the 'natural' world and ecological matters, like climate change, are heavily mediated by language and cultural assumptions that are far from universally objective (Cronon 1996; Escobar 1996; Haraway 2004; Hayles 1995; Kuhn 1970/1962; Latour 2004; Mortimer-Sandilands 2010).[4] Despite being cast in many spaces as scientific metrics, carbon footprint metaphors and the variety of agendas they come to support are exemplary of the various discursive effects that consequentially shape approaches to climate change. We must take seriously poststructuralist warnings about the effects of discourse, especially positivist accounts of the world that fail to reflect on how 'the idea of nature contains, though often unnoticed, an extraordinary amount of human history' (Williams 1980, 67). And yet, 'this is not to say that the nonhuman world is somehow unreal or a mere figment of our imaginations – far from it' (Cronon 1996, 25).

Informed by those who think within the interstices of these paradoxes of natureculture, and by my observations of carbon footprint metaphors, I keep these paradoxes open. For thinking simultaneously about carbon footprints as metaphors *and* about climate change as a pressing issue suggests that just as human societies construct 'nature' as *trope* with words and practices, these societies also construct and manipulate 'nature' as *topos* or 'commonplace' that is shared and co-constituted with non-human actors (Haraway 2004, 65–66).[5] Further, one must find ways of making room for forms of non-human agency – what Jane Bennett calls 'vibrant materiality' (2010) – ways that even as they are inescapably mediated by human discourse, partially and contingently index a larger-than-human world of relations and processes. Ecological metaphors (described below) such as 'carbon footprints' offer the promise of accounting for these connections[6] and, thus, of disturbing anthropocentric approaches to climate change; however, as a critical approach to discourses reveals, these metaphors also risk reifying the very anthropocentric cultural practices – fossil fuel resource extraction, consumer habits of privileged subjects, and market growth – that are central to the problem of climate change.

As studies of metaphor attest, metaphors and discourses do shape worlds (Radman 1997); however, my own approach to the question of (ecological) metaphor gleaned from studying carbon footprints, is paradoxically both to understand this human world-making function of metaphors and also *to explore these metaphors as potential traces of worldly others that exceed humans in all their diverse and contested forms*. In other words, rather than illustrating that *human*-made metaphors unilaterally make the world, I am interested in the ways in which ecological metaphors also potentially communicate the agency of larger-than-human actors who come to challenge a given human way of constructing the world. In order to understand how metaphor may draw novel connections in these urgent larger-than-human concerns, I put carbon footprints metaphors into play in Chapter 2 as 'affective mediators' that trace the paradoxes of natureculture at the turn of the millennium.

While, as William Cronon notes, it is easy to make caricatures of one's adversaries along a nature-culture divide in high-stakes environmental politics, it might be rather more productive to step tentatively forward grappling with the paradoxes of *natureculture* as part of the 'human project of living on the earth in a responsible way' (Cronon 1996, 22). I embark on an extended exploration of the possibilities and foreclosures of this particularly potent metaphor as one who has simultaneous passionate attachments to: an on-going planetary human community rich with internal diversity and aspiring to achieve more equitable relational encounters; biodiverse companion species that condition local and planetary communities and who exist not only for/in the service of humans; and the play of language and metaphor. I humbly ask that the reader think of the tensions that I identify above as paradoxes rather than contradictions. For Donna Haraway, feminist scholar of science *and* postructuralist, the challenge is:

> ... how to have simultaneously an account of radical historical contingency for all knowledge claims and knowing subjects, a critical practice for recognizing our own "semiotic technologies" for making meanings, and a no-nonsense commitment to faithful accounts of a "real" world, one that can be partially shared and that is friendly to earthwide projects of finite freedom, adequate material abundance, modest meaning in suffering, and limited happiness.
>
> (1988, 579)

This is no straightforward task, but it is within these paradoxes that I situate my study of carbon footprint metaphors as one crucial site in which contingent knowledge claims, meaning-making, and the 'real' world interact. Rather than a weak understanding of cultural elements as framing or representational tools in communicating climate change, I insist that cultural elements, such as the carbon footprint metaphor, are powerful sites of struggle in culture, conceived as 'always simultaneously semiotic and material' (Bulkeley et al. 2016, 8). The cultural politics of climate change are embroiled in ongoing struggles about nature and culture that turn on complex issues – tracing carbon footprint metaphors helps to animate and situate these tensions in particular ways that serve to centre the metaphor's promising (and risky) potential to intervene.

Roadmap of the book

In what follows, I set about two related tasks. In Part I, the first chapter situates the elements of carbon and footprint in cultural histories that pre-date the carbon footprint and then briefly describes the emergence of this compound metaphor at the turn of the millennium. The second chapter involves theorizing the links between metaphor, politics, ecology, and 'affect'. The latter is a term that has taken hold in recent scholarship to attend to how the social, the somatic, and in some cases, the ecological are involved in the process of political sense-making as a moving set of force-relations and encounters that are often unaccounted for in 'rational' perspectives of politics (Ahmed 2004; Brennan 2004; Bennett 2010; Massumi 1995; Seigworth and Gregg 2010). This is not to centre instead an "irrational', emotionalized (and feminized) form of affective politics (against cognition), but rather to understand that 'in practice … affect and cognition are never fully separable' and that a political actor's relational 'encounters with mixed forces' (where actors and forces are always larger-than-human) make possible various kinds of political responses (Seigworth and Gregg 2010, 3–4). Seen through this lens, the carbon footprint as it shifts and attaches to various bodies politic, makes possible a diverse and contesting range of responses to climate change.

Part II gives evidence to these various mediations and ambivalent responses through three case studies in which the carbon footprint metaphor appears in Anglo-North American contexts around the turn of the twenty-first century. The three cases have been chosen not only because they show how the carbon footprint metaphor shifts over time, but also because each features a different set of political attachments across various scales that makes possible particular ways of responding to climate change (as well as foreclosing upon other ways of responding). My first case focuses on the carbon footprint reduction lists that largely make possible an individual, liberal humanist response to climate change. The second focuses on a comparative global analysis of carbon footprints of nations, which suggests that responses to climate change must address geopolitical inequities in responsibilities and impacts among people with hugely divergent carbon footprints (as measured impacts). The last case features the carbon footprint of farmed shrimp as a trace of wider larger-than-human relations that are central to responses to climate change. I analyze these carbon footprint metaphors in public texts in order to explore the promises and the risks of the politics they enable. I trace the promises of the footprint metaphor in certain instances as a disruptive force that challenges the norms of anthropocentric, fossil fuel intensive, and geopolitically asymmetrical relationships of power. By contrast, I trace the risks of carbon footprint metaphors as they serve to further authorize these existing anthropocentric and market-driven norms that constitute the urgent issue of climate change and keep global asymmetries in place.

Some existing carbon metaphors – *carbon market, carbon guilt, blue carbon* – are elaborated in this book as they are co-figured with carbon footprint metaphors. Throughout the analysis, I also propose new critical carbon metaphors, including 'carbon citizenship' and 'carbon vitality', as these offer a lens into the kinds of politics that become associated with the carbon footprint metaphors that I analyze. Crucially, I do not claim the carbon metaphors that I propose are more representative or legitimate than others; I, too am mobilizing carbon's tropism as a figure to bring into visibility certain critical associations in the cultural politics of climate change. One of my goals then, is to trace the possibilities of carbon bonding with more radical political and ecological entities and processes.

Notes

1   Images like these – with the question, How Big is Yours? built into the image – are found on numerous sites including: www.fewresources.org/ecological-footprints—human-impact-metrics.html; http://myfootprint.org; www.footprintnetwork.org/our-work/ecological-footprint/, and various blogs such as https://curiositykilledthe-consumer.wordpress.com/2012/05/10/how-big-is-yours (accessed March 1, 2017).
2   Although it arrived in some circles around 2000, as I explain in the next chapter, the carbon footprint burst into public discourse in Anglo-American contexts in 2007.
3   I engage in a deeper discussion of these recent theorizations of metaphor in Chapter 2.
4   Notably, the authors whom I select to describe each of these critical positions (reflexive about constructivism and reflexive about scientific positivism) all employ both science and critical theory in an attempt to find what Hayles (1995) calls 'common ground' in discussing ecological issues. While there still exists debate among these scholars, they all agree on the contributions of some version of post-positivist science and biophysically attentive constructivist critique.
5   Similarly, speaking of climate change discourse, Max Boykoff suggests, 'interpretation and knowledge is constructed, maintained and contested through intertwined socio-political and biophysical processes' (2011, 5).
6   Here, I wish to acknowledge the double meaning of *account* and all of its derivatives as they are used both in the sense of a story and in the sense of an economic-mathematical metric; carbon footprint metaphors carry both of these meanings as they set in motion both: a calculus of tracking and quantifying carbon numbers through environmental economics; *and* an expansion of stories of those who might 'count' in cultural politics of climate change.

References

Ahmed, Sarah. 2004. *The Cultural Politics of Emotion*. New York: Routledge.

Bennett, Jane. 2010. *Vibrant Matter: A Political Ecology of Things*. Durham: Duke University Press.

Borgmann, Albert. 1995. "The Nature of Reality and the Reality of Nature." In: Michael E. Soule and Gary Lease (eds) *Reinventing Nature? Responses to Postmodern Deconstruction*. Washington, DC: Island Press, 31–46.

Boykoff, Maxwell. 2011. *Who Speaks for the Climate?* Cambridge, UK: Cambridge University Press.

Brennan, Teresa. 2004. *The Transmission of Affect.* New York: Cornell University Press.

Bristow, Tom and Thomas H. Ford. 2016. *A Cultural History of Climate Change.* New York; London: Routledge.

Bulkeley, Harriet, Matthew Paterson and Johannes Stripple. 2016. *Towards a Cultural Politics of Climate Change: Devices, Desires, and Dissent.* Cambridge: Cambridge University Press.

Chakrabarty, Dipesh. 2009. "The Climate of History: Four theses." *Critical Inquiry,* 35, 2: 197–222.

Cronon, William (ed.). 1996. *Uncommon Ground: Rethinking the Human Place in Nature.* New York: Norton.

Escobar, Arturo. 1996. "Constructing Nature: Elements for a Poststructuralist Political Ecology." In: Richard Peet and Michael Watts (eds) *Liberation Ecologies: Environment, Development, Social Movements.* London: Routledge, 46–68.

Haraway, Donna. 2004. *The Haraway Reader.* New York, NY: Routledge.

Haraway, Donna. 1988. "Situated Knowledges: The Science Question in Feminism and the Privilege of Partial Perspectives." *Feminist Studies* 14, 3: 575–599.

Hayles, N. Katherine. 1995. "Searching for Common Ground." In: Michael E. Soule and Gary Lease (eds) *Reinventing Nature? Responses to Postmodern Deconstruction* Washington, DC: Island Press, 47–63.

Heise, Ursula K. 2008. *Sense of Place and Sense of Planet: The Environmental Imagination of the Global.* New York: Oxford University Press.

Hulme, Mike. 2014. *Can Science Fix Climate Change? A Case Against Climate Engineering.* Cambridge, UK: Polity.

Hulme, Mike. 2008. "Geographical work at the boundaries of climate change." *Transactions – Institute of British Geographers,* 33: 1.

IPCC. 2001. *Climate Change 2001: The Third Assessment Report of the Intergovernmental Panel on Climate Change.* Cambridge, UK: Cambridge University Press.

Kuhn, Thomas. 1970/1962. *The Structure of Scientific Revolutions, 2nd edn.* Chicago, IL: University of Chicago Press.

Lakoff, George and Mark Johnson. 1980/2003. *Metaphors We Live By.* Chicago, IL: University of Chicago Press.

Larson, Brendon. 2011. *Metaphors for Environmental Sustainability.* New Haven, CT: Yale University.

Latour, Bruno. 2004. *Politics of Nature: How to Bring the Sciences into Democracy.* Cambridge, MA: Harvard University Press.

Luke, Timothy. 2016. "Caring for the Low-Carbon Self: The Government of Self and Others in the World as a Greenhouse Gas." In: Harriet Bulkeley, Matthew Paterson and Johannes Stripple *Towards a Cultural Politics of Climate Change: Devices, Desires, and Dissent.* Cambridge: Cambridge University Press, 66–80.

Massumi, Brian. 1995. "The Autonomy of Affect." *Cultural Critique,* 31: 83–109.

McKay, Don. 2002. "The Bushtits Nest." In: Tim Lilburn (ed.) *Thinking and Singing: Poetry and the Practice of Philosophy,* Toronto, ON: Cormorant Books, 59–77.

Mikaluk, Michael. 2013. "The Forest and the Trees: Sustainability Education and the Anthropocene." Available at: www.michaelmikulak.com/2013/11/27/the-forest-and-the-trees-sustainability-education-and-the-anthropocene/ (accessed May 23, 2017).

Mortimer-Sandilands, Catriona. 2010. "Whose There is There There? Queer Directions and Ecocritical Orientations." *Ecozon@: European Journal of Literature, Culture and Environment* 1, 1: 63.

Morton, Timothy. 2013. *Hyperobjects: Philosophy and Ecology after the End of the World.* Minneapolis, MN: University of Minnesota Press.

Oxford Dictionary. 2017. "Word of the Year FAQ". https://en.oxforddictionaries.com/word-of-the-year/word-of-the-year-faqs/

Radman, Zdravko. 1997. *Metaphors: Figures of the Mind.* New York: Springer.

Rickards, Lauren A. 2015. "Metaphor and the Anthropocene: Presenting Humans as a Geological Force: Anthropocene as Metaphor." *Geographical Research*, 53, 3: 280–287.

Robbins, Paul., 2013: "Choosing metaphors for the Anthropocene: Cultural and Political Ecologies." In: Nuala C. Johnson, Richard H. Schein and Jamie Winders (eds) *Cultural Geography.* Malden, MA: John Wiley & Sons Ltd, 305–319.

Seigworth, Gregory and Melissa Gregg. 2010. "An Inventory of Shimmers" In: Melissa Gregg and Gregory Seigworth (eds). *The Affect Theory Reader.* Durham, NC: Duke University Press.

Sontag, Susan. 1978. *Illness as Metaphor.* New York: Doubleday.

Sontag, Susan. 1989. *Aids and Its Metaphors.* New York: Doubleday.

Tsing, Anna. 2005. *Friction: An Ethnography of Global Connection.* Princeton, NJ: Princeton University Press.

Unitech. 2017. "Carbon Footprint Challenge 2017". Available at: https://createtomorrow-together.com/ (accessed March 1, 2017).

Weaver, Andrew. 2008. *Keeping our Cool: Canada in a Warming World.* Toronto: Viking.

Williams, Raymond. 1985. *Keywords: A Vocabulary of Culture and Society.* Oxford: Oxford University Press.

Williams, Raymond. 1980. "Ideas of Nature." In: *Problems in Materialism and Culture.* London: Verso, 67–85.

Part I
Setting the stage

1 Cultural-material resonances of 'carbon' and 'footprint' and the emergence of the compound metaphor

Following the carbon footprint metaphor as a guide to the high-stakes material and cultural significance of *carbon* at the turn of the millennium offers a glimpse into its valences in seemingly endless contexts. There is a certain dissonance that might be posed by a *carbon* footprint; the actual concern indexed by this metaphor features a set of carbon compounds – not carbon in general (or in isolation) – as well as other greenhouse gases. Clearly, none of these gases has a 'footprint' in the literal sense but the metaphor has strong resonances nonetheless; indeed, these gases are invisible, suggesting that one function of the metaphor is to make visible and tangible something that cannot be seen. Carbon as a scientific term has entered public discourse more recently as a kind of vague signifier that connects to coal and other fossil fuels that are burned and produce unpleasant, even harmful, effects; thus, it may be that the carbon footprint easily stands in as a measure of negative atmospheric effects. However, carbon is also implicated in all kinds of other cycles (materially and metaphorically) that come to influence its modifying role in the footprint metaphor.

My approach to this metaphor's constitutive linguistic elements – carbon and footprint – is to understand them as double-valenced, that is, to see each of these linguistic elements as simultaneously carrying both material and linguistic meanings. In what follows, I explore some of the resonances of carbon and footprint within Anglo-American cultural contexts. These resonances are not exhaustive, but they are meant to suggest some of the central tensions inherent to political solutions to climate change that, in some cases, draw on and reinforce problematic cultural norms and political forms of organization, and in some cases, challenge these norms. While 'footprint' more obviously appears as a metaphor, *carbon* itself has become a preeminent but highly shifty material and cultural signifier of ecological crisis in the late-twentieth and early-twenty-first century.

Allotropic carbon – material and cultural element[1]

A cursory glimpse at carbon's origins as a word and an element reveals an entanglement of 'nature' and 'culture' at its roots. While what we now call carbon has always been a foundational element of planetary life, it was not scientifically identified as such until the late-eighteenth century when chemists began to isolate the various 'elements' of which matter was made.[2] The word, carbon, derives from the Latin for charcoal or 'burning coal' (*carbo*), but different words were used to describe other elemental forms of carbon, like graphite and diamonds,[3] which were not associated with the fuels that people used in antiquity. Carbon is therefore 'modern' as a scientific-discursive element, although ancient in its various manifestations in human history, and prehistoric in its material conditioning of planetary life. Its modern place on the periodic table is one way in which many publics have conventionally come to know about this element. Thus, its use in many discourses grants a certain scientific authority among publics familiar with its place in modern post-enlightenment life in which secular science profoundly shapes worldly understandings.

As a chemical element, carbon exhibits the property of *allotropy*: 'the existence of a chemical element in two or more forms, which may differ in the arrangement of atoms in crystalline solids or in the occurrence of molecules that contain different numbers of atoms' (Encyclopædia Britannica). Allotrope combines the Greek origins of *allo* meaning 'other' and *trope* meaning 'turning toward' or 'affinity to'. Thus, the epistemological contributions of chemistry foreground the tendency of elemental carbon to turn toward other or multiple forms even in its elemental manifestations as: anthracite (coal), diamond, graphite and, more recently, fullerenes and fullerene-related nanotubes (Hirsch 2010; Verdanova et al. 2016). In other words, the embodied forms of carbon as a material element are highly diverse because of the relational encounters and processes in which it is involved.

What is remarkable is that carbon as an element can take on such widely divergent structural forms depending on the arrangement of atoms; each of these forms not only looks different to the naked human eye, but it generates different material effects and affects. The politics and affects associated with diamonds as symbols of wealth, devotion and fraught geopolitical relations, are quite different from those generated by the allotrope of graphite, as an early material used to record information. Arguably much of the 'success' of the human species has been achieved through the elemental form of carbon as anthracite (coal), which was burned by early humans, used extensively by Romans in 100–200 AD for metallurgy (Dearne and Branigan 1995), and, more notably (and ambivalently), fueled the Industrial Revolution. Even as humanity is currently recognizing this human history with coal as a fraught one, we are turning to still other forms of elemental carbon to help power human societies. Recently, the carbon allotrope of graphite has been gathering value as a key component in a growing market for fuel cells and nuclear reactors (Lifton 2012). Meanwhile, the newest discovery of carbon nanotubes apparently holds the promise of 'solving humanity's most pressing problems', including climate change-related ecological matters, according to the Smalley Institute Grand Challenges research group at Rice University.[4] Paradoxically, then, a certain elemental carbon (though strictly in its compounded bonding through combustion with oxygen as CO_2) takes on the burden of being *the* material index of the problem of climate change, even as certain other carbon allotropes, such as carbon nanotubes, promise to fix problems associated with climate change. Understanding this allotropic property of carbon as a chemical element suggests that relations, processes, and bonding capacities matter profoundly in its manifestations, its movements, its promises, and risks.

Notably, carbon as a discursive or cultural element displays a similar polyvalence, taking on different forms and arrangements according to myriad relations and processes. In other words, carbon as a *trope* – a *turn* of phrase or figure of speech – is similarly susceptible to allotropic attachments that manifest in different cultural and material forms (e.g. carbon *as* commodity, carbon *as* index of greenhouse gases, carbon *as* life). This is not to say these discursive forms are 'natural' or elemental; rather they are political, contested, and consequential. For this reason, I do not claim to 'discover' and analyze specific allotropic discursive forms of carbon as arrangements of semiotic carbon atoms, as chemists have done with the chemical element of carbon and its allotropes; to do so would be to black box certain semiotic forms of carbon as more primal than others and to enshrine a one-to-one scientistic representational logic of language that metaphor explicitly overturns. Rather, my purpose for explicitly considering carbon's allotropic character is twofold. First, understanding carbon's non-essentialist allotropic qualities functions to unsettle the ways that carbon footprint metaphors are used to grant authority to questionable practices by virtue of their assumed empirical-quantitative status. Due to carbon's scientific associations, this linguistic element may be used in discourse to legitimate questionable claims (witness climate change denialist Ezra Levant's use of the carbon footprint metaphor to legitimize development of Canada's bitumen sands – described in Chapter 4). Second, explicitly recognizing the semiotic and material *turning* of this element foundationally situates carbon as a kind of *trickster* figure (Girvan forthcoming)⁵ – in both material and metaphorical terms. Carbon has been an indispensably present figure that has shaped planetary life and enabled human progress through technologies of fire, internal combustion engines, and even aeronautical engineering technologies that ironically promise to reduce greenhouse gas emissions of air travel through reductions of airframe weight brought about through the use of lightweight carbon fibre (Timmis et al. 2015). However, carbon is now turning on humans – or perhaps more accurately, dominant human societies are overturning (hydro)carbons – such that carbon seems at times, a duplicitous associate. 'Our' fraught history with this element suggests that, from an anthropocentric perspective, 'carbon represents the best and worst of life' (Miodownik 2006, 6). Of course, paradoxically, the Anthropocene also gestures at 'humanity' as a duplicitous associate – both in terms of certain dominant societies of humans and their disproportionate impact on other humans, and in terms of the human species' generalized effects on our fellow species. However, rather than reading carbon (or ourselves) as duplicitous, the more pressing task is to trace the ambivalent possibilities of certain associations and processes involving carbon. To nuance Mark Miodownik's statement above: *carbon's allotropic associations and processes (including carbon footprint metaphors) present political promises and risks.* Carbon is enigmatically present in cultural-material entanglements as both an enabler and an impediment – both a 'problem' and a 'solution' – teasing out what is being enabled or obstructed, by and for whom, is a central goal of tracing carbon footprint metaphors.

Carbon compounds – material and linguistic

Upon the allotropic formation of carbon as an element, another layer of shiftiness occurs in its compounded forms. Carbon as material actor has a unique ability to 'bind to itself and to nearly all elements in almost limitless variety' (Hirsch 2010, 868). Even as humanity seems to be attempting in earnest to phase out the extraction and combustion of elemental coal/anthracite[6] other compounded forms of carbons are being pitched as bridge fuels in a transition from conventional fossil fuel to renewables. For instance, carbon compounded with hydrogen as CH_4 or methane is the main component of natural gas that is found underground and under the sea. The controversial hydraulic fracturing or 'fracking' method of extracting this bridge fuel is attributed with allowing gains in both energy self-sufficiency and economic growth in the US and elsewhere where conventional oil has not been as plentiful. However, many are questioning the calculus of net decreases in greenhouse gas emissions through this bridge fuel, as recent leaks of methane – a greenhouse gas with a warming effect 25 or more times greater than carbon dioxide – have produced disastrous warming effects[7] (not to mention the subject of air and water contamination and health impacts for those on the frontlines of these operations).

As this massive experiment in up-ending carbon continues, still other forms of compounded carbon are emerging as destructive for much of planetary life as it is presently configured. While *atmospheric* impacts of hydrocarbon extraction and combustion receive the most attention under the banner of climate change, marine impacts attest to how carbon dioxide absorbed by the oceans is rapidly changing the ocean's chemistry. CO_2 combined with water (H_2O) and carbonate ion (CO_3^{-2}) produces H_2CO_3 or carbonic acid; according to the National Oceanic and Atmospheric Administration (NOAA), this chemical reaction has increased the acidity of the ocean by thirty percent since the beginning of the Industrial Revolution (NOAA, nd). While calcium in its partnership with carbonate has enabled the foundational building blocks for shells in sea life and all other life that follows, the rapid up-take of anthropogenic CO_2 by the oceans has severely and negatively affected this relationship. Once thought of as a promising solution to excessive atmospheric CO_2, the ocean's absorption of carbon dioxide and the resulting acidification is now understood as profoundly problematic for marine ecosystems that affect all manner of Earthly life. Seemingly, just as we[8] think we have a handle on carbon's movements and how we might manage them, carbon reveals another attachment or process that hasn't yet been recognized.

Nelya Koteyko and Brigitte Nerlich's investigations of lexical 'carbon compounds' in climate change discourse reveal that linguistic or discursive carbon is equally promiscuous in its compounding attachments (Koteyko 2010; 2012; Nerlich et al. 2012). Using the tools of corpora linguistics, a computer-assisted method of collecting and tracking instances of words in texts to derive abstract rules by which language functions, these scholars track carbon 'comp-ounds' conceived linguistically rather than chemically. Koteyko and Nerlich's studies offer an explicit engagement with the public spaces in which these novel carbon compounds occur as profoundly important sites of politics:

> Carbon compounds in this lexical sense, seem to have overtaken 'eco-compounds' in popularity, that is words which use *eco-* as a prefix to signal various environmental concerns and issues. A whole new language is evolv-ing using carbon as a hub, which needs to be monitored and investigated in order to discover how climate change and climate change mitigation are framed ...
>
> (Nerlich 2012, 32)

The forceful emergence of proliferating carbon compounds constitutes a whole new language (and consciousness), but as these scholars point out, these terms have been adopted without extended critical reflection on how political represen-tations are 'achieved with the help of which lexical means' (Koteyko 2012, 25). In the first of her studies, Koteyko tracks the emergence of carbon compounds in the 1990s and beyond, concentrating on online blog posts as sites of non-expert public conversations that shape cultural politics. In 2007, Koteyko finds 79 carbon compounds in use; perhaps unsurprisingly, in this, the year that the *Oxford English Dictionary* names carbon footprint 'word of the year,' this metaphor is one of the top two most commonly appearing compounds, following 'carbon emissions' (2010).

In a follow-up study, Koteyko analyses how dominant marketplace solutions to climate change are 'discursively enabled and sustained through the use of so-called "carbon compounds"' (2012, 25). Koteyko describes how in the lead-up and follow-through of the Kyoto Protocol, multinational corporations advancing business oriented solutions to climate change created the conditions for certain market-oriented carbon compounds, like 'carbon trading' to dominate. These 'political developments have shifted the focus from the science behind global warming and whether carbon emission could and should be reduced, to who will be doing it and through which economic frameworks' (ibid., 26). The emergence of certain attachments between carbon and markets is commensurate with the creation in the 1990s of what Steven Bernstein calls 'the compromise of liberal environmentalism' that promotes 'liberalization in trade and finance as consistent with (even necessary for) global environmental protection' (2000, 474). As my case studies reveal, the carbon footprint metaphor is entangled within these risky relations of carbon compounds. Koteyko suggests:

> [t]he first carbon compounds to emerge in the English speaking news, such as carbon trading and carbon credits were part of this shift to market-led climate change mitigation. Corporate support for climate measures became evident in the wave of activities and initiatives to manage emissions through product and process improvements, and the exploration of new market

opportunities offered by carbon trading as well as by voluntary offsetting schemes.

(Koteyko 2012, 26)

Similarly, in her article 'Low carbon' Metals, Markets and Metaphor: The Creation of Economic Expectations about Climate Change' (2012), Brigitte Nerlich offers an extended analysis through corpus linguistics of how the lexical compound of 'low carbon' gained prominence in cultural discourses of climate change over time. While the term low carbon was formerly used in specific fields to connote low-carbon steel in manufacturing, it gradually came to take on salience within public climate change discourse in the 1990s when climate change was beginning to enter public consciousness: 'low carbon has acquired new meanings, from signifying quite concretely, the low carbon content of a certain metal to signifying, still relatively concretely, a minimal amount of greenhouse gas emissions, to signifying more abstractly and metaphorically, various (market-based) solutions to climate change' (2012, 38). The discourses of economic benefits and opportunities of 'low carbon', especially in terms of competitive advantage of developing 'low carbon technologies', have particularly taken hold according to Nerlich's analysis (ibid., 40).

These studies offer indispensable attention to carbon compounds in the cultural politics of climate change, especially insofar as they identify and critique the risky market-based associations that come to plague carbon compounds. My study of carbon footprint metaphors picks up on the important critique in order to trace certain tendencies evident in the case studies to favour marketized solutions; however, I also offer a different orientation that centres carbon footprints *as metaphors* that shift and ambiguously create openings as well as foreclosures. Koteyko and Nerlich's approach begins with an important quantitative account of the frequency of certain carbon compounds in their historical emergence and elaborates a taxonomy of these lexical carbon compounds as framing devices as they occur in the media. Rather than counting carbon footprint metaphors and pinning them down as specific framing devices, my approach is to analyze carbon footprint metaphors in their heterogeneous instances, and to locate the metaphorical struggles across these instances as pressing theoretical and practical work in the cultural politics of climate change. I do so in the next chapter by describing these metaphors as 'affective mediators' rather than 'frames', which suggests a more static version of how these compounds might operate. Nonetheless, I find Koteyko's use of 'carbon compound' useful. With its double valence in chemistry and language, the notion of compound facilitates an understanding of how carbon binds with other elements in multiple material and cultural contexts.

Given that carbon, in neither its material nor cultural forms, bonds singularly and monogamously with a specific form or political agenda, carbon compounds must be read as profoundly ambivalent mediators in the cultural politics of climate change. Their ambivalence does not, however, negate their important role; on the contrary, their very shiftiness offers generative insights for moving through the multiple-storied carbon relations that require multiple accounts (beyond simply carbon accounting as a quantitative pursuit). I propose, via my case studies, that one of the political promises of carbon as a trope lies in its capacity to bring into visibility what Jane Bennett calls a 'vibrant materiality that runs alongside and inside humans' but is also avowedly larger-than-human (Bennett 2010, viii). Such a move affords a lively and active force to entities normatively constructed as 'passive matter' (ibid., vii). By contrast, the political risks attaching to carbon's tropological movements feature carbon as an object to be managed and mastered by intentional human agents in human-centric systems that favour certain human groups and societies over others. Paradoxically, even as carbon is recognized as an element that has been disastrously 'up-earthed' by humans through extractive efforts of human mastery that belatedly recognize the power of larger-than-human forces, these same pretensions of mastery are evident in certain proposed solutions for 'managing' carbon. As my analysis demonstrates, such Promethean instrumental solutions risk not only reinforcing existing globally asymmetrical human relations, but they also risk bolstering existing destructive emissions trajectories that worsen the effects of climate change. These promises and risks resonate with the movements of carbon's tropological partner in the compound metaphor of carbon footprint.

Shifting footprints

While carbon has only recently achieved widespread circulation as a modern cultural trope, the trope of the footprint can be traced within a longer cultural history that extends into antiquity. Footprints have been integral to signifying systems of early peoples from all continents of the globe and have come to trace the imprints of beings as diverse as 'early men, giants, heroes, devils, saints, animals, ghosts, witches, fairies and monsters' (Bord 2004, 1). With so many valences signifying both good and evil, ephemerality – when pressed in sand – and permanence – when preserved in stone[9] – the footprint is a mark or trace that is pregnant with possible meanings. Thus, like carbon, footprint is a highly ambivalent trope in political and ecological contexts.

I again focus in what follows on certain dominant Anglo-American cultural resonances of the footprint since these come to shape the dominant spaces in which the carbon footprint resonates. Although dictionary definitions are only part of the story of footprints as metaphors, the *Oxford English Dictionary* offers a glimpse into a range of denotations from 'the impression left by a shoe or a foot on a surface' to 'the area covered by something in particular' to 'the impact on the environment of human activity in terms of pollution, damage to ecosystems, and the depletion of natural resources.' (OED, nd) The latter part of the definition no doubt owes in part to the now normative sense of the *ecological* footprint analysis/metaphor (discussed below). Notably, the OED definitions are particularly humanist in their orientations, although they do also admit human placement within ecosystems. Perhaps its initial appeal to Western humanist subjects – those whose lifestyles are most problematically implicated in climate change – is one of the 'footprint's' initial promises, as I describe in Chapter 3; however, appealing only to this humanist subject position also limits the footprint's more generative capacities. Here, I will briefly gesture at some of these possibilities and limits as they will be further unpacked in the analysis of particular carbon footprint metaphors in the case studies that follow. In order to set up the three case studies that follow, I am interested in focusing on a particular set of tensions revolving around the footprint metaphor's capacity to figure: Western humanist orientations of selfhood; orientations toward material connections with other (humans); and orientations toward a larger-than-human relationality/ecological sensibility.

Humanist footprints in literature and popular culture

The footprint occupies a distinctive, even canonical, place in dominant Western humanist imaginaries. From Lucy's fossilized footprint to 'humanity's footprint' as a sign of a species that has dangerously overshot the Earth's capacity to support us (Dodds 2008), this figure inscribes both the origins and the potential ends of the human as a species. The footprint chronicles a fragile and precarious human-ist species history. The trope of the footprint in Western literary imaginaries traces both the precarity of individual lives and more generally, finitude as a shared human condition. An often-quoted verse in the classic poem *A Psalm of Life* by Henry Wadsworth Longfellow suggests:

> Lives of great men [sic] all remind us
> We can make our lives sublime,
> And, departing, leave behind us
> Footprints on the sands of time

(1838)

In the poem, Longfellow argues against reading life fatally as fleeting and futile and he elevates works of art of 'great men' as part of their enduring legacies, their 'footprints' that are read by others as comforting. In this case a footprint appears as a positive signifier of lasting legacies or bigness (like the tongue-in-cheek 'How Big is Yours?' question that leads in the introduction). Leaving behind a material legacy in the form of literature, art, architecture, technologies, and other works of one's life is thus considered a goal of living, especially in the masculin-ist narrative of 'great men'. The allusion is paradoxical, however, because although the footprint outlives the bodily presence, the mark is on the '*sands* of time', which still suggests a fleeting impression. Such paradoxes of the Western humanist oriented footprint put the carbon footprint metaphor into play in myriad contesting ways. The footprint both: calls attention to a precariousness and ephemerality of humanity that might be signified through the devastating and deadly impact of the human footprint as responsible for producing climate change; and suggests that the footprint might be a comforting legacy, a sign of existence within larger communities over time.

Many other cultural practices relating to footprints similarly attempt to capture or make legacies of what is fleeting in the life of the liberal individual subject. It is this sign of presence of a uniquely celebrated individual, for example, that underscores the practice of making plaster casts or painted prints of babies' feet by many parents celebrating and enshrining the emergence of their offspring. Although such tokens may end up in the detritus of accumulated material over the life-span of that individual, they may seem profoundly important at the time, signifying the emergence of an individual who is linked in a family legacy that endures (and implicitly, one who is linked in the cycle of birth and death). Their presence relays the material evidence of a uniquely celebrated subject and object of love and perhaps the too-fleeting passage of time that renders the size of that small footprint obsolete.

Another one of the most canonical texts in which footprints appear to express this Western humanist imaginary of precariousness is the story of *Robinson Crusoe* by Daniel Defoe (2003/1719). Upon spotting Friday's footprint for the first time after many years on the island as a lonely castaway, Crusoe plummets into a profound psychosis that disturbs both the 'normal' routines of everyday survival in his island life and even his fundamental belief in God:

> It happened, one day about noon going towards my boat, I was exceedingly surprised, with the print of a man's naked foot on the shore, which was very plain to be seen in the sand. I stood like one thunder-struck, or as if I had seen an apparition; I listened, I looked round me, I could hear nothing, nor see any thing; I went up to a rising ground to look farther; I went up the shore and down the shore, but it was all one, I could see no other impression but that one. I went to it again to see if there were any more, and to observe if it might not be my fancy; but there was no room for that, for there was exactly the very print of a foot, toes, heel, and every part of a foot; how it came thither I knew not, nor could in the least imagine. But after innumerable fluttering thoughts, like a man perfectly confused and out of my self, I came home to my fortification, not feeling, as we say, the ground I went on, but terrified to the last degree, looking behind me at every two or three steps, mistaking every bush and tree, and fancying every stump at a distance to be a man; nor is it possible to describe how many various shapes affrighted imagination represented things to me in, how many wild ideas were found every moment in my fancy, and what strange unaccountable whimsies came into my thoughts by the way.

Many postcolonial scholars have commented on Crusoe's colonial, racist reading of the footprint of the 'savage other'.[10] The perspective of the colonizer who has built up an attitude of entitlement to his property and its accompanying resources resonates within many humanist imaginaries, including in some instances of the carbon footprint as I describe below. The footprint in this passage also functions as a figure bound up with existential issues featuring individuals with/against other humans and/or species. The passage hints at the footprint as an 'apparition', one which foundationally shifts the ground upon which Crusoe walks. Significantly, the shift that Crusoe experiences gestures toward a profoundly relational entanglement of presence and absence: *where is the (absent) maker of this footprint, and how does his/her presence on the island threaten to bring about my own absence through death?*

The footprint may not always indicate a threat, but it does carry the force of a presence-absence and self-other set of relations. In this narrative, the footprint also functions as a kind of mirror reflecting back to 'man' an image of identity and difference whereby Crusoe sees in the footprint an image of a fellow human who is at once the same and different. While by the end of the narrative of *Robinson Crusoe*, Friday's presence transforms to one of comfort and community (albeit crucially still within a violent colonial asymmetry), the initial footprint inaugurates a profound shift in consciousness and practices, for Crusoe. As Stephen Curkpatrick affirms, '[p]aradoxically, the footprint provokes a desire to destroy his [Crusoe's] own traces' (2002, 249). Crusoe attempts obsessively to erase his tracks lest this newly identified competitor find him and rob him of his very existence. Friday's footprint therefore functions first, to make Crusoe's own footprints *appear* as one of (at least) two humans on the island, and second, to produce the need to hide his own traces from view. While Crusoe had carved out a self-interested means of subsisting on 'his' island over a number of years (asserting a sovereign autonomy that also functions in the making of a Western subject whose 'footprint' I explore in Chapter 3), the hint of a threatening presence from another human suddenly inaugurates a shift in his perception whereupon he situates himself as one among others with whom he might compete for the resources of the island and even for bare existence itself.

So it may go with carbon footprints. Although a single footprint may provoke no crisis, the accumulated carbon footprint of the human species (again, an internally variegated species with crucially differing sizes of footprints) figures a more daunting prospect that haunts future survival and produces the desire to remove or hide from view these individual traces. The footprint thus not only produces effects that operate irresolvably within and across the complex scales of individuals and species (or subjects and citizens as theorized in Chapters 3 and 4), it also appears paradoxically to figure certain forms of 'self-erasure' that are figured in the instances that follow (for example, the mechanisms of making one's imprint disappear through the market).

The Defoe narrative suggests a particularly problematic reading of 'the other' as not worthy of the same entitlements as the colonial subject narrator of the story. Although 'we' of these Western traditions may think we are *post*colonial when it comes to such starkly unequal narratives of human-human relations like those in *Robinson Crusoe*, we have only to read climate change narratives to see that we are still fully embedded in these kinds of relations. At a time of anthropogenic climate change, the Global North is still often reading as 'threats' other global regions and peoples (in for example, India and China) who are developing through the same hydrocarbon-based means of modernization that have been the norm. Simply put, the discourse goes, *if they had what we have, we would be sentencing ourselves to catastrophic warming.* In other words, 'they' are not entitled to what 'we' have in their modes of development, appetites and lifestyles. Their carbon footprints must be kept lower than say, an average North American.

Footprints as sites of human relationality

Even if one is not familiar with the story of *Robinson Crusoe* or the significance of the fossilized footprint of Lucy, the iconic original ancestor of modern-day humans, footprints also carry familiar and everyday metaphorical associations. Although accumulating footprints can engender feelings of danger as described above, they can also evoke associations with romantic love or even transcendental love as does the popular Christian poem *Footprints in the Sand* (Stevenson 1936),[11] which tells a tale of the footprints of a comforting invisible God walking alongside a human subject/narrator of the poem throughout the course of her life.[12] The footprint can thus function as a site of making room for others with whom we are co-constituted and to whom we may be accountable.

The passage above from *Robinson Crusoe* in its allusion to apparitions reminds that the footprint is a profoundly political 'trace' as a potential opening for conceiving of relationality in a politics of appearance and disappearance. Jacques Derrida figures 'la trace' (one of whose meanings in French is, significantly, 'footprint') as a constitutive presence and absence relation, and therefore, a space highly invested in political relations of visibility and invisibility (1974/1997, 70–72). 'The presence-absence of the trace' suggests 'its play' as a disruption to complete explanations of language, science and any other pursuit that pretends to objectivist accounts (ibid.). Derrida proposes a 'problematic of the trace' suggesting 'that the place of the one and of the other must constantly be in movement' (ibid., 70). Such attention to the movement of relational actors generatively disturbs liberal humanist notions of autonomous, stable selves and marks a world in flux. As a space that literally figures a once-present being to be read by another, a footprint invites a special sensibility to the shifting politics of appearance and disappearance in relational encounters.[13] This sensibility serves as a means of tracing what/who is made present or visible (or not) in certain carbon footprint metaphors.

Anthropogenic climate change as a topic requires thinking constantly about how certain portions of humanity are able to maintain large footprints precisely *because* other portions are maintaining small ones. The world is currently constituted on these very asymmetrical carbon relations. If part of the way the carbon footprint metaphor functions is through measuring relative sizes of footprints as impacts, this (always contingent) measuring of relative difference coupled with the ethico-political space of the footprint marks a key call to action. It is this attribute of the footprint – as a connector between humans and a measure of relative size -that sheds light on a highly problematic set of global relations. As my second case study in Chapter 4 demonstrates, the power of a comparative analysis of nations' footprints is that it lays bare a fundamental asymmetry of global footprints and asks those with larger footprints to relate to others with whom they are connected in terms of these asymmetrical carbon relations and processes.

Footprints as negative ecological impacts

Footprints may evoke positive everyday associations, but the associations that the 'carbon footprint' is *meant* to evoke are negative, rather than positive,[14] reminding on even a mundane level, of messes that are left behind – dirty footprints in clean places – even though they may be unintentional. Carbon footprints suggest that while there is a certain inevitability to human impact on earthly environments, we can do many things to minimize and mitigate the human traces. Thus, the metaphor seems to capture the popular imagination because it suggests both that individuals are bound to have some environmental impact and that they can do various things to mitigate that impact. The footprint metaphor thereby locates a particularly apt site for considering ecological relations. As I elaborate in the next section and throughout the book, the metaphor of the carbon footprint both upholds problematic Western humanist traditions that tie into contemporary liberal environmental logics, and breaks with these same traditions depending on its associations and the politics it fosters.

The *ecological footprint* metaphor was coined William Rees and Mathis Wackernagel through their work on urban sustainability within the framework of ecological carrying capacity (Rees 1992; Wackernagel and Rees 1996). Carrying capacity, conventionally measured in terms of numbers of organisms within a given space, provides a means of hypothesizing the size of a population that can be sustained within a specific region without irreparably damaging the ecosystem. By inverting the notion of carrying capacity, Rees and his then graduate student colleague, Wackernagel, conceived of the amount of land required to sustain a given human community within a material standard as the 'ecological footprint' (measured in hectares) of that community. Revolutionary in its subversion of carrying capacity, this framework allowed an understanding that certain human populations not only exceed their immediate regional basis of sustainability, but that they appropriate carrying capacity from distant lands while exporting ecological degradation.

Notably, Rees and Wackernagel were initially indexing this inversion of carrying capacity through the term 'regional capsule', conceiving of a kind of glass bubble or hemisphere that enclosed a given urban area and considering how big that glass bubble would have to be to support a given regional human population within it (the inspiration they cite for this metaphor is the failed 'Biosphere II' project in Arizona that attempted to recreate an (en)closed self-supporting ecosystem like the Earth) (1996, 9). In a moment that Rees recalls as an 'epiphany' (or what studies of metaphor might connect to the filling of a 'semantic gap' that occurs at the site of emerging metaphors), he swapped in the metaphor of the footprint, as an indicator of land surface area. The origins of this epiphany are interesting. When Rees was given a new tower computer in his office, a colleague asked him how he liked it and he responded (no doubt influenced by his epistemological background in sustainability and land use) 'I especially like it because of the small footprint' (2008). The footprint metaphor resonated with the work he was doing with Wackernagel so they removed the references to the 'regional capsule' as an index and substituted the ecological footprint as 'an *accounting tool* that enables us to estimate the resource consumption and waste assimilation requirements of a defined human population or economy in terms of a corresponding productive land area [my emphasis]' (1996, 9). Although Rees himself acknowledges that the metaphor has been 'powerfully evocative' and partly responsible for the success of the ecological footprint concept he does not delve any deeper into the power of ecological metaphors more generally (2006, 149); the ecological footprint remains widely understood as an accounting tool, in the instrumental terms of its founders.[15] The carbon footprint metaphor also tends to be read as an empirical measure, although close analysis of its uses and appearances in the following analysis reveals that its metaphoricity is productive of numerous cultural and ideological effects. Unlike the ecological footprint, the carbon footprint has no particular author/founder nor steward in terms of what it definitively means/measures.

The notion of the ecological footprint received significant attention within specific circles of interest in the years immediately following the release of the book, *Our Ecological Footprint* (1996), and it continues to gain currency in certain organizational ecological governance circles, but it did not take imaginative hold in certain everyday public spaces the way the carbon footprint would.[16] In fact, it still is not as prevalent as the carbon footprint, within most public contexts, in North America.[17] The reasons for the dominance of the later metaphor pertain in part to the emergence of climate change as a planetary matter of concern, with carbon as its index and also to the singular capacity of carbon footprints to traffic among so many different agendas, especially marketizing ones (as elaborated in all the following chapters of analysis). Both elements of this compound metaphor – carbon and footprint – themselves shift between literal and metaphorical senses; as Rees understood intuitively, the footprint is a powerful metaphorical frame for the ecological footprint metric by virtue of its associations with measured space in land use as well as its associations with grounded ecologies and evocative humanist imaginaries.

Although the quantitative measuring of a carbon footprint is accomplished through weight (tons of carbon dioxide equivalents) rather than by geophysical space (hectares), as with the ecological footprint, the metaphor of the footprint functions to create an imaginative space, or opening, which shifts between a literal measurable entity and a metaphorical quality. This metaphor, then, makes use of the two kinds of associations mentioned in the dictionary for this word: the land area and the (environmental) impact. As studies of metaphor attest, the relationship between the literal and the metaphorical is not as tidy an opposition as one might think (Radman 1997; Franke 2000); indeed, as William Franke evocatively asserts, the *literal itself is figured* by the image of the written letter (2000, 140).[18] The 'footprint' is exemplary of this paradoxical relationship between the literal and the metaphor. While there may exist a strong visual connection between the literal footprint, as a geophysical imprint and environmental (carbon) impact of activities and habits measured by carbon footprint indices, a whole range of other activities – including purchasing consumer goods or offsets – also get figured through carbon footprint metaphors. The 'letter' or sign of the impact-ful footprint is read and deployed in multiple ways with unlikely alliances.

The human footprint also figures prominently within cultural imaginaries and codes of ethics for Western public encounters in 'wilderness'. These imaginaries become complexly entangled with carbon footprint metaphors, sometimes reify-ing problematic humanisms, but also at times challenging them. *Leave nothing but a footprint* is a well-known camping expression, used by twentieth-century scouting organizations (Guides, Scouts, etc.) and for campers more generally, and recently, the expression also appears as an associate of carbon footprint metaphors in certain instances (Energy Results 2011). The *leave nothing but a footprint* edict gestures at a kind of camping/hiking ethics that prohibits damag-ing 'natural' spaces and especially draws attention to the potential for visible human detritus to contaminate what is usually thought of as a pristine wilderness environment. No doubt the footprint in the original camping expression makes strong reference to a literal and physical footprint – a geophysical marker of a former presence – that is thought to be the only impact permitted/unavoidable in the instance of camping or hiking in 'the wilderness'; however, the expression carries a metaphoric meaning as well. Here, the literal geophysical mark and the absence of other common artefacts of human consumption (bottles, cans, etc.) indexes a range of associated practices of a 'responsible' camper. If we look more deeply at what is thought to be the origin of this phrase, these metaphoric circuits appear more clearly: *'Take only memories. Leave nothing but a footprint.'* has been popularly attributed to Chief Seattle or Chief Sealth of the Suquamish Nation in the Pacific Northwest of North America (1780–1866)[19] Beyond a camp-out ethic, this expression also suggests ways of being in the world that are more generalizable to an ethics *against* taking from, or adversely impacting ecosystems (though as this study demonstrates, this is a latent potential conditioned by histor-ical and cultural contexts and associations).

What is notable is that the footprint in this instance attaches a strong visual reference to a literal footprint, but also evokes a footprint metaphorically as a *positive* environmental legacy, one that might be unusual or at least anomalous in Western cultures where ephemerality and 'lightness' of impacts do not generally figure prominently. The legacies of human-built environments are dependent upon an everyday economy of resource extraction and leaving big imprints. From this angle, the *leave only footprints* ethic seems highly fraught in that it fails to acknowledge the many ways in which the 'everyday' non-camping lifestyles of Western privileged subjects also severely impacts ecosystems. Crucially, however, one cannot simply dismiss all carbon footprint metaphors as complicit with this logic of reinforcing the lifestyles of Western privileged subjects. Many of the instances of the carbon footprint metaphor that draw an initial connection to the 'leave nothing but a footprint' expression, clearly appealing to such Western privileged subjects, also then mobilize the carbon footprint to problema-tize the notion that one can ever leave simply a 'footprint' as a geophysical mark when lifestyle and habits are concerned (Energy Results 2011). Paradoxically, then, the affective appeal to this *leave nothing but a footprint* discourse shapes both: 1) how carbon footprint metaphors function to instantiate this very Western liberal subject at the core of individualist solutions to climate change as I describe them in Chapter 3; and 2) how the trope of the footprint also turns critically on these very subjects to bring into visibility problematic lifestyles:

> While making visits to national parks or forest preserves, you'll often be told to 'leave nothing but footprints.' This is always a good policy in these types of situations. However, we often forget, or simply do not know that wherever we go, we actually leave two sets of footprints. Your physical footprint is, for the most part, a harmless indentation left behind wherever you step. Your other footprint is what is known as your carbon footprint, essentially the level of greenhouse gases your lifestyle and activity emit into the environment.
>
> (Energy Results 2011)[20]

This metaphoric shift significantly initiates movement from thinking about visible physical impressions that are unavoidable to countless other everyday impacts that involve lifestyles that involve *some* degree of choice (although, as elaborated in Chapter 3, problems arise in the foisting of all of this responsibility onto individual bodies when larger systems are involved).

Larger-than-human footprints

While footprints can inscribe particularly problematic humanisms, as described above, they also, paradoxically, offer traces for conceiving of larger-than-human relational encounters in material ecologies. Adrienne Mayor and William Sarjeant suggest 'fossil footprints were recognized as traces of living creatures long before petrified bones were perceived as being organic remains' (2001, 143). Such creatures traced through footprints ranged from dinosaurs to oxen to birds to humans and even mythical creatures such as dragons (ibid., 149–152). Although the footprints in question were still being 'read' by early *humans*, their existence and the powerful force they carried did not refer uniquely to humans. Owing to the fact that literal footprints may suggest an impression of an ecological actor in a certain space and time, they offer the unique capacity of tracing forms of presence that are not uniquely human. Tracing carbon footprints in texts suggests that this this capacity connected to 'literal' footprints also extends to the metaphoricity of the footprint as an opening for more-than-human agency. Certain instances of this metaphor, like the 'carbon footprint of shrimp' (Chapter 5) more explicitly trace the presence of ecological actors that are larger-than-human.

Relatedly, the footprint may tell a story not only of an ecological actor leaving an impression, but of a reciprocity of impression-making whereby what is often discursively neutered through the word 'surface' or 'environment' comes to actively participate in the footprint-making process. An impression made in the sand by a walking animal (human or otherwise), for example, presents itself through its co-constitution with its surrounding relations with sand, water, and a host of other actors in place. How deep the impression is and how long it lasts are subject not only to the weight of the footprint-maker but also to the characteristics – permeability, porosity, solidity, etc. – of the relational actors that are co-constituted within the footprint. Many of the footprints of early creatures have recently been located because they were initially made in impressionable volcanic ash that has since become petrified (Mayor and Sarjeant 2001). These properties of the footprint lend to its place as an elemental figure for mediating larger-than-human vital relations. When the footprint not only implies a single actor but also is multiplied to the level of a species and beyond at a time of climate change, this metaphor figures existential questions and shifting consciousness that potentially impart new accounts of larger-than-human conditions. A footprint may not just be a 'surface effect' of what we humans can see with our partial vision, but something much more profound; considering carbon footprints in mangrove ecosystems (Chapter 5), for example, initiates a deeper appreciation for, and humility toward vital relations and processes that we cannot immediately see within these porous places between land and sea.

While the above sketch of cultural and materials resonances of 'carbon' and 'footprints' is by no means exhaustive,[21] what is evident is that these two elements are at play as metaphors in ambivalent cultural and material contexts. Carbon is both value-laden as 'good' as a foundational element to life on Earth, *and* troubling as the stand-in for greenhouse gas-inducing climate change that threatens life as we know it. Footprints can be both problematic *and* comforting, and further, they can both inscribe problematic humanisms *and* trace larger-than-human impressions. Footprints can be tracked for instrumental purposes and capture of the 'objects' they signify or they can be traced as a blurring of subject and object relations with potentially profound effects upon novel understandings of socio-ecological relations. These tensions and paradoxes of carbon and footprint significantly shape their compounded form as the carbon footprint metaphor emerges.

Enter the carbon footprint metaphor ...

At the turn of the millennia in the cultural politics of climate change, an opening to understandings of the mediating role of 'discourse' appears in the IPCC's Third Assessment Report (2001). Working Group III: Mitigation, Section 5.3.8.5 of the report entitled 'Discourse and Symbolism' highlights the need to connect climate change to language through 'discourse', as a political practice that involves power relations. 'Discourse or narrative – the written and spoken word – is one of the most important ways in which governments, business, NGOs, and the media influence each other and build agreement on policy directions' (IPCC 2001). This section of the IPCC report not only newly identifies discourse as a key site to consider for the working group on mitigation, but it also implicitly recognizes *political struggle mediated through language* at the centre of the politics of climate change. For while *scientific* consensus on the problem may have been largely achieved,[22] political consensus on responses to the issue remained and continue to remain far from decided. The IPCC passage acknowledges the need to 'build agreement' on political responses, thus illuminating on-going struggles and tensions that take place through discourse. Importantly, these tensions and struggles do not suddenly appear when the IPCC first acknowledges the role of discourse; these tensions have been part of the conditions in which carbon lexical compounds have existed, as described above. Nonetheless, what was perceived as a new shared consciousness of human impacts at the turn of the millennium led to an opening for new discursive mediators to connect responses to public bodies at multiple scales.

Significantly, this explicitly discursive turn in climate change politics at the turn of the millennium coincides with the entrance of the carbon footprint metaphor that popularly caught the imaginations of publics and took root in the cultural politics of climate change. Compound metaphors involving carbon had been appearing sporadically over the last decade, but they had received little attention as part of these politics, nor had these carbon compounds entered into daily discursive practices of the 'subjects' and 'citizens' – those who have 'foot-prints' and who were involved in the urgent concerns of climate change. This metaphor emerges in part out of a timely quest to affectively describe the surfaces of bodies and collectivities in order to apprehend the ways in which they can respond to these emerging politics. This metaphor, then, in part responds to the question: *how can shifting carbon connections be attached, grounded, and fixed (if contingently so) to bodies across individual, national, and other scales that are part of this urgent issue of climate change?*

The carbon footprint metaphor appears very sporadically in the early 2000s, and achieves a 'viral' quality in 2007 in public discourse with much attention to its novelty.[23] The year in which the carbon footprint becomes the Oxford English Dictionary's 'word of the year' (OED) is 2007 and this is the year that my first textual case studies in what follows (carbon footprint reduction lists) begin to emerge with force. No single person or source has either claimed authorship of this metaphor or definitively identified its source. Finding the exact point of origin of the carbon footprint remains an elusive task. What is clear from looking at its earliest iterations is that those who first use it and attempt to define its contours are suggesting that this metric (not metaphor) contributes to climate change solutions, but who they imply as having a footprint and what they suggest these footprint makers do about it profoundly shapes a diverse range of solutions.

The first carbon footprint metaphor that I have been able to trace appeared on the now-defunct website, safeclimate.net, a project of the Washington DC-based non-profit organization World Resources Institute (WRI).[24] Although the website and its carbon footprint calculator are no longer operational, the traces of carbon footprints linger.[25] On September 1 2001, CIO Magazine, a magazine aimed at Chief Information Officers in Business, reported on the launch of a website, safe-climate.net and its new tool, a carbon footprint calculator[26] aimed at 'helping individuals and organizations calculate and reduce their output of carbon dioxide' (Kaplan 2001, 1). 'SafeClimate.net's main tool is a calculator that measures your "carbon footprint" or the amount of carbon dioxide emitted by your activities or those of your business' (ibid.).

The origins of the emergence of the carbon footprint reveal the tensions built into the politics that ensue from its orientations. While the WRI is a not-for-profit policy-research organization, it has at its origins, the tensions of its founding funders – The MacArthur Foundation, Ford Foundation, and the Rockefeller Brother Fund – whose philanthropic power emerged in large part out of a liberal economic order of profit generation intimately connected to oil extraction and related industries.[27] Further, the WRI has been centrally involved in the promotion of 'offsetting' (a notion and problematic practice to which I return in Chapter 3) carbon impacts through carbon markets (WRI 2010). Thus, its approach to global environmental ('resource') issues and, specifically, climate change is shaped by this liberal economic order of market-driven solutions. Although the carbon footprint calculator and safeclimate.net no longer exist, the fact that this carbon footprint metaphor is next picked up in a business magazine suggests that this footprint is significantly attached to the bodies of organizations that have a stake in preserving the norms of a liberal business-friendly rationality. In the wake of the seeming consensus on anthropogenic climate change at the turn of the millennium, publicists of many major corporations were 'abandoning the claim that there was no global warming problem and shifting to claims about the most business-friendly way to address it' (Weart 2014, 51). This is not to suggest that denial of anthropogenic climate completely vanished; as Weart suggests, 'ExxonMobil continued to spend tens of millions of dollars on false-front organizations that amplified any claim denying the scientific consensus' (ibid., 51–52). The fact that climate change became a more mainstream concern linked with pro-business approaches, however, again highlights the risks of addressing climate change through business-as-usual profit-oriented systems.

I will not dwell on this particular instance of the carbon footprint both because it no longer exists for analysis and because I am interested in the metaphor's viral emergence in the public in 2007. However, I wish to briefly flag this vanishing instance to illustrate this aspect of the carbon footprint metaphor's emergence, which draws on, and risks bolstering, 'the compromise of liberal environmentalism' that was unfolding in the lead-up decade in which climate change politics began to be institutionalized (Bernstein 2000). The Rio Conference or 'Earth Summit' in 1992 was the first meeting out of which emerged the United Nations Framework Convention on Climate Change (UNFCC). Steven Bernstein attributes the particular mechanisms enshrined in the Agenda 21 text from this meeting as a defining moment in history. The first paragraph of the preamble to this lengthy document sets up a context of a watershed moment in which 'sustainable development' becomes the vehicle through which to rectify existing global asymmetries and deteriorating ecosystems:

> Humanity stands at a defining moment in history. We are confronted with a perpetuation of disparities between and within nations, a worsening of poverty, hunger, ill health and illiteracy, and the continuing deterioration of the ecosystems on which we depend for our well-being. However, integration of environment and development concerns and greater attention to them will

lead to the fulfilment of basic needs, improved living standards for all, better protected and managed ecosystems and a safer, more prosperous future. No nation can achieve this on its own; but together we can – in a global partnership for *sustainable development.*

> (UN Sustainable Development Agenda 21 1992, 3 emphasis added)

One hundred and seventy-eight countries signed on to this programme, including the George Bush Senior administration of the United States. This document reveals that emerging agendas of climate change were being tethered to an agenda of 'sustainable development', a notion fraught with tensions. On the promising side, the framework both recognizes the importance of ecosystems and centrally accounts for asymmetrical global relations of power and resources as an object to overcome; however, on the risky side, as many commentators have argued, sustainable development also relies on notions of prosperity that often depend on, or inadvertently result in resource exploitation and unequal power relations (Bernstein 2000; O'Connor 1994). Whereas from the late 1960s 'early attempts to address global environmental problems produced a weakly institutionalized set of norms suspicious of industrialization and economic growth', in the 1990s as the agenda of climate change was coming to the fore, the norms shifted (Bernstein 2000, 465). 'Norms of liberal environmentalism predicate environmental protection on the promotion and maintenance of liberal economic and political order ... [suggesting that] environmental protection, economic growth and a liberal international economy are compatible, even necessarily linked' (465). This compromise has allowed wider participation and interest in the global concerns of climate change throughout the 1990s and beyond; however, predicating climate change solutions upon a liberal economic and political order fails to acknowledge the role of this order in creating the very issues such solutions seek to address.

This study trains attention to the carbon footprint metaphor's critical role in reinforcing such orders; a cultural politics perspective insists on 'attending to cultural sites and dynamics as a critical, if sometimes overlooked means through which consensus is created and hegemonies maintained' (Bulkeley et al. 2016, 18) Carbon footprint metaphors are at times embroiled in these dynamics of upholding such problematic norms. What/who comes into political visibility through footprints is shaped by these institutionalized norms that in turn shape the available responses oriented through the metaphor.

And yet because these cultural politics are always contentious and because the carbon footprint *as a metaphor*, shifts and also defies fixed norms, it will not singularly uphold these hegemonic orders. Most who try to define or take up the metaphor also suggest that its roots lie within the metaphor of the ecological footprint (described above) – a metaphor/metric stewarded by ecologists that deliberately and explicitly highlight and critique human 'overshoot' of a planetary carrying capacity (Wackernagel and Rees 1996). This perspective brought through ecological footprint accounting also strongly critiques a liberal expansionist economic order (even as it forecloses on the promises of metaphor by insisting the footprint is a metric). My case studies trace these tensions and paradoxes within and across the instances of the carbon footprint metaphor.

Before launching into the case studies, I respond in the next chapter to the question of how metaphors foster certain political and ecological orientations and actions. The world-creating effects of metaphors relate to how they make actors and actions visible, what attachments they foster, and whether they are taken to be contingent, rather than representational.

Notes

1   A version of the section 'Allotropic carbon – material and cultural element' appears within Girvan, A. 2017. "Trickster Carbon: Stories, Science and Postcolonial Interventions for Climate Justice", Journal of Political Ecology. Vol 24, 2017.

2   Carbon. Dictionary.com. *Collins English Dictionary – Complete & Unabridged 10th Edition*. HarperCollins Publishers. Available at: http://dictionary.reference.com/browse/carbon (accessed July 12, 2013).

3   See, for example: diamond. Dictionary.com. *Collins English Dictionary – Complete and Unabridged 10th Edition*. HarperCollins Publishers. Available at: http://dictionary.reference.com/browse/diamond (accessed July 12, 2013).

4   "Smalley Institute Grand Challenges: Nanoscale Science and Technology." Rice University. Available at: https://sci.rice.edu/node (accessed June 2, 2017).

5   I am alluding to the traditional tales of tricksters – Anansi stories from West Africa via Jamaica and Brer Rabbit stories from Central and Southern Africa and the American South –which I have experienced through my Jamaican family background. As I highlight in a forthcoming article, (Girvan 2017) tricksters come off in these stories ambivalently as, at times, heroic and other times villainous. This kind of 'trickster' agency is also theorized by Donna Haraway as a means of 'giving up mastery … making room for surprises and ironies at the heart of all knowledge production [since] we are not in charge of the world.' (1988, 184) Understanding carbon in this way as an allotropic trickster is born of both personal experience with trickster stories, and the impulses of feminist science studies that temper a scientistic apprehension of carbon as the only way of knowing about this element.

6   A crucial period for legislating the phase-out of coal in the US was marked from 2015 to 2016 with the Clean Power Plan (2015); China made a similar commitment in 2015 as did certain provinces in Canada (Ontario) and states (Oregon). In 2016, Vietnam's Prime Minister also announced the phasing out of coal.

7   Conley et al. (2016) suggests that the Aliso Canyon California methane leak in 2015 to 2016 has contributed enormous radiative forcing effects equivalent to the annual effects of half a million passenger cars. This leak, which has produced the largest climate impacts of all such leaks in US history, will put California far behind its emissions targets for the year. The 97,100 metric tons of methane leaked from this one single source is equivalent to the annual emissions produced from the Ch_4 sector in a medium-sized European country.

8   Again, the 'we' here is a troubled we, not a universal one, since not all humans share this enlightenment myth of managing carbon for once and for all.

9   Janet Bord compiles stories and images of footprints that are imprinted in stone as signs of permanence of beings, be they saints or demons, or animals. In Aztec culture, there was a 'belief that a deity or divine personage could leave some of their power behind in their footprints' (Bord 2004, 7).

10 See, for example, Carey 2009; Chakraborty 2003; Peneze, 2008 for postcolonial readings of Defoe.

11 There is also a popular Leona Lewis song from 2008 that was loosely based on the Stevenson poem. Available at: www.azlyrics.com/lyrics/leonalewis/ footprintsin thesand.html (accessed June 6, 2017).

12   The two sets of footprints in the sand register this steadfast companionship and trans-cendental love. Questioning God as to why there is, in the subject's time of greatest need, only one set of footprints in the sand, God responds by saying that during a time of particular need, God himself was carrying the subject. Available at: www.foot prints-inthe-sand.com/index.php?page=Poem/Poem.php (accessed June 2, 2017).

13   This emphasis on appearance and vision is admittedly fraught with discourses of 'ableism', which place primacy on the human sensory capacity to see. Nonetheless, with Bennett, Rancière and Derrida, I claim a politics of appearance/disappearance as necessary even as I wish in future work to disturb its sensory exclusivity and to insist more on the partiality of vision.

14   The positive associations do not entirely disappear, as I suggest below in the section describing the discourses of 'leave only footprints'.

15   See for example the Global Footprint Analysis' description. Available at: www.foot-printnetwork.org/en/index.php/GFN/page/at_a_glance/ (accessed June 2, 2017).

16   Using the tool, Google NGram Viewer, one can see the kinds of hits elicited by a search of ecological footprint yield specialized titles for organizations, such as *The Ecological Footprint of Cities* (1998) and *The Ecological Footprint of Hostel Tourists in Ontario and Quebec* (2008), whereas, the carbon footprint elicits titles such as *How to Reduce Your Carbon Footprint* (2008) and *Reducing your Carbon Footprint on Vacation* (2008). Available at: http://books.google.com/ngrams/graph?content= carbon+footprint%2C+ecological+footprint&year_start=1990&year_end=2013& corpus=15&smoothing=3&share= (accessed May 12, 2013).

17   This claim is corroborated by the Google search Trends function, which tracks frequency of results for the two terms. Available at: www.google.com/trends?q= carbon+footprint%2C+ecological+footprint (accessed March 24, 2011).

18   An 'ironic predicament is, in fact, written into the very term *literal,* itself based on the metaphor of the written character, the letter, being used to stand for a certain kind of meaning. The letter is itself nothing but a figure, a concrete image, for this kind of literal meaning that is purportedly devoid of figurativeness' (Franke 2000, 140).

19   Though it is difficult to definitively acertain this connection, the phrase is commonly cited as Chief Seattle's in various places on the web (e.g. http://quotationsbook.com/ quote/26014/#sthash.LBpeKP57.dpbs).

20   This text is found on a variety of websites including the Israeli Foreign Affairs website. Available at:http://israelforeignaffairs.com/watch-where-you-step-under-standing-your-carbon-footprint/ (accessed May 12, 2013).

21   Crucially, not all of these will resonate with all readers, nor will I have gestured at all of the interpretations of footprint metaphors that readers will bring to their readings. In discussions with readers of this text, each reader might favour a different interpre-tation of what footprint metaphors might evoke. While I cannot do justice to all of these metaphorical allusions, their very plurality confirms the struggle in which carbon footprint metaphors are embroiled.

22   This is not to say that 'consensus' means unanimity; crucially, some of the same lobbies involved in the GCC have remained on the scene to query consensus. In 2009, for example, the 'Climate-gate' scandal during which some IPCC scientists were found to have selectively chosen certain data, provided fuel for the fire of deniers of anthropogenic climate change. Nonetheless, as Oreskes suggests, these 'well-financed contrarians' are a very small minority (2007, 77).

23   See Google trends for searches of carbon footprint at: www.google.com/trends?q= carbon+footprint%2C+ecological+footprint&ctab=0&geo=all&date=all&sort=0

24   The Miriam Webster dictionary suggests that the first known use of the phrase occurs in 1999 but I have not been able to find this (www.merriam-webster.com/ dictionary/ carbon%20footprint).

25   A web search for Safe Climate's carbon footprint calculator yields the following message that depicts the slipperiness of carbon footprint (calculators): 'WRI does not

currently support or endorse any carbon footprint calculators. The methodology and accuracy of these tools may vary, and are the responsibility of the organization that hosts each one' (WRI Safe climate).

26　Although carbon footprint calculators do not comprise one of my three case studies, I do discuss them as co-productive of 'carbon subjectivity' along with carbon footprint reduction lists in Chapter 3.

27　In particular, the Rockefeller Bros fund was built at its origins through oil extraction. The Rockefeller brothers co-founded Standard Oil whose successors in the wake of anti-monopoly rulings include Esso, Chevron, Exxon and Mobil. Of course, the Ford Foundation legacy was created through the mass production of automobiles. While the MacArthur Foundation was not built expressly on fossil fuel industries, billionaire-philanthropist John D. MacArthur built his wealth through the finance capital of large real estate holdings in Florida and through his insurance company (www.macarthur.org/about/our-history/).

References

Bennett, Jane. 2010. *Vibrant Matter: A Political Ecology of Things*. Durham, NC: Duke University Press.

Bernstein, Steven. 2000. "Ideas, Social Structure and the Compromise of Liberal Environmentalism." *European Journal of International Relations* 6, 4: 464–512.

Bord, Janet. 2004. *Footprints in Stone: The Significance of Foot-and Hand-Prints and Other Imprints Left By Early Men, Giants, Heroes, Devils, Saints, Animals, Ghosts, Witches, Fairies and Monsters*. Marlborough, UK: Heart of Albion Press.

Bulkeley, Harriet, Matthew Paterson and Johannes Stripple. 2016. *Towards a Cultural Politics of Climate Change: Devices, Desires, and Dissent*. Cambridge: Cambridge University Press.

Dearne, Martin J. and Keith Branigan. 1995. "The Use of Coal in Roman Britain." *The Antiquaries Journal* 75: 71–105.

Derrida, Jacques. 1974/1997. *Of Grammatology*. Translated by Gayatri Chakravorty Spivak. Baltimore, MD: Johns Hopkins University Press.

Dodds, William. 2008. *Humanity's Footprint: Momentum, Impact and our Global Environment*. New York: Columbia University Press.

Encyclopædia Britannica Online, "allotropy". Available at: www.britannica.com/EBchecked/topic/16560/allotropy (accessed March 7, 2017).

Energy Results 2011. "Watch Where You Step: Understanding Your Carbon Footprint." Available at: www.articlecity.com/articles/environment_and_going_green/article_1150.shtml (accessed June 2, 2017).

Franke, William. 2000. "Metaphor and the Making of Sense: The Contemporary Metaphor Renaissance." *Philosophy and Rhetoric* 33, 2: 137–153.

Hirsch, Andreas. 2010. "The Era of Carbon Allotropes." *Nature Materials* 9: 868–871.

IPCC. 2001. *Climate Change 2001: The Third Assessment Report of the Intergovernmental Panel on Climate Change*. Cambridge, UK: Cambridge University Press.

Kaplan, Simone. 2001. "Leave a Smaller Footprint." *CIO Magazine*. September 1, 2001.

Koteyko, Nelya. 2010. "Mining the Internet for Linguistic and Social Data: An Analysis of 'Carbon Compounds' in Web Feeds." *Discourse and Society* 21, 6: 655–674.

Koteyko, Nelya. 2012. "Managing Carbon Emissions: A Discursive Presentation of 'Market-driven Sustainability' in the British Media." *Language and Communication* 32, 1: 24–35.

Lifton, Jack. 2012. "Graphite and Rare Earth Metals for the 21st Century." *The Gold Report*. Available at: www.theaureport.com/pub/na/graphite-and-rare-earth-metals-for-the-21st-century-jack-lifton (accessed March 7, 2017).

Longfellow, Henry Wadsworth. 1838/1893. *The Complete Poetical Works of Longfellow.* Boston: Houghton Mifflin Company.

Mayor, Adrienne and Sarjeant, William A.S. 2001. "The Folklore of Footprints in Stone: From Classical Antiquity to the Present." *Ichnos: An International Journal for Plant and Animal Traces.* 8, 2: 143–163.

NOAA (National Oceanic and Atmospheric Administration). nd. "What is Ocean Acidification? The Chemistry." Available at: www.pmel.noaa.gov/co2/story/What+is+Ocean+Acidification%3F (accessed June 5, 2017).

Nerlich, Brigitte. 2012. "'Low Carbon' Metals, Markets and Metaphors: The Creation of Economic Expectations about Climate Change Mitigation." *Climatic Change* 110, 1–2: 3.

Nerlich, Brigitte, Nelya Koteyko and Brian Brown. 2010. "Theory and Language of Climate Change Communication." *Wiley Interdisciplinary Reviews. Climate Change* 1, 1: 97–110.

O'Connor, Martin (ed.). 1994. "On the Misadventures of Capitalist Nature." In: *Is Capitalism Sustainable?* New York: Guilford.

OED. Available at: www.oxforddictionaries.com/definition/american_english/ footprint ?q=footprint (accessed March 7, 2017).

Rees, William E. 1992. "Ecological Footprints and Appropriated Carrying Capacity: What Urban Economics Leaves Out." *Environment and Urbanization* 4, 2: 120–130.

Rees, William E. 2006. "Ecological Footprints and Bio-capacity: Essential Elements in Sustainability Assessment." In: Jo Dewulf and Herman Van Langenhove (eds) *Renewables-Based Technology: Sustainability Assessment*. Chichester, UK: Wiley.

Rees, William E. 2008. "Epiphany, Serendipity, and the Genesis of the Ecological Footprint analysis." Public Lecture. February 10, 2008, Environmental Professional Series: YMCA: Vancouver BC.

Stevenson, Mary. 1936. "Footprints in the Sand" Available at: www.footprints-inthe-sand.com/index.php?page=Poem/Poem.php (accessed June 2, 2017).

Timmis, Andrew J., Alma Hodzic, Lenny Koh, Michael Bonner, Constantinos Soutis, Andreas W. Schäfer and Lynnette Dray. 2015. "Environmental impact assessment of aviation emission reduction through the implementation of composite materials." *The International Journal of Life Cycle Assessment* 20, 2: 233–243.

United Nations Sustainable Development. 1992. "Agenda 21." Available at: http://sustainabledevelopment.un.org/content/documents/Agenda21.pdf (accessed June 2, 2017).

Verdanova, Martina, Bohuslav Rezek, Antonin Broz, Egor Ukraintsev, Oleg Babchenko, Anna Artemenko, Tibor Izak, Alexander Kromka, Martin Kalbac and Marie Hubalek Kalbacova. 2016. "Nanocarbon Allotropes—Graphene and Nanocrystalline Diamond—Promote Cell Proliferation." *Small* 12, 18: 2499–3509.

Wackernagel, Mathis and William E. Rees. 1996. *Our Ecological Footprint: Reducing Human Impact on the Earth. Vol. 9*. Gabriola Island, BC; Philadelphia, PA: New Society Publishers.

Weart, Spencer. 2014. *The Discovery of Global Warming* (on-line extended and up-date version of published book). Available at: www.aip.org/history/climate/index.htm (accessed June 2, 2017).

World Resource Institute. 2010. "The Bottom Line on Offsets." www.wri.org/sites/default/files/pdf/bottom_line_offsets.pdf (accessed June 2, 2017).

2 *Mise-en-scène*

Metaphor, affect, politics, ecology

In the analysis that follows, I situate carbon footprint metaphors as 'affective mediators' in order to explore how footprints attach to certain bodies in orienting responses to climate change. I will explore the complexities of affect below, but I first briefly situate the notion of mediator from discourse and communications studies that insist that the mediations of language (here metaphor) are never neutral, but are recursively involved in the formation of worlds (Dryzek 2005; Fairclough 2001). This active notion of mediation renders visible a politics constituted within and through language rather than simply reading language as an instrumental tool. The following section will situate metaphor in this world-making interplay. I also wish to build on popular notions of mediation as an active process of opening dialogue in dispute or struggles, although as I illustrate through the cases of carbon footprint metaphors, there is a political imperative involved in keeping these struggles open rather than aiming for dispute 'resolution'. By resisting the totalizing imperative to ultimately 'resolve' the specifics of the who/what/ how that are indexed through the carbon footprint metaphor, one might gesture toward a different orientation of mediation whereby larger-than-human actors may continually register in process. The forces and processes that come together within each instance of the carbon footprint metaphor reveal specific ways of perceiving the issue of climate change and how to address it. As mentioned in the previous chapter, a certain tendency exists to mobilize such forces instrumentally toward specific human-centric and market-oriented solutions; carbon footprint metaphors indeed risk being mobilized in this way. And yet, by acknowledging that 1) metaphors shift and 2) these metaphors are involved in mediating processes that involve larger-than-human relationalities, one can also affirm a role for this metaphor as affectively mediating larger-than-human forces. The benefit of drawing on the affect theories and political theories that I do below is that they do not insist on prescribing a specific ontology of the body or of political actors that might come to count through this metaphor. The interacting terms of mediation that I tease out below are metaphor, affect, politics, and ecology.

Why (and how) metaphor?

The effects of carbon footprints metaphors derive, in large part, from their very metaphoricity. While metaphors have conventionally been conceived as frill, extraneous to signification 'proper', they occupy a more central and everyday place in creating ways of knowing about the world and in shaping worlds themselves. I begin here with an initial contingent working concept of metaphors, which will be fleshed out throughout the book through the particular cases of carbon footprint metaphors I study. Of the two approaches to metaphor identified by Dennis Sobolev within studies of metaphor – 1) identifying structures of metaphor and 2) exploring functions (2008, 905–906) – my own project falls into the latter agenda. That is, rather than sealing metaphor in a tight definitional construct in order to say what metaphor definitively is, my purpose for this study is to theorize how one particular metaphor – the carbon footprint, itself a multiplicity – produces effects, and to begin to understand some of these effects (and affects). To understand how it produces these effects, however, one cannot completely avoid drawing attention to *what* may be identified as metaphor.

With Sobolev (2008), Ricouer (1977) (and even going back to Aristotle[1]), I contend that metaphors are formally identifiable when considered explicitly through some relationship of resemblance – either pre-existing or created within the metaphor itself – that highlights certain attributes of a given entity when seen through another. Through this poetic function, 'carbon footprints' thereby index greenhouse gases (another metaphor) as climate *impacts* (yet another metaphor) when seen through the footprint as a marker of an impact or impression. The above loose definition of metaphor, however, instantly produces other necessary conditions like 'difference' since the entities being drawn together must also be somehow dissimilar for metaphors to work; such absent terms and tensions are central to the effects of metaphor which works by connecting together unlikely things. This is a central feature of the functioning of carbon footprint metaphors: their effects are generated in part, by the yoking of unlikely things. *How is it that carbon and footprint get yoked together, despite their un-likeness?* I identify the general feature of yoking that situates carbon footprint metaphors within a 'politics of aesthetics' (Rancière 2004) in which metaphors fundamentally help to constitute worlds, rather than simply describing things in a poetics that is conceived as devoid of political (and ecological) importance.

Aesthetics for Jacques Rancière is not limited to the domain of art, but rather, refers more generally *and politically* to the organization of 'material arrangements of signs and images, between what is seen and what is said, between what is done and what can be done' (2004, 39). In other words, reflecting on aesthetics reminds us of the ways in which 'composition' takes place in politics through words (metaphors), and what they bring into visibility which, in turn shapes the actions that flow from such arrangements. While metaphors have long been recognized for their forceful power in the literary arts, this force has not conventionally been cast as political. Although Rancière does not explicitly focus on metaphors in his politics of aesthetics, he outlines a connection between political statements and 'literary locutions', which describes a crucial relationship between politics and metaphor:

Political statements and literary locutions produce effects in reality. They define models of speech or action but also regimes of sensible intensity. They draft maps of the visible, trajectories between the visible and the sayable, relationships between modes of being, modes of saying, and modes of doing and making. They define variations of sensible intensities, perceptions and the abilities of bodies.

(2004, 39)

As my analysis of carbon footprint metaphors brings to light, these metaphors produce effects through prescribing roles and models for speaking and acting in the cultural politics of climate change. Each of these metaphors provides a range of possibilities (and forecloses upon others) in ways that profoundly shape politics and ecologies, but these ways are usually overlooked because of the everyday quality of metaphors.

A politics of aesthetics of metaphors compels understanding metaphors not as exceptionally used language against 'proper' language (as do Aristotle and certain other 'Fathers' whose canonical political texts are based on Aristotle's legacy[2]), but as everyday mediators that are pervasive, inescapable, and bundled up with ways of knowing about the world that in turn shape the world (Chilton 1996; Lakoff and Johnson 1980). Many of the hundreds of metaphors that we use each day are not recognized as such simply because they have been conventionalized.[3] There is simply no way in which to communicate literally in both everyday life and even within scientific disciplines without the use of metaphors (Larson 2011; Kuhn 1970/1962). Like many metaphors that are popularized in everyday cultural spaces, such as the media, the carbon footprint metaphor has become naturalized as a 'representational' concept to account for emissions impacts. This conventionalization, however, does not entirely deprive the carbon footprint of its metaphoric power; on the contrary, as I will show in my analysis, it, or rather *they,* continue to yoke together unlikely things and generate consequential cultural practices, without explicitly drawing attention as metaphors. Metaphors can thereby covertly generate equivalencies where none previously existed. This means that the associations generated also risk becoming conventionalized and closed off as practice, against the promising openings that these metaphors may afford.

Paradoxically, what makes metaphors *seem* exceptional is that in their emergence (and as they yoke together unlikely things), they can effect a kind of disruption to the order of what is assumed to be the normal function of language. As Paul Ricouer suggests, metaphors involve suspending or altering 'reality' such that the whole referential function of language is marked by ambiguity (1977, 224). In resolving the tensions involved with a temporary dissonance between two unlike entities in order to make sense of a metaphor, new relational orders are created. This is what Radman (1997, 7) calls the 'world-making' function of metaphors. What is more, as Denis Sobolev (2008, 917) suggests, metaphors emerge in response to a 'semantic gap', where no language exists to respond to a given set of circumstances. This is one of the key functions of carbon footprint metaphors: they emerge alongside novel understandings of climate change in the gap of: *now that we know about it, what are we to do?*

As my analysis reveals, how these metaphors respond to this gap depends on the different instances of the metaphor and the varying sets of associations and practices yoked within it. Various worldly possibilities are enabled by different instances since metaphors are shifty mediators. As Paul de Man insists, 'not only are tropes, as their name implies always on the move – more like quicksilver than like flowers or butterflies which one can at least hope to pin down and insert into a neat taxonomy – but they can disappear altogether or at least appear to disappear' (1978, 18). In these moments of appearance of disappearance, metaphor's world-making function is obscured from view. The various carbon footprint metaphors I analyze exemplify this movement of tropes in different times and space, and how they often 'appear to disappear' as metaphors. In the many examples of carbon footprint metaphors in discourses that I have traced, very few mention the carbon footprint as a metaphor at all (Brainard 2008; Berners-Lee 2011; Nerlich 2012). Those that do mention the metaphorical aspect of the carbon footprint, generally do so only in passing and then move on to what the carbon footprint definitively measures or *means*. A certain quantitative authority is granted to the carbon footprint when the explanation does not recognize its metaphoricity, but makes claims such as 'Carbon footprint *sums up* the impact of human activities …' (Grant 2008, 4) or 'A carbon footprint *is the amount* of carbon dioxide …' (Yarrow 2008, 6) (emphasis added). The power of the carbon footprint metaphor derives in part from this disappearance of appearance of metaphor. Rather than making a claim to neutralize these powerful effects by re-exposing its metaphoricity, my goal is to re-charge the carbon footprint explicitly as a metaphor and thereby re-assert its power as a shifty mediator in the cultural politics of climate change. Much of the promise of this metaphor relies on novel understandings of metaphors and explicit recognition of what they might offer in these cultural politics by creating openings for unaccounted human and non-human actors to appear.

The carbon footprint metaphor's shifting mediations in these politics reveal a final key function of metaphor, suggested in the work of Susan Petrilli. She offers metaphor, in its constant movement, as an ethical or political opening to 'the other':

> Metaphorization is a movement of perpetual displacement that leads sense outside the sphere of the common place, of plain meaning. The metaphorical dimension of signifying processes evidences that meaning is not something that can be grasped for once and for all, but is a question of opening to the otherness of sense, to the logic that animates it.

(2006, 77)

By shifting from meaning or representation to 'sense', Petrilli highlights the contingency of understandings through language that may be taken as commonplace. Metaphor, from this perspective, reveals sense-making as an on-going dialogic process that features relational encounters and processes that shift through these encounters. Definitive meaning is not grasped, but explicitly deferred through metaphor. As Marshall McLuhan's evocative twist on a line of Robert Browning poetry suggests: 'a man's [sic] reach must exceed his grasp or what's a metaphor?' (1964, 7).[4] *If recognized for their metaphoricity*, carbon footprint metaphors do offer this potential of opening out to otherness in a way that troubles a fixed (and human-centric) account of stable, knowable entities that can be named and managed for once and for all. 'Tropes swerve, they defer the literal, forever, if we are lucky; they make plain that to make sense we must always be ready to trip' (Haraway 2004, 2). I explore the carbon footprint metaphor's promise in its ability to 'trip up' given human, managerial, market-oriented norms through fostering more humble connections with larger-than-human relations and processes. I also supplement this promising angle on metaphors with a critical perspective that attends to the risks of certain agendas in which carbon footprints reinforce the norms of a given order of the world, rather than challenge it by allowing new actors to appear.

To sum up a provisional working definition of metaphor from the contours outlined above: metaphors function pervasively in everyday spaces by yoking together unlikely things in circumstances where existing language fails; they thereby create worlds that may shift in different instances. As new metaphors emerge in a semantic gap, they offer the promise of bringing new entities or sensibilities into view, but because they are 'shifty', and situated within wider discourses as cultural practices, metaphors also carry risks of reinforcing problematic exclusions when they are forgotten as metaphors. These are the features of metaphor's functioning that I have chosen to highlight from extant literature on metaphors because these features relate specifically to carbon footprint metaphors. I wish to further extend the importance of thinking of metaphor in an ecological key as a particularly important intervention at this time of heightened socio-ecological crises.

'Ecological' metaphor

While some theorists of metaphor have formatively centred the importance of *social* context in understanding how metaphors achieve meaning and how metaphors and society recursively shape each other (Chilton 1996; Sontag 1978; 1989), there has been limited explicit work to date on the recursive relations between metaphor and the larger-than-human world.[5] Although there has been no shortage of ecological metaphors circulating in dominant societies in recent decades – 'population bomb' (Ehrlich 1968/1997), 'tragedy of the commons' (Hardin 1968), 'Gaia' (Lovelock 1972), 'silent spring' (Carson 1962), 'Spaceship Earth' (Fuller 1969; Boulding 1966), and 'Earth in the balance' (Gore 1992) to name a few – these have received little scholarly attention *as metaphors,* nor has metaphor attained a place of importance within political ecology. One exception is found in the work of Richard A. Underwood, who explicitly identified metaphor as a site of ecological intervention in 1970 when he stated, 'the ecological crisis is one primarily and fundamentally of metaphor … the resolution of the ecological crisis depends, then, upon the extent to which life-giving metaphors can be restored to our communal life' (1970, 154). While Underwood's imperative may seem simplistic in its quest to 'restore life-giving metaphors' without clear elaboration of what that might mean, he did hint at a crucial agenda for metaphorical interventions and socio-ecological change on a metaphorical level that has rarely been taken up to date.

A second notable exception to the marginalization of metaphor in ecological scholarship is environmental scientist Brendon Larson's *Metaphors for Environmental Sustainability* (2011). In this highly elaborated work, Larson examines a series of what he calls 'feedback metaphors', that is, 'scientific metaphors that harbour social values and circulate back into society to bolster those very values' (22). He examines the feedback metaphors of 'progress', 'competition', 'barcoding', and 'meltdown' in each chapter to demonstrate how each determines both a certain approach to the material-ecological world, and the practices surrounding proposed solutions to environmental crises. For example, in his chapter on barcoding as scientific taxonomizing of species, Larson demonstrates how metaphor, technology (emerging hand-held devices that barcode 'life' in the name of bio-diversity conservation), and material practices converge to reify a consumerist approach to biodiversity where 'the solution to a problem lies in a product' (139). 'Thus the metaphor is not just rhetorical embellishment: instead it drives a particular vision of the world and how it should be. The metaphor is not just language but an encouragement to people to act on the world in a certain way and to develop certain capacities rather than others' (138). The question driving Larson's analysis is 'whether the metaphors we use in environmental science nurture sustainability' (96).

My own approach to metaphors is sympathetic with Larson's perspective on metaphors as potentially 'driving particular visions of the world' and activating certain capacities while deactivating others, but my analysis differs from Larson's in four important ways. First, my focus is mostly on the popular everyday discourses and uses of carbon footprint metaphors as well as some policy-oriented discourses,[6] rather than on their uses specifically in environmental science. Although carbon footprint metaphors are connected to a scientific approach aimed at quantifying emissions, they stray so far from scientific discourses and appear in such a wide array of popular discourses and public contexts (unlike, for example the DNA barcoding metaphor and practice enacted by environmental scientists as identified by Larson[7]) that apprehending them as everyday mediators of natureculture in their origins is necessary.

Second, rather than proposing a group of four feedback metaphors (progress, competition, meltdown, and bar-coding) that shape all the other metaphors that follow, as Larson does, I explore the effects of one metaphor – the carbon footprint – that reveals itself to be a tense family of plural metaphors. This extended treatment allows carbon footprint metaphors themselves in their shifting emergent appearances to lead the directions I take in my analysis. Although I do come to some similar conclusions as Larson about how carbon footprint metaphors often risk securing marketized approaches to the environment, carbon footprint metaphors themselves have surprised me in their shifting accounts of larger-than-human relations and processes that matter (as I describe in Chapter 5). As Lawrence Buell suggests, the non-human environment has often been perceived as a context or a 'framing device' of human activities and artefacts, but '… human artefacts [themselves] … bear traces' of non-human agencies (2005, 25).

Attunement to these traces and active presences requires reading and sensing with metaphors differently, actively seeking out the traces of non-human agency even though (especially because) such traces offer no stable ground. In other words, carbon footprint metaphors reveal that one must be cautious of positing metaphorical feedback loops that can always be reified in human terms, for these may not present the whole story. Importantly, neither does *this* analysis of carbon footprints claim to represent the whole story; rather, it illustrates that when metaphors are recognized as bearing larger-than-human traces, these metaphors expressly reveal a flawed partiality of understanding in attempting to grasp and represent the whole story in dominant human terms. As Donna Haraway reminds, our understandings are always based on 'situated knowledges' that can only ever be partial perspectives (1988). This explicit and sustained understanding of partial perspectives enabled by metaphors thereby opens up to a potentially more inclusive (of human and larger-than-human) worldly politics. Once again, however, one must be attentive to the shiftiness of the carbon footprint figure whose allegiance does not lie singularly within such inclusionary projects.

Such shiftiness leads to the third point of divergence from Larson's work. The title of his book, *Metaphors* for *Environmental Sustainability* (emphasis added) asserts an agenda for finding the 'right' metaphors. This tendency is echoed in geographer Paul Robbins' very brief treatment of metaphor, entitled 'Choosing Metaphors for the Anthropocene' (2013). Robbins swiftly moves through a number of nature/culture theories built on metaphors including 'adaptation', 'systems', 'networks', and 'epidemics' and suggests that 'each such metaphor is a cultural expression and a necessary simplification that allows certain kinds of insights into how people interact with the world around them' (2013, 316). While crucially important in drawing attention to metaphor's material implications, such perspectives on metaphors tend to treat them as a set of singular entities from which we can choose the right ones to properly orient human actions. My extended treatment of carbon footprint metaphors suggests that their very metaphoricity allows them to shift in different contexts for a variety of agendas such that one cannot render a verdict in all cases as to whether *the* carbon footprint metaphor is *for* or *against* 'sustainability' (a notion that, in itself, is notoriously metaphorically shifty). Metaphors are as ecologically responsive as their specific practices, and attachments, permit. As this story of carbon footprints illustrates, in a world as diverse and complex as this, with multiple cultures, discourses, and ecological actors, it is not simply a singular instrumentally conceived metaphor itself that does this work; rather it is through the lively, shifting interactions and associations that are carried over by ecological metaphor in different contexts that political and material effects take hold. These practices and orientations enabled through specific carbon footprint metaphors in specific contexts are the focus of my attention in this book.

While I am aware that ecology itself is a contested and evolving term that may be used metaphorically to describe relations in corporations, organizations, and networks of all kinds, I am using the notion *ecological metaphor* to highlight the kind of metaphor that explicitly orients thoughts, feelings, attachments, and actions vis-à-vis the living world conceived not solely in human terms.[8] This is to again insist that while the way 'we' come to know and express the world is certainly mediated by human language, non-human actors exert influence on the need for linguistic and metaphoric innovation and intervention in cultural and material contexts. The emergence of ecological metaphors (and the ways in which these shift after their initial emergence) is related to historical and material-ecological conditions that demand novel accounts. It is in the form of precipitating semantic gaps that non-human actors or forces might appear in human discourse. How these actors appear in language is subject to cultural conditioning, but I would like to suggest that humans might not be the sole authors of metaphor if one concedes that metaphors also arise out of ecological conditions; thus metaphors might be thought of as both culturally *and ecologically* conditioned. In fact, my purpose for using this term is to explicitly highlight that *ecological* metaphors are utterly emblematic of entangled relations of 'nature' and 'culture' in this epoch of heightened crises. The ecological metaphor 'invasive species,' for example, no doubt carries over a socially-constructed human military logic that bears scrutiny (Larson 2011). Its emergence, however, signals an ecological interaction that both exceeds the human by suggesting a certain intrusion into an order (or perception of order) and paradoxically, centrally implicates the human (colonial) author of this problem as one who introduces new species into geoclimatic regions where these 'invasive' species spread at the expense of 'native' species (another metaphor). It is certainly imperative, as Larson insists, to debate whether the invasive species metaphor and its associated xenophobic practices of 'advocating with fear' are the appropriate responses to this phenomenon (2011, 161);[9] however, the point that any ecological metaphor emerges at all (however faulty and subject to critique) to figure this process reveals an active presence of non-humans as an impingement upon given human accounts. Ecological metaphors like the carbon footprint, similarly introduce a host of interacting entities, both human and non-human, that require novel accounts at this historical juncture. These metaphors are not deterministic representational accounts of 'objective nature' and thus, they bear scrutiny, but as my analysis demonstrates, neither can they be said to be entirely human constructs, which makes them unique mediators of entangled larger-than-human relations.

My final point of divergence from Brendon Larson's *Metaphors for Environmental Sustainability* is one of terminology. While Larson uses the term 'environmental metaphors', I choose the term ecological metaphor for three reasons. First, ecology is potentially available to implicate humans *within* the term than is environment, which at times suggests 'setting' or backdrop to human activity. As Timothy Morton suggests: 'The very word *environmentalism* is evidence of wishful thinking ... a case of some "thing" that surrounds us, that environs us and differs from us' (2007, 141). Second, and relatedly, ecology seems to resonate with a certain 'aliveness' and relationality between species in a way that environment does not, as environment is often conceived as a kind of inert, stable space. Third, and most crucially, in keeping with the analysis that follows, the term ecology itself implicitly connotes a space for making visible certain actors who have not yet been accounted for, but who are relationally important. A given ecology as a network of humanly recognizable relations may, at times, be 'policed' by ecologists or land managers who attempt to define its contours as ecological communities, bioregions, or even conservation/national parks. These practices, however well-intentioned, seem always ambivalently marked by particular lively relations and emergent properties that do not follow such managerial logics. While these managerial practices of ecology bear scrutiny, I contend that the notion of ecology has the potential to focus attention on 'the part that has no part' (Rancière) in an anticipation of actors that exceed the givens of a particular (human) understanding of an ecological system at any point in time.[10]

Ecological metaphors – those that bear traces of non-humans and that consequentially orient, dis-orient and re-orient thoughts, feelings, attachments, and actions vis-à-vis the larger-than-human world – particularly bear scrutiny for their worldly effects. Given the unprecedented pace of ecological change at the turn of the millennium,[11] metaphors that trace naturalcultural relations must be recognized as crucial figures. As a particularly potent and timely ecological metaphor, the carbon footprint metaphor makes certain relations visible and outlines contours through which to think, feel, and act in relation to the politics of climate change; thus, it is intimately bound up with an aesthetics of worldly politics. The associative work of metaphor carries over effects that are not only poetic and semantic, but also political and biospherical. Metaphors do this work, I argue, through affective means.

Metaphor and affect

Theories of metaphor and theories of affect that explicitly engage with political questions share many traits, not least of which are how they insist that each – metaphor and affect – function politically through 1) binding entities/bodies together in contingent linkages and 2) movement. From the perspective of metaphor studies, acknowledging that both 'carbon' and 'footprint' carry histories of cultural meaning and exert their own metaphorical force suggests that the compound metaphor is caught up within metaphorical relations that bind to create resemblances or yoke together distinct entities with profoundly political effects. As the cultural case studies that follow suggest, the meanings shift as carbon footprint metaphors turn toward or bind with different entities. Different worlds may come into visibility through each of this metaphor's diverse iterations. For metaphor studies scholar, Dennis Sobolev, 'the question is not whether the terms of a given metaphor are similar (they are in one sense or the other), but whether this similarity plays a central role in the production of meaning' (2008, 909). This creation of resemblance then, is key to metaphor; however, paradoxically, the relationship is dependent upon dissonance and contradiction. The fact that metaphors are generally not easily paraphraseable suggests that they initiate a relationship between entities that are in some kind of contradictory relationship. As Paul Ricouer suggests, 'the interplay of resemblance ... consists in the initiation of a *proximity* between formerly 'remote' meanings' (1977, 230). This is the process whereby 'carbon' (as a stand-in for all greenhouse gases) comes to be seen as having a 'footprint' despite the initial dissonance generated by bringing these two entities together.

Generating proximities between meanings is not just a matter of semantics as a representational act, but an act of political world-creation. This is the site of what William Franke calls the 'uncanny onto-linguistic power' of metaphor (2000, 143). Metaphors help bring worlds into being through fostering attachments and creating/reinforcing cartographies of what is visible. As Paul Chilton elaborates, security metaphors circulating around the time of the 'Cold War' did more than just name or represent an existing geopolitical situation. Discursive analysis of key policy and public texts reveals that these metaphors helped to draw the maps of the visible geopolitical world as a 'house divided,' thereby both playing into material realities of the tensions between Western Bloc and Eastern Bloc countries, and also significantly shaping these tensions (1996). Similarly, carbon footprint metaphors not only describe/ represent the climate change impacts as their definitions suggest, but they also function to shape how to view these impacts in the world and, crucially, what to do about them in diverse and complex ways. This force is called an 'onto-linguistic power' in Franke's words because it involves not only reinforcing existing worlds, but creating new ones. Metaphor encompasses a:

> dynamic capability of bringing absolutely new possibilities of significance – and even the possibility of sense itself – into existence. The metaphorical significances thus created would be not just variations on literal significances but absolute metaphorical creations of significance that set teetering all previously established, presumably stable, literal meanings and even beings.
>
> (Franke 2000, 144)

Franke's formulation is suggestive of an understanding of metaphor not as a signifying power, but as an 'affective' one that isn't necessarily attached to, or instrumentally wielded exclusively by human subjects. Extended to the cultural politics of climate change, this power is evocative: might not metaphors that attempt to account for ecological relations vis-à-vis carbon offer the potential to 'set teetering' the stability of representational accounts that feature in these politics? Might they shift understandings of who appears in these politics in terms of differentially conceived human actors and, if we acknowledge their metaphorical force, might these metaphors even shift the terms of 'beings' that count in these politics beyond the exclusively 'human'? The affective mediations of carbon footprint metaphors would suggest that we keep attuned to this promise, even as we critically examine the attendant risks of these metaphors in their reification of both geopolitically asymmetrical human relations and human-centric fossil fuel-dependent systems. If metaphor, like affect, as I describe it below, bears a 'thoroughly immanent neutrality' (Seigworth and Gregg 2010, 10), such neutrality does not render metaphor politically neutral. Understanding this metaphor as an affective mediator entails a 'generative pedagogic nudge aimed at a body's becoming an ever more worldly sensitive interface, toward a style of being present to the struggles of our time' (Seigworth and Gregg 2010, 12).

Given the abstract nature of climate change as something that is both everywhere and nowhere, a serious consideration of the carbon footprint's mediating role appropriately attends to *affect* as a field of forces and relations that connect bodies in larger-than-human worlds. 'Climate change appears to detach knowledge from meaning, distancing received scientific facts from the thick textures of lived experience' (Bristow and Ford 2016, 6). Mediators of affect that tentatively and contingently connect this abstraction to lived experience are crucial in this context. Recent political theories of affect have been decisive in establishing affect not as feminized emotion that resides in a human subject and that is gendered in opposition to rational cognition, but as a moving force or set of forces and relations that draw bodies together or away from each other (Ahmed 2004; Bennett 2010; Gregg and Seigworth 2010; Massumi 1995; 2002). Affect therefore does not properly belong to or reside in any particular subject/body but rather moves through relational encounters and 'shape[s] the very surfaces of bodies' (individual and collective) that appear in politics (Ahmed 2004, 4). In this respect, affect theory is not occupied with determining what a body is (ontology), but rather how bodies surface, and how they affect and are affected by other bodies. This line of thinking comes from Spinoza's formative and oft-quoted line 'No one has yet determined what the body can do' (1959, 87). How bodies and collectivities – both human and non-human – are drawn together and affect each other through capacities to act is a profoundly political aspect of climate change. In my analysis, I show that by drawing certain bodies together and alienating other bodies, the carbon footprint metaphor plays a central role in this politics of affect.

While theories about metaphor and theories about affect overlap in many respects, some distinctions must be made in order to understand how affect theory contributes to my analysis of metaphors as mediators of affect. My approach to affect, following a combination of affect theorists in the 'vitalist' tradition (Bennett 2010; Massumi 2002) and those in the tradition of analyzing affective relations in texts and discourse (Ahmed 2004; Ngai 2005; Woodward 2009), is to insist that a politics of affect might encompass, but not be reducible to, emotion or something captured in discourse. Understanding the complex mediations of carbon footprint metaphors entails attention to both linguistically (metaphorically) rendered human subject-centric affects/feelings (like guilt) and to those affects, still metaphorically mediated, that are less capable of being pinned to definitive personalized and human subject-centred circuits (like 'carbon vitality' as I elaborate in Chapter 5). The reduction of affect to an exclusively human-subject-centred emotion (like guilt) signals one of the risks of the carbon footprint, for as I describe in my analysis, the politics that ensue are shaped by certain problematic liberal human subject-centred concerns. Whereas when the metaphor functions as an opening or threshold onto affect in the vitalist or Spinozian sense, it is arguably most politically promising in its capacity to figure larger-than-human relations that orient responses. From this branch of affect theory, Brian Massumi suggests that affect gestures at a *'connecting thread of experience'* that runs prior to, throughout, and after the 'sociolinguistic fixing of quality or experience which is from that point onward defined as personal' (Massumi 1995, 88). Whereas emotions are captured linguistically and may follow conventional 'narrativizable action-reaction circuits', affect is something less deterministic for Massumi (2002, 28). I concur with Massumi on the need to understand affect as encompassing more than emotion as it is captured in language, especially in the cultural politics of climate change where human language (and also emotion) must always be read as partial in its re-presentations of larger-than-human worlds. Affect, formulated as 'intensities' in this Spinozist tradition, is considered a vital force that exceeds human subjects and is immanent to *every* body, including the non-human.

The role of what may be called 'weather' as a political force of relations and processes is one example of a politics of affect that is not easily rendered in language. The force of 'weather' or 'meteorological events' in cultural politics of climate change is difficult to capture because weather is not directly correlatable to climate change, and so to even begin to talk about this relationship requires a difficult discursive dance between a scientific logic of knowable causation along with the principle of uncertainty symptomatic of the abstraction of climate change as statistic. This dance is situated within a cultural politics of climate change that seems to demand indisputable scientific proof 'translated' into public discourse in order to justify making the significant socio-ecological transitions that are called for. Rendering these paradoxes linguistically seems an impossible task; and yet, as those who are savvy to cultural politics of climate change will attest, 'weather' does exert a profound force or intensity within the politics of climate change. (Boykoff 2011; Hulme 2009; Weaver 2008).[12] This is but one example of the many important larger-than-human sets of force relations that get short shrift in the politics of climate change. While humans as situated actors with partial perspectives cannot account for, or count on specific, knowable trajectories of such larger-than-human force relations, we can orient ourselves to anticipate and make room for these relations to appear. Indeed, place-based Indigenous knowledge systems build such sophisticated orientation into the fabric of relational living through foundational principles such as 'all our relations', which always connect larger-than-human kin (LaDuke 1999). While Anglo-American colonial systems of representation tend to reify the human/non-human binary to the detriment of socio-ecological health, ecological metaphors can offer potent sites through which to entertain larger-than-human presence. This is one key example of the importance of bringing a politics of affect into conversation with climate change, which pushes on the limits of what have been understood as human systems, including the system of 'representational' language.

With Woodward, however, I do not dismiss the importance of linguistically rendered feelings or emotions as potential sites of analysis since as she states, 'we live in a mixed economy of feelings, one characterized by both the psychological emotions and intensities, and my point is that they often stand in a dialectical relationship to each other, with the narrative of our experience a crucial capacity' (Woodward 2009, 25).[13] These two positions on affect, expressed by Woodward and Massumi, inform two aspects of my hybrid reading of affect. First, with Woodward, Sarah Ahmed, Sianne Ngai, and others who follow a discursive approach to understanding affect, I contend that narratives of experience, which are inescapably linguistically rendered,[14] do offer crucial insights in understanding a politics of affect. Many political affects are undeniably created and mediated within and through language. Sarah Ahmed illustrates how affect pulls the bodies of 'white' subjects together into British nationhood and away from immigrant/refugee 'outsiders' who are seen as making injurious claims upon the nation for support; understanding these politics of affect entails attending to discursive circuits of 'hate' that appear in the media, and in other public texts (2004). Ahmed considers 'the role of hate in shaping bodies and works through the way hate generates its object as a defence against injury' (42). Ahmed's work also informs my method of understanding texts as affective 'contact zones' for critical analysis as described below.

In order to understand the affective work of carbon footprint metaphors, I explore how critically understanding certain socio-linguistically captured feelings such as individual subject-centred 'carbon guilt' allows for the narration of the appearance of certain bodies and worlds and the disappearance of others. Such an analysis brings into visibility this metaphor's complicity in bringing fraught solutions to climate change that rely on a reduced or captured interpretation of the issue and reproduce a liberal order of environmentalism, which leaves intact global asymmetries and fossil fuel intensive systems. In Chapter 4, I explore what I call 'carbon fellowship' to trace citizen-oriented feelings affectively mobilized through carbon footprint metaphors; while in some instances such affects draw together and make visible differentially responsible and impacted human bodies, other examples of this fellowship brought about through carbon footprint metaphors connect nation-bound citizens into affective relations and processes that both distance global others, and insist that support for carbon-intensive resource extraction is a key condition of being a 'good' citizen.

The second aspect of my interpretation of affect aligns more closely with the vitalist branch of affect theory, which centrally recognizes the limits of discursively rendered affects as outlined above in the words of Massumi. Affect, he suggests, can be something less determinate than what can be captured in language. Thus, attending to affect might entail what Jane Bennett describes as the impossible task of 'giv[ing] voice to a vitality intrinsic to materiality' (2010, 30). Tracing such a vitality of ecological materiality is especially essential for understanding relations in the politics of climate change, which inescapably and centrally entails larger-than-human circuits (as opposed to the *human* social circuits of hate that Sarah Ahmed traces). Paradoxically then, I make sense of these vital connections and processes through language (as do affect theorists), but through an explicitly metaphorical language that suspends the representational logic and mastery of human representation. Gesturing toward 'pre-personal intensities' (Deleuze and Guattari 1987) or circuits of associations and moving processes is an especially necessary move in attending to larger-than-human relations that exert force in the matter of climate change. I elaborate on the possibilities of the affective force of what I call 'carbon vitality' (Chapter 5), following Bennett and William Connolly on vitality as a necessary antidote to human-centric rationality and instrumentalism (Bennett 2010; Connolly 2013). This metaphorically-rendered affect is only partially captured, but remains deliberately fuzzy as a notion in order to account for moving relations and processes.

Affect does not entail the 'generic figuring of "the body" (*any* body) but, much more singularly, endeavoring to configure *a* body and its affects/affectedness, its ongoing affectual composition of a world, the *this-ness* of a world and a body' (Seigworth and Gregg 2010, 3). Rather than generically configuring *the* carbon footprint metaphor, I am interested in teasing out certain specific affective relations brought into political visibility through diverse instances of carbon footprint metaphors in their worldly compositions.

To bring metaphor and affect into conversation is to begin by understanding paradoxically, that affect is involved in language, but it is also constrained by language because language involves a (contingent) closure to create meaning and to represent, while affect encompasses more than what can be captured by language. Metaphor, as a linguistic entity that has only a tenuous claim on representation (*if* it is recognized as metaphor), keeps this place of contingency even more open, and thus, might be thought of as more susceptible to affective forces and movements. To return to the words of William Franke, the force of metaphor offers the potential to 'set teetering all previously established, presumably stable, literal meanings and even *beings*' (2000, 144) (emphasis added). This teetering away from stable meanings and beings enables metaphor to make visible larger-than-human circuits of being. A 'connecting thread of experience' that has yet been unuttered or sensed may thereby be carried over by metaphor as metaphor plays a 'key role in expressing what exceeds conceptualization altogether' (ibid., 147). While the carbon footprint metaphor in many contexts tends toward a literal meaning/interpretation, as a metaphor it remains affectively charged by the excesses that continue to escape its conceptualization or literalization. This metaphor moves toward the edges of existing articulations of the world and beyond the actor-beings that are already represented in its calculus. This creative power of metaphor draws these connecting threads into a politics of affect. Metaphor, then, as an entity that suspends the referential function of language (Ricouer 1975, 224–225), has a special role to play in the affective politics of climate change.

As metaphors are tropes that turn, analysis requires attending to the particularities of each textual instance of the carbon footprint metaphor rather than asserting their definitive function. This is not to suggest, however, that this metaphor and metaphors in general are free-floating signifiers; their *onto-linguistic power* comes into play with past histories of association that shape the possible worlds they can make. In what follows, I draw attention to certain tendencies and 'naturalized' associations that cut across many instances of the carbon footprint. Again keeping in mind that affect plays to no particular agenda, but 'bears an intense and thoroughly immanent neutrality' (ibid., 10), it is important to trace the affects of these particular instances of carbon footprint metaphors that offer both promises and risks (with both promises and risks often emerging from the same instance or text as it moves and shifts to connect to different worlds). Carbon footprint metaphors act in part through this interplay of: semiotic capture of effects and affects by connecting footprints of specific bodies (be they individual, national, human, non-human) to a planetary carbon calculus that is associated with other bodies (for instance, carbon markets, but crucially, not only these); and the movement beyond such affects toward other bodies not yet accounted for.

Openings as promises; dominant norms as risks

I return to Rancière's politics of aesthetics in order to tease out the promises and risks of what is mapped out through varying carbon footprints. Who comes to appear as an active political actor through carbon footprint metaphors, evokes what Rancière signifies as 'la partition du sensible' (the distribution of the sensible) (2004).[15] This framework describes 'the system of self-evident facts of sense perception that simultaneously discloses the existence of something in common and the delimitations that define the respective parts and positions within it' (2004, 12). The 'something in common' that is described by this distribution is nothing less than a particular world order that prescribes the actors, roles, ways of acting, and the relations between these.

Rancière's critical illustration of the distribution of the sensible begins with Aristotle's notion of the speaking citizen who takes part in politics. 'Aristotle states that a citizen is someone who has a part in the act of governing and being governed. However, another form of distribution precedes this act of partaking in government: the distribution that determines those who have a part in the community of citizens' (2004, 12). For Rancière, although Aristotle's elaboration of all citizens' rights to participate in governance seems an inclusionary principle enabling democratic engagement, a prior partitioning out of the voiceless ('slaves', women, artists, etc.) that undergirds the notion of citizen consequentially limits public engagement. Rancière's gestures reveal that even in those institutions that claim to be democratic, certain dispositions are already written into these institutions (who can participate and how) such that exclusions are made. In other words, this system provides a kind of 'map' or shared way of seeing the world or a particular part of it. The notion of 'partition' also signals interplay between the normative system as it paradoxically *permits* the participation of those who register within it by being heard or seen within this system, just as it *bars* from participation those who do not register:

This partition should be understood in the double sense of the word: on the one hand, as that which separates and excludes; on the other, as that which allows participation. A partition of the sensible refers to the manner in which a shared common (*un commun partagé*) and the distribution of part and shares (*parties*), itself presupposes a distribution of what is visible and what not, of what can be heard and what cannot.

(Rancière 2010, 36)

The partition of the sensible is alternately translated from French into English as either 'partition of the sensible' or 'distribution of the sensible' since the notion of partition in French connotes both: 'partition' as a walling off or separation, *and* 'distribution' in the sense of sharing out (partager) or distributing among participants. For the sake of consistency and because of its possible resonances with distributed networks of sentience/affect that are larger-than-human, I favour the use of 'distribution of the sensible' to signal this political relation; however, I linger on the above quotation momentarily to tease out what might get lost in translation with the loss of the notion of partition. The *partition* of the sensible as outlined in the above translation both functions to exclude and provides the terms of political engagement. A partition is no doubt meant to exclude, but it is premised upon the notion of introducing an artificial barrier that did not exist; partition in this phrase signals that something has already been constructed or composed, and thus, that it may be subject to forces that un-do/re-work it. In other words, as Rancière notes, a partition requires boundary control that is bound to be thwarted from time to time because its very existence suggests forces that exceed it, forces that cannot be contained. 'The whole democratic process is about the displacement of that boundary' (2010, 58). Thus paradoxically, the existing partition of the sensible sets up the conditions for its own displacement. This movement toward a not-yet (not ever completely) achieved inclusion of all is 'politics' for Rancière. '*Politics* means the supplementation of all qualifications by the power of the unqualified' (ibid., 58). I extend the notion of the supplemental power further below as I position the carbon footprint metaphor within this interplay of closing off of, and opening up to, supplemental political-ecological actors that exceed the given account of carbon footprints.

There is a limit to the metaphor of a walled-off partition when extended into too 'literal' an interpretation of a wall in English because it forecloses upon the other important aspects of 'la partition'/distribution as in 'sharing out'; this second aspect of Rancière's notion is equally important. In order to get a share of something, to participate in the distribution, a participant must *appear* and this involves what Rancière suggests is an 'aesthetics at the core of politics that has nothing to do with … the perverse commandeering of politics by a will to art, by consideration of the people qua work of art' (2004, 13). Rather aesthetics for Rancière is 'the system of *a priori* forms determining what presents itself to sense experience' (ibid.) What or who appears as present to sense experience in this system is not based on 'self-evident facts', but a world-making aesthetics; Rancière thereby returns the element of 'construction of common objects' that is at play in politics (2009, 72). In other words, a normative distribution of the sensible involves a kind of authoritative *putting into place* of qualified actors attributed with certain roles. These givens and proper roles, taken as shared ways of seeing or sensing the world, establish a normative distribution of the sensible with built-in exclusions. Such exclusions are, in fact, composed aesthetically by 'delimiting the sphere of the political … shrinking the political stage' and through 'a "purification" of politics' that results in the 'eviction' of those deemed inadmissible (2010, 54). For Rancière, however, politics cannot ultimately be so neatly purified because the active presence of those excluded inevitably challenges and displaces the boundaries drawn.

Carbon footprint metaphors are integrally woven into these political relations of foreclosures and openings described by Rancière as they:

> can be implemented in opposite ways depending on the sense of the 'common' in which they are framed. They can circumscribe the sphere of the political and restrict political agency to an activity performed by definite agents endowed with the appropriate qualification; or they can give way to forms of interpretation and practice that are democratic, which invent new political places, issues and agents from the very same texts.
>
> (Rancière 2010, 54)

The movement of carbon footprint metaphors sets in motion 'another setting of the stage, producing different relations between words, the kinds of thing that they designate and the kinds of practices they empower' (ibid., 54). In Chapter 3, for example, I analyze carbon footprint reduction lists as mechanisms through which 'carbon subjects' (largely Western privileged humanist individuals) are hailed into specific modes of action within the cultural politics of climate change. While this call to certain subjects through the carbon footprint metaphor offers the promise of having these subjects *appear* to take responsibility for their disproportionate role in contributing to climate change, the call also in part reinforces problematic norms in which individualist and consumer-based solutions to climate change prevail. This normative distribution of the sensible prescribes roles and relationships for certain actors who have carbon footprints, but leaves many other actions and, crucially, other human and non-human actors out of the (ac)count.

For Rancière, this existing normative distribution of the sensible does not shut down politics, which is an inherently disruptive process; a supplementary power (in his problematic terms, 'power of the people') in excess of the normative distribution always comes to challenge the givens. Politics then, hinges on a form of perpetual democratic movement that incites iterative emergence of 'the part of those who have no part' (2010, 70). Rancière suggests that the essence of politics is 'an infinite openness to that which comes – which also means, an infinite openness to the other or the newcomer' (2010, 59). As carbon footprint metaphors are involved in the inherently disruptive processes of politics and ecologies through which previously unaccounted actors appear, certain carbon footprint metaphors can be seen as enacting novel distributions of the sensible or *re-distributing the sensible* such that 'newcomers' appear. With the help of Rancière's thought, I theorize a means of accounting for the ways in which carbon footprint metaphors become yoked to certain practices and mechanisms in the cultural politics of climate change and the ways in which they also potentially disturb these practices through new attachments. That is to say that these metaphors are involved in both processes of reifying norms and processes of un-doing these very norms as new actors emerge to challenge the givens of the metaphor as it is understood.

Using Rancière's thought in this way, however, is not without its complications. Indeed, ecological metaphors animate Rancière's distribution of the sensible in particular ways that expose the limits of his own humanist assumptions within a notion that never reaches beyond the human at the centre of his elaboration of politics. Reading Rancière within and against himself entails understanding the ways in which he exerts his own form of boundary control by 'delimiting the sphere of the political' (2010, 54) to the human species – the *power of the people*. Nonetheless, his thought remains ripe for opening up his own boundaries (with the help of Jane Bennett below). My claim is that carbon footprint metaphors act in this way as (co-)constituted elements of cultural politics of climate change. These metaphors risk delimiting the sphere of politics to specifically fraught human systems and agents who already 'qualify', thereby foreclosing upon political participation; however, as my analysis highlights, these same metaphors (though in different contexts with different co-constituents) also offer the promise of new interpretations, agents, and politics.

I am re-contextualizing *ecological* actors that emerge through carbon footprint metaphors within a Rancièrian play of emerging political actors via Jane Bennett who insists on an explicit place for non-human actors against what Bennett calls Rancière's own 'prejudice':[16]

> Though Rancière objects to the "Platonic" prejudice against the demos, which positions commoners as defective versions of men in possession of logos, to imagine politics as a realm of human activity alone may also be a kind of prejudice: a prejudice against a (nonhuman) multitude misrecognized as context, constraint or tool.
>
> (Bennett 2010, 108)

Nonetheless, Bennett insists that Rancière's own theory of how politics entails disturbance from forces that are 'irreducible to the particular bodies' that fall within the existing order, 'invokes flow through nonhuman bodies' (108). 'Rancière implicitly raises this question: Is the power to disrupt really limited to human speakers?' (108). Jane Bennett's quest to sense the politics of a 'vital materiality' in the world thus entails taking Rancière seriously beyond his own limits.

My own *mise-en-scène,* however, insists (beyond Bennett) on the role of (carbon footprint) metaphors as potential parts in this process of iteratively adding actors who come to challenge a given order in a collective. While Bennett does insist on elaborating a role for larger-than-human actors that emerge to challenge a given political order, she does not permit an explicit role for metaphors or aesthetics in her accounts as does Rancière. Therefore, my cross-pollination of Rancière and Bennett permits each to supplement the other as a way of making room for both aesthetics and larger-than-human affects as necessary in my approach to unpacking the promises and risks of carbon footprint metaphors in the cultural politics of climate change. If Rancière's theorization is meant to insist upon the aesthetic order at the heart of all politics, it also simultaneously addresses and re-connects the fundamental split dividing aesthetics and politics that began with Plato and Aristotle and still today effects a partitioning of what is thought proper to aesthetics and politics, seen as independent spheres. This rift parallels the way in which Aristotle, in his trademark taxonomic logic, launched a legacy of *putting metaphor in its place* by presenting a certain regime of intelligibility or a normative distribution of the sensible that metaphor has always exceeded.[17] Since Aristotle's definitions of metaphor in *Rhetorics* and *Poetics*, metaphor has conventionally been cast within political thought as literary frill, or at worse, in the political philosophy of Thomas Hobbes (whose own theorizations of the *leviathan* and the *body politic* are unabashedly metaphorical), an 'absurdity' or 'danger' to be avoided at all costs (1651/1891). The tendency has been for *The Poetics* to have informed an evolving field of literary studies, and *The Rhetorics* to have been marginalized within the study of politics and philosophy. This conventionalized dismissal of a political place for aesthetics is the way through which metaphors, such as the carbon footprint *appear to disappear.*[18] To attempt to banish metaphor from language because it is unfaithful to hubristic human attempts to properly represent, is to pretend human mastery of the world is possible.

The events and processes taking place during this turning of millennia surely invite responses that temper notions of human mastery and faithful representation. Poets thinking along a nature-culture axis offer a key intervention in this regard. As poet, Don McKay, suggests, 'one metaphor for the excitement of metaphors is to say that they are entry points where wilderness[19] re-invades language, the place where words put their authority at risk, implicitly confessing their inadequacy to the task of representing the world' (McKay 2002, 71). Although the notion of 'wilderness' is problematic – as a metaphor that gestures toward an impossible 'outside' of human involvement and one that consequentially enacts colonial dispossession (Cronon 1996) – McKay's gesture remains an important one. Metaphor denies the quest for mastery within human representational systems through putting at risk the authority of words. There exists a charged force to metaphor, what McKay calls the 'energy' associated with the 'sheer muscle required to speak a lie in the interests of truth, and leap between two distant regions of experience' (61). To put words' authority at risk therefore means enabling a certain opening, a constant questioning stance vis-à-vis human apprehension: *Can 'we' call 'It' (x) that (y), and if so, what 'truths' or realities are 'we' creating through the lies of yoking together unlikely entities? Further, once a metaphor emerges, how does it shift and what associations does it carry with it?* These are profoundly political questions that reveal the constant work of creating worlds that a politics of aesthetics brings to visibility. At a time when climate change paradoxically both points to the folly of human mastery *and* offers new opportunities to enact hubristic solutions, returning the shifting and disrupting force of metaphor is crucial. This study locates metaphor explicitly within a tension-ridden affective form of politics by other means.

Texts as contingent 'contact zones'

In order to attend to the political struggles and particularities of diverse carbon footprint metaphors in what follows, I analyse a variety of public texts that offer contexts in which to contingently ground these footprints. 'Metaphors have no context-free, constant, core meaning that could then be applied differently in different contexts. Their meanings are completely context dependent and, in effect, context-created' (Franke 2000, 146). As I have been teasing out, the contexts in which carbon footprint metaphors emerge are not limited to textual relations with other texts, but are shaped by these wider political contexts and norms that might include 'past histories' (Ahmed 2004, 13) and larger-than-human impingements upon the attempt at stable meanings within these metaphors.

To tease out affective mediations using linguistically rendered texts might seem a contradiction, given the 'vitalist' imperative to attend to affects that are pre-discursive; importantly, however, even vitalist theories of affect theorize *through language* as an inescapable conundrum. Notably, such theorists think at the limits of language and use metaphorical language that defies easy representation.[20] When I tease out associations among 'carbon footprints' and other novel carbon compounds such as 'carbon subjectivity', 'carbon citizenship', and, especially, 'carbon vitality', in what follows, I am foundationally situating these *as metaphors* that bring into visibility key struggles in the cultural politics of climate change. Like Sarah Ahmed (2004), Kathleen Woodward (2009) and others who analyze texts to elaborate a politics of affect, I do not claim that affect is *in* the texts that make up my case studies (just as affect is not resident in human subjects); rather I consider these texts to be 'contact zones' (Ahmed 2004, 14) that draw together particular actors, histories, norms, disruptions, and movements. As contact zones, texts reveal that affective associations are performative since these texts 'involve speech acts which depend on past histories, at the same time as they generate effects' (ibid., 13). Ahmed suggests contact as a way of understanding how 'the public and the personal, the individual and that social … take shape through each other, or even how they shape each other' (14). Textual contact zones reveal this active shaping of individual bodies and collectivities.

In what follows, I attend to the generation of bodies – individual, collective, human, and non-human – with/through 'carbon footprints'. As Ahmed insists, figures of speech such as metaphors are crucial in the generation of effects in these contact zones because they leave traces of 'how different "figures" get stuck together, and how sticking is dependent on past histories of association that often "work" through concealment' (ibid.).[21] Metaphors may thus smuggle in problematic normative associations when they disappear as metaphors. Although Ahmed's project remains tethered to a *human* circulation of affects, she hints at an embodied materiality that is alive through texts: 'words are not simply cut off from bodies, or other signs of life' (13). As such, *words*, have a profoundly material relation to *worlds* and their ecologies. Each impinges upon the other; just as words shape worlds, so do worlds (in all their lively contingency and specificity) shape words in often unanticipated ways.

Although this metaphor traffics among familiar themes and associations it also, as I have begun to elaborate, generates new previously un-figured associations. Thus, in attending to the affects circulating within and through carbon footprint metaphors, it is important to allow for an as-yet unfolding history at a time of climate change, one which is not yet over-written by an all-encompassing and definitive logic (i.e. either an all-encompassing logic of global capital or its similarly all-encompassing critiques). Based on Spinoza's refrain, 'No one has yet determined what a body can do' (1959, 87), affect theories keep this notion of not-yetness of bodies and networks in play. Bodies are not ontologically sealed immutable beings; they only come to be sensed through relational encounters and processes that result in new bodies or 'assemblages', themselves subject to shifting relations and processes (Deleuze and Guattari 1987). Neither is *the* carbon footprint metaphor definitively sealed as a device that tracks pre-scribed bodily imprints of pre-scribed bodies; rather, as the textual contact zones that I analyze reveal, this footprint metaphor attaches to and traces shifting bodies. I wish to explore the radical implications of: *no one has yet determined what a carbon footprint can do*.

Notes

1   Since Aristotle's definition, the notion of resemblance has been key to understanding metaphor. Although metaphor scholars in the mid-twentieth century attempted to steer away from the notion of resemblance, noting that the metaphor often *creates* a similarity that does not exist prior to the creative act this relationship of (created) resemblance is nonetheless part of how metaphors obtain significance. The notion of resemblance need not imply object-to-object similarities within the terms of metaphor, but rather similarities between *relations* to other objects. For Sobolev, 'the question is not whether the terms of metaphor are similar (they are in one sense or the other), but whether this similarity plays a central role in the production of meaning' (2008, 909). This (creation of) resemblance then, is key to metaphor; however, paradoxically, this relationship is dependent upon dissonance and contradiction. The fact that metaphors are generally not easily paraphraseable, suggests that metaphors initiate a relationship between entities that are in some kind of contradictory relationship. As Ricouer suggests, 'the interplay of resemblance ... consists in the initiation of a *proximity* between formerly 'remote' meanings' (1977, 230). The workings of metaphor thus initiate a disturbance and call for a contingent or partial resolution of this disturbance through the yoking together of sometimes unlikely things.

   This work of yoking together should be not be interpreted as a definitive enclosure around a given metaphor, for metaphors often obtain significance through a degree of openness. This claim productively tempers an overly deterministic account of metaphors in general as a certain structure, and it will also productively temper the potential pitfalls of attempting to read the carbon footprint metaphor as an expression of a singular orientation toward climate change.

2   Thomas Hobbes' scorn for metaphors for example is evident in the following passage from *Leviathan* (itself ironically, an extended metaphor): 'And whereas all bodies enter into account upon divers consideration, these considerations being diversely named, divers absurdities proceed from the confusion, and unfit connexion of their names into assertions ... the sixth [cause of absurd assertions is] the use of Metaphor, Tropes, and other Rhetoricall figures, in stead of words proper. For though it be lawfull to say, (for example) in common speech, *the way goeth, or leader hither, or thither, The Proverb says this or that* (whereas wayes cannot go, nor Proverbs speak;) yet in reckoning and seeking of truth, such speeches are not to be admitted' (Hobbes 1981, 114–115).

3   When one thinks of computational 'networks', for example, one cannot help but mobilize a number of metaphors that are entanglements of computational and 'natural' worlds as they interact: 'digital environments'; 'distributed intelligence'; 'smart metres'; 'World Wide Web.' Even on the mundane level of everyday responses to the question, 'How are you?,' one can respond metaphorically with: 'I'm feeling down/up/ under the weather/over the moon/blue/burned out/wiped/done/out of my element/over the hump', and so on.

4   McLuhan's original line is 'Ah, but a man's [sic] reach should exceed his grasp, or what's a metaphor?' and the Browning line from the poem, Andrea del Sarto, is: 'Ah, but a man's [sic] reach should exceed his grasp, or what's a heaven for?' Available at: www.poetryfoundation.org/poem/173001 (accessed June 5, 2017).

5   For a few exceptions see: William J. Mills "Metaphorical Vision: Changes in the Western Attitudes to the Environment." *Annals of the American Association of Geographers*, 1982, 237–253; Brendon Larson (2011); Star Muir, "The Web and the Spaceship: Metaphors of the Environment." *ETC A Review of General Semantics*, Summer, 199451(2): 145–152.

6   In Chapter 4, for instance, one of my examples is from global climate governance circles.

7   Larson (2011, 127–150).

8   Thus, while 'cold war' for example, is a critically important political metaphor that no doubt carries implicit ecological implications and effects, I am not calling such metaphors 'ecological metaphors'. By contrast, I am indexing metaphors like 'invasive species' and 'tragedy of the commons', which explicitly conceive of larger-than-human relations, with the notion of 'ecological metaphor'.

9   Brendon Larson takes on this invasive species metaphor in an entire chapter of his book (2011, 160–193). He suggests that other metaphors such as 'ecosystem saturation' (189) might shape different approaches than the all-out battle suggested by 'invasive species'. Hobbs, Higgs and Hall (2013) suggest the notion/metaphor of 'novel ecosystems' as a way to engage with complexity rather than 'invasive species', which reifies an essentialist binary of 'native' vs 'invasive'.

10   The term ecology does not escape critical debate in extant literature. Martin O'Connor (1988, 147), for example, speaks of the 'inherently duplicitous' terms like 'ecological balance'; 'taking everything into account' that traffic between economic and ecological agendas. Such debates are relevant to the spirit of my inquiry, but must be bracketed for now in favour of providing a contingently stable meaning of *ecological metaphor*.

11   Even Marxist theorist, David Harvey who criticizes the 'naturalist' politics of environmentalism concedes that 'the environmental transformations that are now underway are larger scale, riskier, and more far-reaching and complex in their implications ... than ever before in human history' and thus require engaging with paradoxes (Harvey 1998, 5).

12   This is not to say that the connecting thread of experience of 'weather' always leads to movement to act on climate change. The event of cold weather also presents the opportunity to confirm bias against the thesis of anthropogenic warming.

13   Whether one attributes a difference in degree (Ngai 2005) or kind (Massumi 2002) between affect and emotion, there is a recognized connection between the two – either a discursive 'capture'-type relation in Massumi or a 'dialectics' in Woodward.

14   Although here I would nuance this statement by saying that different 'languages' and semiotics come into play as well as 'words', such that visual arts, music, and the like also narrativize experiences.

15   I will supplement this notion with the interventions of Bruno Latour (2004) and Jane Bennett (2010) who insist that political actors (or 'actants', in Latour's terms) include larger-than-human forces that exceed Rancière's theorizations of political actors.

16   When Jane Bennett explicitly asked of Rancière in a face-to-face encounter 'whether he thought that an animal or a plant or a drug or a (non-linguistic) sound could disrupt the police order' (another phrase he uses for the normative distribution of the sensible), his answer was 'no' (Bennett 2010, 106).

17   In *The Poetics* (1997), under his trademark taxonomic logic, Aristotle names four kinds of metaphors used in Greek tragedies: 'A metaphor is the application [to something] of a name belonging to something else, either (a) from the genus to the species, or (b) from the species To the genus, or (c) from a species to another species, or (d) according to analogy.' I take two fundamental premises from Aristotle's theorizations. First, by positioning normal language as a kind of proprietary relationship between a 'thing' and its rightful 'name', Aristotle asserts metaphor as a kind of deviation to this normatively conceived labelling function of language. Although he does allow four different categories of metaphor in *The Poetics*, Aristotle's conceptualizations do not stray far from his take on metaphors as 'the application of a noun which *properly* (my emphasis) belongs to something else'. While his first theorizations also gesture at the important attributes of resemblance and dissonance (to be discussed below) at the heart of metaphor, there has been a tendency to emphasize Aristotle's take on metaphor as *exceptional* language layered onto or supplementing *proper* language rather than a view of metaphor as constitutive of language, thought, and inescapably, of politics, in ways that are deeper than a rhetorical art of persuasion. Metaphors, I argue are too pervasive to be deemed 'exceptional', but their disturbing (tensive) qualities are what makes them seem exceptional and what makes them both powerful and subject to marginalization at the same time. Their 'disturbing' quality emerges from this regime in which they are understood as undermining the misapprehended labelling function of language, itself an enduring, though contested, distribution of the sensible of language. However, rather than conceive of this disturbance negatively, I affirm a role for certain metaphors as explicit disturbances of a normative distribution of the sensible.

18   Another example appears in Bruno Latour's *Politics of Nature* (2004); he evocatively suggests the composition of the world on human and non-human actors involves 'adding voices to the choir' when the process may not always be as 'harmonious' as the metaphor suggests.

19   McKay names the wilderness 'the placeless place beyond the mind's appropriations' (2002, 62).

20   Perhaps most iconically, Deleuze and Guattari (1987) toggle between metaphors for bodies that seem 'organic' and those that seem machinic – 'rhizomes', 'bodies without organs', and 'machinic assemblages' – to present a new conceptual vocabulary for gesturing at and deliberately intermingling themes of technology and ecology.

21   Ahmed's goal of understanding and critiquing the affective generation of racialized bodies is utterly dependent upon historical understandings of racial hierarchies that have been naturalized.

References

Ahmed, Sarah. 2004. *The Cultural Politics of Emotion*. New York: Routledge.

Aristotle. 1997/335 BCE. *Poetics*. London, UK: Penguin.

Bennett, Jane. 2010. *Vibrant Matter: A Political Ecology of Things*. Durham: Duke University Press.

Berners-Lee, Mike. 2011. *How Bad are Bananas?: The Carbon Footprint of Everything*. Vancouver: Greystone Books.

Boulding, Kenneth E. 1966. "The Economics of the Coming Spaceship Earth". Available at: http://dieoff.org/page160.htm (accessed June 5, 2017)..

Boykoff, Maxwell. 2011. *Who Speaks for the Climate?* Cambridge, UK: Cambridge University Press.

Brainard, Curtis. 2008. "Consider the 'Carbon Footprint.'" *Columbia Journalism Review*. Available at: www.cjr.org/the_observatory/the_carbon_footprint.php?page=all (accessed June 25, 2008).

Bristow, Tom, and Thomas H. Ford. 2016. *A Cultural History of Climate Change*. New York; London: Routledge.

Buell, Lawrence. 2005. *The Future of Environmental Criticism: Environmental Crisis and Literary Imagination*. Malden, MA: Blackwell.

Carson, Rachel. 1962. *Silent Spring*. Boston, MA: Houghton Mifflin.

Chilton, Paul. 1996. *Security Metaphors: Cold War Discourse from Containment to Common House*. New York: Peter Lang Publishing.

Connolly, William. 2013. *The Fragility of Things*. Durham, NC: Duke University Press.

Cronon, William. 1996. "The Trouble with Wilderness, or, Getting Back to the Wrong Nature." *Environmental History* 1, 1: 7–55.

Deleuze, Gilles, and Felix Guattari. 1987. *A Thousand Plateaus*. Brian Massumi (trans.), Minneapolis, MN: University of Minnesota Press.

de Man, Paul. 1978. "The Epistemology of Metaphor." *Critical Inquiry* 5, 1: 13–30.

Dryzek, John S. 2005. *The Politics of the Earth: Environmental Discourses*. Oxford University Press.

Ehrlich, Paul R. 1968/1997. *The Population Bomb*. New York, NY: Ballantine Books.

Fairclough, Norman. 2001. *Language and Power, 2nd edn*. London: Longman.

Franke, William. 2000. Metaphor and the Making of Sense: The Contemporary Metaphor Renaissance. *Philosophy and Rhetoric*, 33, 2: 137–153.

Fuller, R. Buckminster. 1969. *Operating Manual for Spaceship Earth*. Carbondale, Ill: Southern Illinois University Press.

Gore, Al. 1992. *Earth in the Balance: Ecology and the Human Spirit*. Boston, MA: Houghton Mifflin.

Grant, Nancy. 2008. *The Pocket Idiot's Guide to Your Carbon Footprint*. Toronto: Penguin Books.

Haraway, Donna. 1988. "Situated Knowledges: The Science Question in Feminism and the Privilege of Partial Perspectives." *Feminist Studies* 14, 3: 575–599.

Haraway, Donna. 2004. *The Haraway Reader*. New York: Routledge.

Hardin, Garrett. 1968. "The Tragedy of the Commons." *Science*, 162, 1243–1248.

Harvey, David. 1998. Marxism, Metaphors, and Ecological Politics. *Monthly Review* 49, 11: 17.

Hobbes, Thomas. 1651/1981. *Leviathan*. London: Penguin

Hobbs, Richard, Eric Higgs and Carol Hall. 2013. *Novel Ecosystems: Intervening in the New Ecological World Order*. Chichester, UK: Wiley-Blackwell.

Hulme, Mike. 2009. *Why We Disagree about Climate Change: Understanding Controversy, Inaction and Opportunity.* Cambridge, UK: Cambridge University Press.

Kuhn, Thomas. 1970/1962. *The Structure of Scientific Revolutions, 2nd edn.* Chicago, IL: University of Chicago Press.

LaDuke, Winona. 1999. *All our Relations.* Cambridge, MA. South End Press.

Lakoff, George and Mark Johnson. 1980/2003. *Metaphors we Live by.* Chicago, IL: University of Chicago Press.

Larson, Brendon. 2011. *Metaphors for Environmental Sustainability.* New Haven, CT: Yale University.

Latour, Bruno. 2004. *Politics of Nature: How to Bring the Sciences into Democracy.* Cambridge, MA: Harvard University Press.

Massumi, Brian. 1995. "The Autonomy of Affect." *Cultural Critique* 31: 83–109.

Massumi, Brian. 2002. *Parables for the Virtual: Movement, Affect, Sensation.* Durham, NC: Duke University Press.

McKay, Don. 2002. "The Bushtits Nest." In: *Thinking and Singing: Poetry and the Practice of Philosophy* Tim Lilburn (ed.), 59–77. Toronto, ON: Cormorant Books.

McLuhan, Marshall. 1964. *Understanding Media.* New York: McGraw Hill.

Morton, Timothy. 2007. *Ecology without Nature.* Cambridge, MA: Harvard University Press.

Nerlich, Brigitte. 2012. "'Low Carbon' Metals, Markets and Metaphors: The Creation of Economic Expectations about Climate Change Mitigation." *Climatic Change* 110, 1–2: 3–52.

Ngai, Sianne. 2005. *Ugly Feelings.* Boston, MA: Harvard University Press.

Petrilli, Susan. 2006. "Meaning, Metaphor, and Interpretation: Modeling New Worlds." *Semiotics* 161, 1/4: 75–118.

Radman, Zdravko. 1997. *Metaphors: Figures of the Mind.* New York: Springer.

Rancière, Jacques. 2004. *The Politics of Aesthetics.* Gabriel Rockhill (trans.), London, UK: Continuum.

Rancière, Jacques. 2009. *The Emancipated Spectator.* London, UK: Verso.

Rancière, Jacques. 2010. *Dissensus: On Politics and Aesthetics.* London, UK: Continuum.

Ricouer, Paul. 1975/1977. *The Rule of Metaphor.* Toronto: University of Toronto Press.

Robbins, Paul. 2013. "Choosing metaphors for the Anthropocene: Cultural and Political Ecologies." In: Nuala C. Johnson, Richard H. Schein and Jamie Winders (eds). *Cultural Geography.* John Wiley & Sons Ltd, Malden, MA: 305–319.

Seigworth, Gregory and Melissa Gregg. 2010. "An Inventory of Shimmers." In: Melissa Gregg and Gregory Seigworth (eds). *The Affect Theory Reader.* Durham, NC: Duke University Press.

Sobolev, Dennis. 2008. "Metaphor Revisited." *New Literary History*, 39, 4: 903–929.

Sontag, Susan. 1978. *Illness as Metaphor.* New York: Doubleday.

Sontag, Susan. 1989. *Aids and Its Metaphors.* New York: Doubleday.

Spinoza, Baruch. 1959/1677. *Ethics.* New York: Dutton.

Underwood, Richard, A. 1970. "Towards a Poetics of Ecology." In: Richard E. Sherrel (ed.) *Ecology: Crisis and New Vision.* Virginia: John Knox Press, 144–154.

Weaver, Andrew. 2008. *Keeping our Cool: Canada in a Warming World.* Toronto: Viking.

Woodward, Kathleen. 2009. *Statistical Panic: Cultural Politics and Poetics of Emotion.* Durham, NC: Duke University Press.

Yarrow, Joanna. 2008. *How to Reduce Your Carbon Footprint: 365 Simple Ways to Save Energy, Resources, and Money.* London, UK: Duncan Baird Publishers.

Part II

Case studies

Introduction

A tale of three footprints

In the following chapters, I elaborate my analysis of carbon footprint metaphors through three instances of carbon footprint metaphors found within recent texts that have popular or public currency (including books, websites, and news articles). This analysis clearly does not comprise a comprehensive corpus of these metaphors, but rather features case studies of three different forms of usage of carbon footprint metaphors that each offer key insights. There are compelling reasons for focusing on the three aspects or cases of the metaphor that I highlight in the three central chapters. In focusing on carbon subjectivity in Chapter 3, I am drawing attention to the way that this metaphor shapes individuals as the locus of climate change interventions; in focusing on carbon citizenship in Chapter 4, I am foregrounding the way the metaphor shapes wider geo-political (but still particularly human) connections as the scale of action; and, in focusing on carbon vitality in Chapter 5, I am drawing attention to the instances in which carbon footprints make clear manifold connections between humans and non-humans as key to the politics of climate change. Each of these case studies could be thought of as a different story of carbon footprints that has a kind of internal coherence of its own, and a discreet theoretical support of their elaboration. When combined in a series, however, each productively troubles a singular reading of *the* carbon footprint.[2] An implicit chronology accompanies the analysis since each of the chapters describes a case or cases of carbon footprint metaphors that are roughly two years apart, beginning in 2008 and ending in 2012. These three have been chosen from an extensive collection because, each in turn, demonstrates how the metaphor shifts over time and in different contexts such that new associations and practices are potentially brought into view.

Each of these contact zones offers different theoretical registers through which to engage an analysis that attends to the promises and risks inherent to each carbon footprint metaphor. In Chapter 3, Carbon subjectivity, I explore the promises of the emergence of carbon subjectivity as a new apprehension of the ways in which human individuals are connected to the matter of climate change, but I also highlight the risks of the subsumption of carbon under the logic of the '*visible* hand' of the market (for it certainly requires a very explicit and visible mechanism to make it so). Here the emergence of carbon subjects is commensurate with the viral spread of carbon metaphors that can be viewed as supporting this marketized logic and disseminating it to the many individuals who in turn support the system. Feeling guilty and dispensing with this guilt, I argue, are intimately connected to how carbon is made visible to carbon subjects in these instances of the carbon footprint metaphor. Orienting the footprint in this way risks reifying an anthropocentric economic system that externalizes the vast elements of non-human 'nature' until this economic system belatedly recognizes their human value (as ecosystem services, which is taken up in Chapter 5).

Chapter 4, Carbon citizenship, explores instances of the carbon footprint metaphor that propose a new sense of political community. I draw into play notions of shared ecological and political space and citizenship as the metaphor fosters connections to fellow carbon footprint makers who are distant, in terms of both geographies and of relative carbon footprint 'impacts'. The rights and responsibilities of asymmetrically culpable and variably impacted sets of human fellows touched by these carbon flows bring into sight a different distribution of the sensible through this metaphor. This aesthetic recomposition may feature a politics of distributive justice for the people of the planet; and yet, its association with some of the struggles inherent to 'citizenship' (as a theory and a practice) risk limiting the sphere of the political to problematic nation-bound discourses and practices that end up, once again bolstering asymmetrical economic development.

As I elaborate in my fifth chapter, these metaphors also offer the potential to explicitly present larger ecological matters through their larger-than-human traces. Chapter 5, Carbon vitality, features an instance of the carbon footprint metaphor as it connects (farmed) shrimp of Southeast Asia (and the up-rooting of mangroves) to the dinner tables of an increasing human population with a taste for shrimp once considered a rare luxury. Here the up-ending of 'blue carbon' – that which is stored in living coastal ecosystems – reveals a complex ecological relationality vis-à-vis carbon that this form of aquaculture significantly disregards. Bringing into visibility blue carbon as an index of the important marine life systems in the life of the planet, this carbon footprint metaphor promises to make marine life count in new ways; however, bringing such marine life into human accounts of the carbon footprint metaphor also risks domesticating them within carbon accounting schemes whose goals are encumbered by marketized capital.

Although each of these tales of three footprints begins with a particular instance of the metaphor and suggests a particular interpretation based on its context and a certain theoretical engagement that will vary in each chapter, there is necessary traffic between these contexts and interpretations (both within my dissertation and within public discourse). Carbon footprint metaphors do not exist in a vacuum; rather they are mutually imbricated intertextually such that they obtain significance from each other and also from other discourses[3] that may even have little to do with climate change and human responsibility. The chapters that follow are thus explorations of somewhat re-contextualized or 're-mixed' carbon footprint metaphors such that some of their metaphorical struggles are staged for novel understanding of potential effects. Similarly, there is a certain amount of theoretical re-mixing across the chapters (e.g., subjectivity, citizenship, affect theory) such that these notions throw into relief particular processes, actors, and relations at play within carbon footprint metaphors. In one sense, the theoretical line in each chapter may appear as a continuum that begins with the carbon footprint of the individual subject in Chapter 3 and attempts to push the boundaries from the individual subject to the connected citizen in Chapter 4 and then finally through Chapter 5 to the carbon footprints implicating larger-than-human ecologies; yet as my analysis reveals, the plot is not so linear and uncomplicated. Whereas stepping from the carbon footprint of a subject to those of connected human citizens and then further to those that explicitly connect humans and non-humans implies a promising intervention in the cultural politics of climate change, a certain risk for these emerging actors to be re-cast in a normative distribution of the sensible exists. What follows as analysis then should be thought of as much as politico-aesthetic re-composition, rather than a singular course of interpreting the effects of instances of the carbon footprint metaphor; these interpretations figure ecological metaphors as important sites of political struggle at a time of climate change.

Notes

1   With thanks to Eric Higgs for a conversation in the early stages of my research. His work on the ambivalent entanglements of nature and culture, and indeed his 'tale of two wildernesses' in the book *Nature by Design* helped to inform my set of case studies as a 'tale of three footprints', where each footprint offers both promises and risks, depending on its attachments and orientations.

2   One could write an entire book on carbon footprint metaphors as 1) mechanisms of 'carbon subjectivity' *or* 2) gestures at global 'carbon citizenship' *or* 3) sites of emerging ecological actors brought into discourse, *or* myriad other singular internally cohesive readings; however, to do so would be to miss the shifty sites of tension as these metaphors have come to appear in the years since they emerged.

3   This latter type of intertextuality has been called 'interdiscursivity' by those in the Critical Discourse Analysis tradition. See, for example, Fairclough (1992, 117).

3   Carbon subjectivity

In 2007, when the carbon footprint metaphor went viral in Anglo-American contexts, carbon footprint reduction lists were also beginning to proliferate. The lists that I analyze in this chapter bring 'carbon subjects' into view by affectively hailing certain individuals to situate themselves within the crisis of climate change and to act in ways that the lists promise will be easy and beneficial to the individual. Carbon subjects are, in theory, individual people who are aware of climate change as a pressing matter of concern in which they themselves are implicated and feel an affective pull to respond to varying degrees. Yet the idea of carbon subjectivity is a complex one, both in theoretical and practical terms, and its unfolding associations present both promises and risks. *Carbon* subjectivity in this chapter elaborates a theoretical framework for understanding evolving mechanisms for making carbon appear and connecting these mechanisms to individual carbon footprint makers.

Evolving cultural sensibilities around carbon may be traced to how a potent metaphoric carbon bonds with other elements to affectively connect to individuals in the politics of climate change. The contact zone of carbon footprint reduction lists illustrates that bringing carbon into view is a complex undertaking that simultaneously involves (among other things): identifying carbon as the lynch-pin of a new political concern for these individual subjects via its scientific apprehension; problematizing the existing patterns and relationship with carbon for these subjects; and directing carbon subjects to self-manage through affective appeal to their guilt. I use subjectivity to describe this visceral package of effects because this term encompasses both mind and 'gut', that is, the arousal of both consciousness about carbon, and feelings that accompany this consciousness. This chapter explores both the promises of carbon subjectivity and the risks of particular associations that offer dispensation of the guilt of carbon subjects through carbon markets. Here, the reduction of 'affect' to the subject-centered or subjective emotion, of guilt, also emerges as a problematic re-centring of the human just at a moment when a more humbling ecologically embedded sense of humanity may arise. While the *mise-en-scène* featured in the previous chapter asserts this metaphor's affective *potential* to mediate larger-than-human relations, this case reveals a particularly human-centric social emotion of carbon guilt, an affect that moves toward a particular reification of a liberal consuming Western self and risks effacing other key human asymmetries and more-than-human relations and processes. Thus, while I acknowledge that affectively connecting climate change to individuals through the footprint metaphor may be necessary, I also highlight the limits of subject-oriented practices that structure 'the field of possible action for individuals' (Paterson and Stripple 2010, 346).

How do I become a carbon subject? Let me count the ways ...

As an important textual genre to emerge when the carbon footprint metaphor was first proliferating in public spaces, the list enumerating ways to reduce one's carbon footprint enables a particular means by which certain individuals become connected to the planetary concern of climate change. I am identifying the list as a 'genre' – a new but quickly recognizable form of address that follows the same patterns or conventions in addressing subjects. To supplement conventional associations of genre with a category of literature, music, or art, I bring the insights of contemporary genre theory that 'connect a recognition of regularities in discourse types with a broader social and cultural understanding of language in use' (Freedman and Medway 1994, 1).[1] In other words, I am suggesting a degree of shared form, content, and importantly, *cultural practices*, around these lists that pertain to the fact that certain individuals are historically coming to identify as having carbon footprints and considering a suite of individual-oriented responses. The following (Fox 2013) is an excerpt from one short example on-line of many much longer lists, including full-length print-based book lists:

10 Actions You Can Take Today to Reduce your Carbon Footprint:
1   Change your light bulbs
2   Unplug your gadgets
3   Take public transit or carpool
4   Choose a laptop over a desktop
5   Filter your own water
6   Adjust your curtains and thermostat
7   Buy local food
8   Plant a tree
9   Print or digital, be mindful reading the news
10   Choose energy-efficient kitchen appliances

The brief description that follows each item on the preceding list on-line also features cost-reduction (a characteristic of this genre), suggesting that these lists help to reinforce and shape a certain liberal consuming subject as a carbon footprint maker at the centre of climate change. I will pick up on these risks of carbon subjectivity in a later section, but first, I will explore the promises offered through bringing certain responsible individuals into accounts of climate change through this list genre.

This genre varies slightly across on-line environments versus conventional print texts, and according to the agenda of the creators of each list, but a sufficient number of common elements suggest it as a fairly cohesive genre that builds on a pervasive societal 'list mania' enumerating (and often ranking) all aspects of life.[2] Importantly, the print-based books, which I excerpt in my analysis, offer a wider range of practices than those in the list above, but the range of activities remains oriented toward a particular consuming subject. These books include: *How to Reduce Your Carbon Footprint: 365 Simple Ways to Save Energy, Resources and Money* (Yarrow 2008); *The Environmental Equation: 100 Factors that Can Add to or Subtract From Your Total Carbon Footprint* (Shimo-Barry 2008); *101 Ways to Reduce Your Carbon Footprint* (Bomholdt 2010); *Pocket Idiot's Guide to Your Carbon Footprint* (Grant 2008); and *You Can Save the Planet: A Day in the Life of Your Carbon Footprint* (Hough 2007).

I particularly attend in my analysis to the important introductory statements in these book lists as they map out an unfolding landscape of carbon subjects vis-à-vis climate change by connecting the bodies of these individuals to the problem and orienting the kinds of solutions subjects may undertake. Recalling Rancière's notion of the distribution of the sensible, these introductory statements present 'facts' that 'simultaneously disclose the existence of something in common', in this case, climate change as a matter of planetary concern, 'and the delimitations that define the respective parts and positions within it', in this case, carbon subjects and the roles and positions they may occupy (Rancière 2004, 12). The bulk of the lists appeared in 2007 to 2009, the early days of the viral existence of carbon footprint metaphors. While the publication of these prescriptive lists has slowed somewhat, their historical importance remains in the launching of carbon subjectivity. Recalling that metaphors emerge in semantic gaps, this carbon footprint list genre is particularly important because it responds to the urgent question, *what is to be done about climate change?*, by giving individuals a sense of meaning and control through a set of micro-practices that will presumably add up to mitigation results.

Keeping in mind the precept from metaphor studies that contexts matter, I do not claim that this list genre produces monolithic effects, but rather that when these discreet lists are taken together and multiplied in various public contexts, they foster a certain generalized orienting response to climate change; this response is individualized and privatized, often calling on the actions of home-owners as they go about their everyday activities. Such lists commonly prescribe: changing the lightbulbs, adjusting the thermostat and planting a tree, among a suite of options (Bohmholdt 2010; Yarrow 2008). Many of the lists from 2007 to 2008 also suggest offsets[3] (a point that will be addressed later). Taking these texts as contact zones that authorize particular orientations and foreclose upon others, I trace the specific political practices that these lists enable. First, I briefly draw attention to an unfolding theoretical understanding of carbon subjectivity, and then elaborate on its promises and risks that I wish to highlight as central to the effects of the carbon footprint reduction lists.

The emergence of carbon subjectivity heralded through carbon footprint metaphors describes an ambivalent affair in both practical and theoretical terms. Among a long tradition of political theories of subjectivity that describe a process of individuation through social or political forces, I am building on Foucauldian notions that insist there is no pre-existing category of 'the subject' as a thinking, knowing, transcendental, or psychologized individual who enters into a political arena in a generalizable way, but that specific 'positions of subjectivity' arise as effects of discourses and practices in a political and historical arena (Foucault 1969/1989, 60–61):[4]

> In the proposed analysis, instead of referring back to the synthesis or the unifying function of a subject, the various enunciative modalities manifest his [sic] dispersion. To the various statuses, the various sites, the various positions that he can occupy or be given when making a discourse. To the discontinuity of the planes from which he speaks. And if these planes are linked by a system of relations, this system is not established by the synthetic activity of a consciousness identical with itself, dumb and anterior to all speech, but by the specificity of discursive practice. I shall abandon any attempt, therefore, to see discourse as a phenomenon of expression – the verbal translation of a previously establish synthesis; instead, I shall look for a field of regularity for various positions of subjectivity.
>
> (1969/1989, 61)

'Carbon subjectivity'[5] emerges at the turn of the millennium as a novel and ambivalent 'position of subjectivity' brought about through discursive (and metaphoric) practice in the politics of climate change. Foucault's analytic attention is occupied with how individuals with certain political positions discursively emerge on a political 'plane'. Against conceiving of a fixed structure or naturalized system connecting these planes and the subjects within them, Foucault insists that such systems are constructed through discursive practice. This aspect of Foucault's thought resonates with Rancière's notion of distribution of the sensible that draws attention to how 'political statements and literary locutions' draw maps of a visible system and prescribe roles and dispositions for those in this system (2004, 39); however, certain differences also exist between the two.

Unlike Foucault, Rancière asserts an aesthetics at work within the distribution of the sensible and, thus, his thought fosters attention to the composing work of *metaphors* and how they affectively pull bodies together as I have described in the previous chapter. Another key difference is Rancière's naming of 'subjectivity' as the active force of newcomers appearing to disrupt a normative distribution of the sensible. Rancière suggests that:

> the political process of subjectivation … continually creates 'newcomers', new subjects that enact the equal power of anyone and everyone and construct new words about community in the given common world … Subjects … are 'newcomers', who allow new objects to appear as common concerns, and new voices to appear and be heard.
>
> (2010, 59–60)

Rancière describes subjectivation as a process whereby agents come to have a say in politics, to potentially interrupt an existing construction of the world. Foucault does not accord subjectivity such a role, but rather sees it as an effect; thus Foucault, in contrast with Rancière, is occupied with historical specificities, the everyday micropolitics of how various subjects come to be through discourse. For Foucault, understanding how 'subjects' like medicalized or sexualized bodies come to occupy these subject positions in a particular time and place entails tracing the specific discursive practices of and historical struggles of these times and places (1978/1990; 1969/1989).

Drawing attention to a generative metaphorical struggle over subjectivity itself in these theorizations on the theme by Rancière and Foucault (as well as those who take up Foucault's notion of governmentality and Judith Butler who takes up subjectivity more broadly[6]), I am interested in exploring the sympathies and tensions between understanding carbon subjects as 'newcomers' and understanding carbon subjects as 'discursive effects'; the promises and risks of the affective pull of carbon footprint metaphors emerge in this interplay that I will tease out below. I propose, with Rancière, that 'the opening of an interval for political subjectivation' (2010, 69) enacted through calling on individuals with carbon footprints offers the potential to make visible previously obscured actors or 'newcomers' that have had no explicit part within the politics of climate change; with Foucault, however, I also attend to the discursive practices that define the roles and fill in the content of what these 'newcomers' can or cannot do. In what follows, I bring the notion of carbon subjectivity as a Rancièrian opening into conversation with Foucauldian notions of 'governmentality', which describes an ambivalent process of how these subjects come into political play to manage their own carbon, 'directing their conduct, constraining their actions and reactions ...' (Foucault 2008/2004, 2).

The promise of reconfiguring the power and responsibility of individuals

The promise of carbon subjectivity affectively launched through an appeal to reduce one's carbon footprint hinges on its ability to bring certain responsible individuals centrally into the politics of climate change.[7] During the decade of 1990 to 2000 when climate change visibly emerged as a planetary public concern, a certain regime of climate change politics began to take hold. While the previous planetary abstraction of climate change (and carbon) had been brought 'down to Earth' in certain ways, climate change remained largely abstract for individuals in their daily lives. The political bodies of the Intergovernmental Panel on Climate Change (IPCC) and Kyoto Protocol-enabled carbon markets inscribe roles for scientists, architects of global governance and policy, national governments, environmental economists, global corporations, and some local organizations but they left individual people out of political accounts. In the forward to the book, *101 Ways to Reduce Your Carbon Footprint* (Bomholdt 2010), Bill Burtis, Manager of Communications for the non-profit Clean Air-Cool

Planet, suggests: 'People aren't taking action to do something about global warming because they feel powerless' (10). Citing a general trend of climate change communications and (in)action following an IPCC report that sets up the solution through a proposed new bill (in an American context), Burtis states:

> But bills and wonderful ideas like deserts full of solar cells and algae, while they make great goals and terrific targets, lack a crucial ingredient: We can't do them. We – the people who have to keep our heads out of the sand; who have to listen to the tales of feedback loops, floods, droughts, starvation, and war; who have to stay in this in order to get Congressional delegations to pass a climate bill and governors to allow off-shore wind and state legislature to pass renewable energy incentives – we need things we can do. They need to be simple, easy, inexpensive, normal, unweird things.
>
> (ibid., 11)

Burtis expresses a common feeling of debilitation and dis-connectedness from the massive planetary problem of climate change and its proliferating and cascading effects. This, in Burtis' testimony, is the genius of the book, *101 Ways to Reduce your Carbon Footprint*; the list empowers certain individuals who want to do something about climate change by allowing them to appear in these politics. While Burtis' phrase 'we – the people' in the above quotation deserves critical attention, I will suspend this judgment of the liberal environmental subject momentarily in order to attend to a necessary shift that occurs. This shift generates 'another distribution of the sensible, another setting of the stage, in producing different relations between words, the kinds of thing that they designate and the kinds of practices they empower' (Rancière 2010, 54). Rather than reinscribing the normative sense of climate change in which, as Burtis suggests, disaster narratives predominate and certain experts occupy the positions of authority to speak about and act upon climate change in a global order, this new affective connection of a carbon footprint to individual people marks an *opening for political subjectivication* of these individuals. Such individuals must be explicitly connected to climate change politics to register, to have a say, and to act in these politics. Crucially, the carbon footprint metaphor in these lists enables certain subjects to see their own 'footprints' attached to the topic of climate change and to do something about these impacts. In a world partly constructed on a discursive and political exclusion of the relationships between carbon, various publics, and their constituent individual actors, conventional terms of political subjectivity and the norms of daily individual life are tested with the advent of anthropogenic climate change. The metaphor of the carbon footprint promises to address this semantic and political gap by registering the mark of an individual carbon-emitting human at the centre of climate change. The emergence of carbon footprint metaphors thus initiates, in language, this new form of subjectivity to challenge the given terms of politics. The kind of newcomer that emerges in this discourse is an emitting individual who is susceptible to examining his or her daily practices vis-à-vis climate change and *potentially* shaping these practices differently. I am not suggesting that these largely privileged Western individual subjects do not already appear in politics writ large, but rather that they are being invited to appear differently in climate change politics by thinking of themselves as carbon producers who have a responsibility to reduce their carbon production. The emergence of a carbon subject thus entails connecting the politics of climate change to an individual who shares in how carbon is accounted for (and managed); the discursive practices of carbon footprint reduction lists further bolster the terms of carbon subjectivity.

As I describe below, there exists a certain sympathy between the initial discursive hailing of a carbon (governmentalized) subject and what Rancière calls the 'opening for a space of political subjectivation' for these individuals in the cultural politics of climate change. Before I describe these sympathies, I first draw attention to how these carbon footprint reduction lists might lend themselves to a Foucauldian analysis of 'governmentality' through which carbon subjects come to self-govern.

The textual contact zones of these carbon footprint reduction lists do not issue from a central authority that forcefully charges and threatens individual subjects to self-manage; rather, they emerge from various public fora and institutions such that individuals willingly participate in the call to become subjects. The many extended book lists, for example – *How to Reduce Your Carbon Footprint: 365 Simple Ways to Save Energy, Resources and Money*; *The Pocket Idiot's Guide to Your Carbon Footprint*; *The Environmental Equation: 100 Factors that Can Add to or Subtract from your Total Carbon Footprint* and others – are popular books that must be purchased or borrowed from libraries voluntarily by emerging carbon subjects who are conscious of climate change as a problem and upon whom an affective appeal to connect to mitigation efforts works. Similarly, the on-line lists are generally accessed through an intentional act on the part of individuals. Carbon subjects, then, are part of a complex circuit of power. As Foucault's historical analysis demonstrates, in contemporary times, power does not singularly issue from a centralizing authority or (sovereign) power of state government over the subjects it rules, rather, power operates in a diffuse network, flowing through various non-state and state institutions, as well as *through the bodies of individual subjects themselves*. Thus, rather than top-down governmental forms of authority that make or discipline political subjects through force (or penalty of death in previous historical times), Foucault conceives of a dispersed 'governmentality', a new kind of rationality that enjoins individuals themselves to freely submit to forms of self-discipline according to the specific rationalities at work (2004/2008).

Matthew Paterson and Johannes Stripple have taken Foucault's well-known governmental formulation of the *conduct of conduct* into the realm of climate change politics by suggesting that we must now conceive of the 'conduct of carbon conduct':

> a government of people's carbon dioxide emission that does not work through the authority of the state or the state system, but through people's

governing of their own emissions. Different regimes of 'carbon calculation' operate so that individuals either work on their emission-producing activities or to 'offset' their emissions elsewhere. The conduct of carbon conduct is therefore a government enabled through certain forms of knowledge (measurements and calculations of one's own carbon footprint), certain technologies (the turning of carbon emissions into tradable commodities), and a certain ethic (low-carbon lifestyle as desirable).

(2010, 347)

In their analysis of this evolving ambivalent governmentality, Paterson and Stripple caution against reproducing a simple critique of a misplaced individualism written into the governmental forms of conduct of carbon conduct and instead suggest a more-nuanced account of how 'knowledge', 'technologies', and a 'certain ethic' work together to shape this conduct as part of a larger dynamic of climate change politics. This nuanced perspective suggests that while there is reason to critique a singular focus on individualism in these politics, some focus on individual loci of control and the market is, in fact, necessary. 'Sure the creation of markets does so in a way that pursues commodification, but such commodification cannot logically exist without individuals. Power operates through individual practice, not over and against it. At the same time, such remaking of individual practice involves reconstructing collectives themselves' (Paterson and Stripple 2010, 344). Understanding the affective mediations of carbon footprint metaphors entails understanding how individuals are being drawn together to produce collective responses with a variety of ambivalent effects.

In the above quotation, Paterson and Stripple suggest the carbon footprint as a measure located within the realm of 'knowledge' in this locus of governmentality. This characterization is partly accurate since subjects do use the metrics of carbon footprint calculators to inform their knowledge, as I describe further below; however, the normalization of the carbon footprint as a quantitative metric also bears scrutiny. My analysis of the carbon footprint *metaphor* (not only calculus) suggests that through these lists, this metaphor affectively mediates relations between all three of these sites, bringing knowledge to subjects about the problem of climate and measuring their impacts, providing 'certain technologies' of tradable carbon commodities as mechanisms to lower *your carbon footprint*, and featuring a 'certain ethic'/morally coded affect of lowering one's carbon impacts (though this ethic is ambivalently connected to the affect of carbon guilt as I describe below). I will draw these out with specific examples from the lists below, but first I will remain for a moment on the promise involved in this form of governmentality.

Problematizing carbon conduct

As Paterson and Stripple insist 'government is a problematizing activity. Issues and concerns have to be made to appear problematic' (2010, 345). The knowledge that launches this form of governmentality for carbon subjects, affectively mediated through carbon footprint lists, begins with self-reflection about one's conduct in relation to an identified problem, in this case, climate change. While there is reason to examine certain liberal environmental practices that 'structure the field of possible action for individuals' (ibid., 346), the fact that liberal subjects are coming to question their conduct at all with the advent of climate change, offers a generative opening. Such a problematization of one's own conduct, especially with regard to the practices of carbon subjects vis-à-vis climate change creates what Paterson and Stripple call a 'dynamic of awareness raising which gives resources to individuals to change practices' (345). The promise for Paterson and Stripple in this account, is the very act of connecting individuals to a problem in which they are implicated. 'Problems are not pregiven, but have to be constructed and made visible. This process can occur in different ways in different sites and by different agents' (346). In this case, metaphor itself is a site through which problems are constructed and made visible through worldly acts of yoking. The mediations of carbon footprint metaphors, especially these carbon footprint reduction lists, help to make the problem of climate change newly visible within the daily lives of individual carbon subjects.

Many of these carbon footprint reductions lists lead with a problem statement about anthropogenic climate change before connecting the problem to the bodies of individuals with footprints. After briefly defining a carbon footprint as 'the amount of carbon dioxide (CO_2) emitted as a direct or indirect result of an activity', Joanna Yarrow's book-length list follows with the heading, 'What's the problem?' (2008, 6). This section defines greenhouse gases, their beneficial historical impact upon planetary living conditions, and the unprecedented historical scale of contemporary human impacts:

> Since the Industrial Revolution, human activity – primarily through the burning of fossil fuels ... – has been releasing CO_2 that was absorbed over millions of years at a rate far faster than it can be reabsorbed, and it's building up in the atmosphere. At the moment, CO_2 is being released about three times faster than it can be reabsorbed. Every second, human activity emits another 770 tons – enough to fill 140 Olympic-size swimming pool.
>
> (2008, 6)

After making climate change visible as an unprecedented historical problem in pace and scale, in a following section, 'What can we do about it?', Yarrow connects to the individual scale of the footprint:

> The fact that almost every area of human activity contributes to our carbon footprint might sound like an overwhelming problem. But the good news is that this gives us scope to reduce our footprint in almost every aspect of our lives ... Governments worldwide are debating how best to regulate emissions, and businesses are beginning to take responsibility. But the issues are so enormous ... that change at every level is crucial.

As individuals, there are numerous things we can each do to reduce our carbon footprints – in our everyday actions and in our wider sphere of influence as consumers, voters, and global citizens. We all have the power to significantly reduce our footprint by making low-carbon choices.

(2008, 8–9)

Yarrow makes reference to the global scales at which action has been directed thus far, but notes that an individual scale must also be addressed. Resonating with Yarrow's words and the comments of Burtis above in Bohmholdt's book list, Paterson and Stripple suggest that a shift to individuals marks a necessary re-orientation in climate change politics. During early efforts to address climate change, 'the focus of action had been on states and firms but in the early 2000s this started to be complemented by a focus on individual practice' (2010, 341). Newly recognizing that political subjects have carbon impacts or 'footprints', means acknowledging a prior exclusion in the conventional terms of political subjectivity; thus, the emergence of carbon footprints constitutes the carbon subject, not a real individual or set of individuals, but a category or un-acknowledged relationship between individual subjects and carbon. Making these associations clear – how individuals are connected on the issue of climate change – is part of the promising work of the texts that enable carbon subjectivity to take hold through appeals to carbon footprint makers.

A characteristic of carbon subjectivity expressed through carbon footprint metaphors in the list-genre is a certain quasi-scientific engagement with 'carbon selves', which has developed as a result of the ways in which carbon has become visible for a wider public at a time of climate change. This is part of the 'governmental' knowledge generation that allows for the conduct of carbon conduct for subjects. Among the first published books in 2007 to 2009 for lay-publics (following the on-line versions) that brought carbon subjects into existence through the carbon footprint metaphor, a certain opening statement in these book lists features a scientific engagement with the element of carbon as it relates to climate change, industrialization as the combustion of carbon, and to the footprint of each individual on the planet. *The Pocket Idiot's Guide to Your Carbon Footprint* (2008), for example, briefly defines carbon footprint and then situates it within a discussion of the element of carbon and the carbon cycle of the planet.

Let's get started with a look at the *carbon cycle*. Carbon appears in many forms throughout the planet. Carbon is a part of every living thing, even dead things that are decomposing. Carbon is an *element*. Carbon molecules can be alone, or they can move around to combine with other elements. In one form or another, carbon is under our feet in the soil and rocks, around us in the plants and animals and people we live among, in the foods we eat, and in the air we breathe. Carbon is one of the building blocks of life … Carbon is the sixth most abundant element in the universe.

(Grant 2008, 4–5)

Reading like an introductory science lesson on carbon, this section situates carbon as a foundational planetary element to which a planetary 'we' are already *subject* as we enter the planetary scene as a species. Similarly, *How to Reduce Your Carbon Footprint: 365 Simple Ways to Save Energy, Resources and Money* (2008) names a carbon footprint 'as the amount of carbon dioxide emitted as a direct or indirect result of an activity' and then contextualizes this new definition within a planetary carbon cycle that precedes humans but foundationally facilitates their entrance onto the planetary stage. The book-length lists often feature some description of 'the good greenhouse', the non-anthropogenic heat-trapping gases that, along with foundational element of carbon, 'makes life on our planet possible' (Grant 2008, 9).

The next problematizing move implicates human activity since the Industrial Revolution. These carbon footprint lists thus reinforce the idea that the planetary scale of recent climate change, attributed to contemporary human civilization itself, suggests nothing less than the need for a massive intervention in what have come to be normal patterns of human life for a dominant many at the turn of the millennium. 'Our' relationship to carbon has been largely identified as the one that is off kilter; the landmark and oft-cited study of Revelle and Suess (1957) is exemplary of this identification:

> Human beings are now carrying out a large-scale geophysical experiment of a kind that could not have happened in the past nor be reproduced in the future ... we are returning to the atmosphere and oceans the concentrated organic *carbon* stored in the sedimentary rocks over hundreds of millions of years.
>
> (19, emphasis added)

As Spencer Weart (2014) insists, the above excerpt has gained recent currency in a wide variety of texts; such statements have helped shape a cultural imaginary around climate change, relationality, and processes vis-à-vis carbon. Thus, it is at the 'carbon-level' that intervention has been proposed. Intervening, however, may be difficult for those for whom carbon dioxide and other greenhouse gases still remain largely abstract. For many lay-people, until the emergence of climate change consciousness, 'carbon' as a named element was not as explicitly relevant to daily life. Linking this allotropic element to the metaphor of the footprint as a symbol of imprints/impacts affectively connects this scientific abstraction to the day-to-day experiences of subjects. This form of scientific apprehension of carbon as it relates to climate change is reduced in complexity for a lay-audience, so paradoxically, carbon gets both discursively reduced *and* generalized, which allows it to function for a variety of agendas. The scientific 'facticity' involved in representing the problem initiates a sense of authority that is carried over in the subsequent 'mobilizing of individual subjectivity and individuals' capacity to govern themselves' (Paterson and Stripple 2010, 346).

Crucially, however, the specific metaphoric capacity of the 'footprint' also helps to mediate the visible and invisible relations in these politics such that certain actors and relations appear (and others do not); thus, while the carbon footprint comes to be normatively understood as a metric, its powerful metaphoricity is also affectively at play in drawing out what/who comes into visibility and what is problematized. In the introductory pages of the *Pocket Idiot's Guide to Your Carbon Footprint,* for example, Nancy Grant explains, '[y]our carbon footprint is invisible – you can't look down at the kitchen floor and see it the way you might notice snow[8] from your boots ... but this imaginary symbol represents the focus of intense interest today' (Grant 2008, 3). By carrying over these associations of footprints as messy imprints and encouraging subjects to use their imaginations, these carbon footprint reduction lists present an opening for yoking together the unlikely entities of carbon and footprints; attaching these carbon footprints to the bodies of carbon subjects brings these messy imprints of individuals into view. 'Unfortunately, no one has yet invented a cheap, reliable, easy-to-read, all-purpose environmental impact gauge. But you can use your imagination to visualize how your actions affect the natural world' (ibid.). The carbon footprint provides the 'imaginary symbol' for visualizing impacts in the absence of such an 'all-purpose environmental impact gauge'. Such statements reveal a pivotal point about carbon footprint metaphors as entities that reveal an aspiration beyond what is apprehensible. This aspiration again recalls Marshall McLuhan's evocative pun, as mentioned in the Introduction: 'a man's [sic] reach must exceed his grasp or what's a metaphor?' (1964, 7). The carbon footprint in this instance expresses a reach exceeding a grasp, where the grasp would be a metric or gauge that is not yet available (nor ever will be, as I insist). The grasp is towards a scientific, quantitative, all-in definitive calculation in this instance, but the reach is an always-partial account that requires the imagination to fill in. The risks of the political 'filling in' of the content of this metaphor for carbon subjects also require critical attention, as I elaborate below, but I would like to linger on one further promise enabled through the metaphor's affective drawing together of bodies.

The political promise of carbon subjectivity enabled through carbon footprint metaphors consists in its potential not only to connect carbon to responsible individuals, but also to connect these individuals to a comparative planetary calculus of footprints. While it is important to note that the appeal in this new form of subjectivity is generally made to a Western consuming liberal subject, arguably *these are the very subjects that most need to appear in a governmental frame of problematizing their carbon conduct.* Such a calculus, which becomes visible through the metaphor in the first instance, reveals a profound disparity in existing freedoms to emit among carbon footprint makers; identifying carbon subjects with carbon footprints potentially brings to light such disputes over freedom to emit greenhouse gases associated with certain lifestyles and the relative (in)equality in the distribution of these freedoms. The genre of lists that establishes carbon subjectivity through carbon footprint metaphors may function to bring these inequalities to light, revealing that some are more subject to the appeal to carbon subjectivity than others. In the introductory section of her book, *How to Reduce Your Carbon Footprint*, Joanna Yarrow states:

People all over the world are emitting CO_2 at unsustainable rates. But some of us are worse than others. The average European emits around 11 tons per year, while the average American emits over 22 tons – more than 5 times the world average (4 tons). In contrast, in sub-Saharan Africa the average footprint is less than 0.8 tons per person.

(2008, 8)

Similarly, in her introduction to *101 Ways to Reduce Your Carbon Footprint*, Andrea Bohmholdt suggests, 'as a nation, Americans tend to consume more energy per person than do residents of any other country' (2010, 15). Attention to pre-existing, but somewhat more urgently pressing global inequalities, is enabled by the calling to account of carbon subjects through carbon footprint metaphors.

Crucially, as these lists reveal, not everyone appears equally as a carbon subject; the appeal to carbon subjects to reduce their carbon footprints is not an appeal to a carbon subject in sub-Saharan Africa where 'the average footprint is less than 0.8 tons per person' (Yarrow 2008, 8). In terms of a Rancièrian opening for subjectivation, these subjects with already low carbon footprints do not really appear to have a 'say' in the micropolitics of a daily carbon footprint inventory (changing lightbulbs, lowering thermostats, etc.). And yet, paradoxically, they do appear to trouble or question the gargantuan footprints of those in the Global North. When a comparative calculus is featured, this knowledge of widely divergent carbon footprints potentially plays a part in the governmental problematization of carbon conduct (I more thoroughly develop how the carbon footprint metaphor brings these inequalities into view through the frame of 'carbon citizenship' in the following chapter). A prolonged attention to disparities, however, remains an unfulfilled potential within the carbon subjectivity initiated through carbon footprint reduction lists. Most other publicly directed carbon footprint books or lists of the same era do not contain explicit statement of inequities of a systemic kind (be they oriented at nations, or sectors, or lifestyles, etc.) and even the two mentioned above do not develop this notion of inequity beyond an initial cursory statement. Some texts, in fact, feature the uniqueness of *your* carbon footprint; the *Pocket Idiot's Guide to Your Carbon Footprint* insists that, 'your situation is unique – and that's where this book can help you. Instead of trying to come up with nationwide averages … we look at numbers that will have value in your particular case. A carbon footprint is definitely not one-size fits all' (Grant 2008, 21). This kind of statement metaphorically connecting a carbon footprint to a kind of shoe-shopping enterprise that is highly individualized, reveals a normative liberal environmental order in which carbon subjects appear as domesticated privileged consumers.

Attention to such discourses compels understanding the ambivalent shifts of the metaphor even within this list genre (itself a sub-set of a diverse and shifting range of instances of carbon footprints). The carbon footprint is generally elaborated in the lists in both qualitative and quantitative terms in its appeal to carbon subjects. Words like 'impact' in many definitions partially suggest a qualitative mode of engagement where carbon subjects theoretically embrace a will to reduce emissions and make gestures to improve their legacy, while words like 'amount' or measure speak to a quantitative mode. Crucially however, even when these lists propose a quantitative definition or metrics, the metrics are notoriously variable. In *The Pocket Idiot's Guide to Your Carbon Footprint*, Nancy Grant suggests 'the size of your carbon footprint may become one of the most important *numbers* [emphasis added] in your life in the twenty-first century', but then she goes on to suggest a few pages later that the number and complexity of the calculations would take a long time to compute 'Something else makes calculating your carbon footprint even trickier. It has two parts!' (2008, 8, 18). Grant then proceeds to explain the 'primary' and 'secondary' carbon footprint of an activity, whereby the primary carbon footprint consists of the direct impacts of an activity and the 'secondary carbon footprint consists of the greenhouse gas impact of the things that are an indirect part of this activity [or product]' (ibid., 19). The secondary footprint is notoriously tricky to calculate definitively, especially with the partial knowledges coming from certain hegemonic human actors and their instruments that represent only a partial picture of the actors, relations, and processes involving carbon. These relations and processes cannot be easily isolated and understood in a transcendent and objective way.[9] In short, the infinite number of possible calculations exposes the carbon footprint as (among other things) an aspirational quantifier that will never reach a definitive mark, but rather, will offer trace effects that are politically and ecologically crucial in a shifting world.

Some call to quantify carbon footprint analysis more rigorously (Berners-Lee 2011), yet the metaphor is evasive and owes allegiance to no singular metric or interpretation. Carbon footprint metaphors operate in these qualitative and quantitative tensions. The book *How Bad Are Bananas: The Carbon Footprint of Everything* (Berners-Lee 2011) is a more recent manuscript in the list genre that, in some places, encapsulates these kinds of tensions; significantly, it is the only one among the lists that explicitly uses the term 'metaphor':

> I'm using the word *footprint* as a metaphor for the total impact that something has. And I'm using the word *carbon* as shorthand for all the different global warming greenhouse gases. So I'm using the term *carbon footprint* as shorthand to mean the best estimate that we can get of the full climate change impact of something.
>
> (Berners-Lee 2011, 5)

Berners-Lee's definition implicitly acknowledges some key elements. First, he affirms that the (carbon) footprint is a metaphor, which suggests a certain critical semantic gap between the assumed direct representational equivalence of language and what it nominates. While he does not explicitly name the element of carbon as a metaphor, he implies that it works metaphorically (or 'metonymically' as a part used to express an associated whole) by suggesting it as 'shorthand' for all the various greenhouse gases. Acknowledging the carbon footprint's metaphoricity therefore hints at a certain non-representability that will defy even his own efforts to pin it down definitively. Further, he states 'I'm using the word' each time he defines a term, thus acknowledging the wide range of practices that surround carbon footprint metaphors. Using the personal pronoun 'I' positions Berners-Lee as one of many who use the carbon footprint metaphor for a variety of purposes.

Another element of the definition, the term 'shorthand' underscores the elliptical and metaphorical nature of 'carbon' in the footprint metaphor. As a stand-in for a host of greenhouse gases, carbon here discursively reduces not only these other greenhouse gases, but also a range of other ecological actors that will not be counted, except if they weigh in on a carbon scale. 'Best estimate' in the above definition further highlights the imprecision that both plagues this metaphor as a metric and allows it to powerfully proliferate for a number of competing agendas. A best estimate may be a grasp for a number, but one that by definition remains highly contingent and only suggestive of a certain variable range that is subject to change. In short, Berners-Lee's definition returns the metaphoricity to the carbon footprint, points to its qualitative and quantitative mixture, and suggests that it can never be an accurate measure. What is slightly ironic, however, in what follows in the text, is that Berners-Lee demands more rigour in its quantitative use. He suggests that the 'phrase carbon footprint' (now no longer cited as a metaphor) encounters abuse by missing out on 'some or even most of the emissions caused' (6). He even goes so far as to suggest another metaphor, 'carbon toeprint', for this kind of 'abusive' analysis of partial emissions (ibid.). Never quite permitted to be completely qualitative (how can carbon really be a quality?), but failing all the while to be quantitatively rigorous in the ways demanded of it, the carbon footprint metaphor when explicitly analysed, performs a kind of splice that troubles treating climate change from either an exclusively qualitative or exclusively quantitative point of view. A key aspect of carbon subjectivity suggested by these lists is that the qualitative and the quantitative can be mobilized in the cultural politics of climate change to create effects and affects for different agendas.

Carbon footprint metaphors trace these tensions between aspirations of quantitative metrics and the 'filling in' of imaginaries for carbon subjects. Crucially, however, an explicit engagement with the imaginary is often what is left behind in accounts of carbon footprints, so the imaginary and political 'filling in' of content is both initially needed, and then cast off in these lists as they then derive a certain authority from what seems scientific, objective, and beyond examination. Thus, while the conduct of carbon conduct mediated through these lists relies on what appear to be knowledge and facts about climate change and its connection to individuals, this conduct is, from the outset mediated by both facts and values.

Thus, ambivalently, the emergence of carbon footprint metaphors in these lists enables carbon subjects *to appear* to draw attention to carbon relations, processes, and inequities and to distribute responsibility, but then risks foreclosing upon these very politics. What remains, as I describe in what follows, is a feeling of guilt on the part of certain individuals along with a range of possible practices for dispensing with that guilt. My purpose for naming a carbon subject here is to accentuate this theoretical frame that keeps open the question or 'dissensus' (Rancière 2010) that founds the naming or appeal to individuals through carbon footprint metaphors, as a mechanism for individuals to appear as producers of carbon impacts; individual lay-people had not yet been accorded a central role in these politics.[10] Yet as these individual carbon subjects appear and become associated through carbon footprint metaphors with specific practices generated through the list, this theoretical frame of carbon subjectivity also prompts a critique of the risks of who appears and how they appear to conduct their carbon conduct. Many of these practices function to bolster the perpetuation of a carbon subject who is constituted upon these very unequal relations with global others. While there is every reason to recognize carbon as a constitutive element of life and to problematize the practices of individual culpable carbon-emitting subjects, there is also reason to examine how the emergence of a guilty carbon subject involves naming and *taming* such that footprints can be domesticated and managed in specific ways that reify existing inequities and systems of ecological degradation. Although Paterson and Stripple draw attention to the making of governmental subjects as enabled partly through 'a certain ethic (low-carbon lifestyles as desirable)' (2010, 347), the tensions involved in the mechanisms for reducing one's carbon footprint reveal a wide range of interpretations of how to achieve 'low-carbon' lifestyles. These diverse interpretations are enabled by the ways in which carbon footprint reduction lists affectively generate 'carbon guilt' and its dispensation.

The risky practices of guilty subjects

While the association between carbon and guilt has gained popular currency in the past few years (Gans 2012; McFeatters 2007; Millward 2007), little attempt has been made to understand how the carbon footprint metaphor affectively initiates and mediates this feeling. Carbon guilt suggests what Kathleen Woodward might call a 'psychological' feeling that is captured in language 'with the narrative of our experience a crucial capacity' (Woodward 2009, 25). Naming this novel affect, or psychological feeling of carbon guilt, allows a narrative elaboration of a contemporary experience that connects the bodies of liberal governmental carbon subjects through certain practices. Like Woodward, I attend here to 'feelings as sensitive and telling sensors that register emerging shifts in social and cultural formations' (ibid., 7). As carbon has become visible through its scientific apprehension and then distributed to individuals through a variety of mechanisms, including the prominent carbon footprint reduction lists, becoming subject to carbon has entailed a novel sense of guilt on the part of certain privileged individuals. Such individuals, if over a certain age, might recall a time when one might have for example, gone for a destination-less 'joy-ride' in a car without feeling guilty about carbon emissions.[11] The freedom to emit greenhouse gases with impunity even extended to air travel, what is now known to be a particularly potent climate-changing site of emissions. With the novelty of public knowledge of the carbon impacts of such fossil-fuel intensive lifestyles, largely normalized in the Global North, has come carbon guilt, a feeling intimately linked to a dominant form of carbon subjectivity in which certain subjects are connected in an enigmatic multiscale globalized and yet domesticated and privatized calculus of carbon. The subjects susceptible to carbon guilt are generally home-owners in the Global North with fossil fuel-dependent vehicles and lifestyles, that is, subjects whose practices of consumption are centrally implicated in the crisis of climate change. These are the people who are hailed within many lists that invite 'you' to change the light bulbs, install energy-efficient windows, or buy a hybrid or electric car.

Instrumental in these lists is the appeal to 'you', which inaugurates the guilty carbon subject, an individual who is newly recognized as part of the problem (and thus, solutions) in the cultural politics of climate change. 'You' are invited and told how to reduce 'your' carbon footprint. Popular book titles such as *How to Reduce Your Carbon Footprint, 101 Ways to Reduce* Your *Carbon Footprint,* and *The Pocket Idiot's Guide to Your Carbon Footprint* exemplify the kinds of lists that proliferate in conventional and on-line media in this genre. This call to 'you' and the response – to buy the book list/follow the on-line list and act in a variety of ways to reduce your carbon footprint – entails what Judith Butler might describe as a psycho-social circuit of power that produces (guilty) subjects (1997).

In *The Psychic Life of Power*, Butler's chapter entitled 'Conscience Doth Make Subjects of Us All', works within and against Louis Althusser's formulations on the interpellation of individual subjects into a symbolic order by an authority. (Butler 1997, 106–131; Althusser 1971). In Althusser's well-rehearsed formulation, the police on the street calls 'Hey you there!' and an individual pedestrian, in turning to respond to this power of authority/law, becomes subject to it, through interpellation (Althusser 1971). Against such a conception of a centralizing notion of power, and building on Foucauldian notions of distributed power that flows through individual bodies as well as institutions, Butler suggests that what is missing from this account is the psychic process within the individual that would prompt them to turn to this authority in the first place. 'What conditions and informs that response? Why would the person on the street respond to 'Hey you there!' by turning around? ... guilt and conscience operate implicitly in relation to an ideological demand, an *animating reprimand*, in the account of subject formation' (1997, 112–113). This is one of the paradoxes of subject formation for Butler: guilt or an 'animating reprimand' ambivalently offers the very guarantee of social and political recognition of subjects in this case.

In a similar vein, paradoxically, carbon subjects come to register and have a say in the cultural politics of climate change through an 'animating reprimand' that names them as guilty. 'The average European emits around 11 tons per year, while the average American emits over 22 tons – more than 5 times the world average (4 tons)' (Yarrow 2008, 8). 'You' are interpellated through the finger-pointing exercise in which 'you', the disproportionate emitter (with the American 'you' as the worst) are named as having a footprint unbecoming 'the planet's ability to reabsorb CO_2' (Yarrow 2008, 8). Crucially, this finger-pointing is not achieved through a regulatory authority of law that exerts power over subjects, but through the conscience of a guilty governmental subject who willingly submits to the pull mediated through carbon footprint reduction lists in examining their carbon conduct. While clearly not all of the fault falls on the shoulders of these individual carbon subjects, but rather accrues more systemically to broader social and economic orders, the feelings of carbon guilt engendered by the calculation of one's footprint are intensely individualized and domesticated, inviting personal atonement from carbon subjects on an atomic or household level.

Where and how carbon becomes 'visible' and manageable in their daily lives largely dictates how carbon subjects can allay their guilt and, in turn, bolsters certain orientations toward climate change solutions. I'd like to explore three key aspects of this feeling of carbon guilt.

- First, this feeling involves a repetitive everyday calculus of these subjects and their actions, whereby repeated performance further bolsters the effects of carbon subjectivity.
- Second, this feeling is launched simultaneously with an appeal to cost-saving on the part of the carbon subject, thereby yoking financial concerns with carbon footprint reduction.
- Third, even when all attempts are made by carbon subjects to lower their carbon footprints in this daily calculus, they will remain guilty subjects since they still will not have lowered their personal carbon footprints enough; some other mechanism will be necessary to dispense with the guilt. The mechanisms of offsets connect these guilty subjects to the nascent carbon markets as a key solution to climate change.

Iterative everyday acts of reflexive guilty carbon subjects

The trope of the carbon footprint in these lists offers myriad opportunities for subjects to atone for their feelings of carbon guilt. Those who turn toward the feelings engendered through this trope in these lists enact a form of carbon subjectivity whereby the many suggested behaviours and actions imply an individual or household calculus of everyday life. Advising on everything from the length of your morning shower and how to do your grocery shopping to using a 'rake or an electric leaf blower instead of a gas-powered one' (Government of British Columbia 2008, 117), the lists suggest that your carbon footprint is implicated in everything on a certain domestic front. You are invited (or in some cases, admonished) to participate, save money, and enjoy doing your part through managing your carbon footprint (Yarrow 2008).

Some of the implications of these daily activities are easier to understand than others. Line-drying one's clothes when one can, instead of using a clothes tumble dryer, for example, is suggested in most of the lists. The clothes dryer is fairly well-known as a particularly energy-intensive appliance, so mapping the idea of 'carbon-intensive' onto this appliance seems an easy stretch. The calculus in this case is fairly straight-forward: drying your clothes on a line is a carbon, energy (and money, as the lists promise) saver, but myriad other activities related to household activities whose carbon is so embedded, often defy easy carbon accounting.[12] There is good news, however, according to Joanna Yarrow: 'The fact that almost every area of human activity contributes to our carbon footprint might sound like an overwhelming problem. But the good news is that this gives us scope to reduce our footprint in almost every aspect of our lives' (2008, 8).

The sheer number of ways to reduce your carbon footprint on a checklist flattens out a range of diverse actions as if they were equivalent (having a shorter shower = buying an electric leaf blower instead of a gas-powered one) (Government of British Columbia 2008). Particularly amongst the extended lists, which often feature some gimmicky number of actions or behaviours – 52, 100, 101, or 365 ways to reduce your carbon footprint – such a high count necessitates looking at the carbon implications of a multitude of minor and major household undertakings as if 'you' are really going to do one of these a day, or one a week in a systematic, check-list kind of way (Government of British Columbia 2008; Shimo-Barry 2008; Bohmholdt 2010; Yarrow 2008). These gimmicks reinforce the element of fiction or constructedness in the notion of carbon subjectivity. It matters little to this evolving form of subjectivity if every reader does each or few of the inventory; there is no test at the end of these lists to determine whether you can join 'the club' of carbon footprint-reducing subjects. 'You' are already in the club by responding to the hail (buying the book, reading the list on-line, performing a few of your duties as prescribed on the list). Nor even does it matter whether everyone reads these lists: enough people and organizations, including governments (Government of British Columbia 2008) subscribe to the value of these lists such that they become a powerful element in the formation of carbon subjects. What *does* matter is the domestic and repetitive nature of the tasks that ensures: first, that carbon subjects are now recognized as individuals who can combat climate change on the home front; and second, that the many tasks require an iterative performance of carbon subjectivity that reinforces this domestic, individualized handling of climate change.

As Judith Butler notes, subject formation as an on-going process is achieved through repetition or performativity:

> performativity cannot be understood outside of a process of iterability, a regularized and constrained repetition of norms. And this repetition is not performed *by* a subject; this repetition is what enables a subject and constitutes the temporal condition for the subject. This iterability implies that "performance" is not a singular "act" or event, but a ritualized production, ritually reiterated under and through constraint …
>
> (1993, 95)

Insisting that there is no pre-constituted subject nor ever a definitively achieved subject, but only a ritualized production that shifts according to historical conditions, Butler emphasizes the repetitive nature of subject production. The many repetitive daily acts suggested in the carbon footprint reduction lists and the proliferation of such lists, reinforce recognition of individual subjects within a given social/political and historical order through which carbon subjectivity unfolds. Butler suggests such an order as a 'domain/field of intelligibility' that, in part, constrains how subjectivity is performed (1990, 24). For Butler, 'gender' is that field of intelligibility, for climate change politics, I propose, 'carbon' presents the shifty field of intelligibility or what Foucault (1969/1989, 61) might call the 'planes' from which a subject speaks and acts. Notably, carbon as a cultural element/trope in discourse (like gender) does not refer to an essential and unitary materiality or body; rather, carbon allotropically turns towards other non-essentialist bodies and entities. This turning means that a variety of practices enable the performance of carbon subjectivity. As I describe below, however, certain wider cultural norms come to constrain these affective connections.

This process of carbon subjectivity involves both psychic (or subject-internal) and social circuits of power whereby iterative calls to carbon subjects shape the discursive practices as acts of individuals in larger on-going public performance. The ambivalent process of carbon subject formation enables subjects to be recognized (or 'to count') within the shifty field of political intelligibility with respect to 'carbon'. Subjects must then respond repeatedly to the lists that hail them as responsible or 'guilty' and perform an array of activities or duties that function both to make them feel less guilty in their own psychic terms and to outwardly appear to be contributing to a climate change solution. The list features an on-going animating reprimand from a social/political and psychic order through which subjects respond reflexively. One can address one's carbon guilt repeatedly and continually in potentially so many ways, thus reinforcing an ambivalent circuit of carbon subjectivity.

Functioning as a support to this repetitive calculus of the list is the on-line carbon footprint calculator that emerged alongside or within these lists. Some of the book-length lists have a primitive carbon calculator inside (Shimo-Barry 2008, 8–9), while others propose that the first step in reducing your carbon footprint should be to go to one of the on-line calculators that they suggest (Bohmholdt 2010, 15–16). These calculators are quantitative and yet not precise, and they also involve iterative calculations. After an initial survey of 'your' habits and practices, 'you' are invited to come back after tweaking aspects of your daily life and return to check out the new numbers. Andrea Bohmholdt suggests in *101 Ways to Reduce Your Carbon Footprint*:

> Once you have calculated your carbon footprint, document it and use it as a baseline number. After you have implemented the suggestions from this book, calculate your carbon footprint again. Then subtract your new carbon footprint from your baseline carbon footprint to determine the net reduction of emissions. You'll be amazed how all these minor changes add up.
>
> (2010, 16)

The metrics typically involve a complex calculation of household energy consumption, travel habits, dietary preferences, and consumer habits; however, even as these calculations are complex, they also involve 'calculative choices which can serve to render visible some things and invisible others' (Paterson and Stripple 2010, 350). Paterson and Stripple note two exemplary problems of complexity in these calculators that require 'calculative choices' to resolve. The first pertains to 'embodied energy' in products, or what I have referred to above through Grant (2008) as the 'secondary carbon footprint', which leads to an impossibly infinite number of calculations (including, for example, the transportation choices of the employees who worked in the production of an item that is consumed by the carbon subjects calculating their impact). The second issue they note arises in the calculation of airline emissions, which are notoriously complex in that they also entail a calculation of the 'mutiplier' effect on emissions based on the altitude of travel (Paterson and Stripple 2010, 350). These complexities are resolved, they suggest, through calculative choices that 'systematically underestimat[e] the overall emissions individuals help to produce' (ibid.). Such calculative choices are not typically visible to carbon subjects who trust in the math and continue to perform their duties.

The more one is hailed to perform some of these actions and behaviours, the more one comes to identify as a carbon footprint-making subject governing one's own carbon conduct. Performance does not have to entail endless iterative attempts to quantify your carbon footprint through a carbon calculator (who does that anyway?), but it may involve thinking about the infinite tasks of daily life in the novel terms of carbon, and also considering the suggestions offered as footprint-reducing mechanisms. One carbon footprint calculator, for example, asks for a complex home energy audit requiring inputs from energy bills; at the bottom of the page, appears a tip about reducing your home energy carbon footprint ('put rugs on your floors' in order to make your feet feel warmer and thus prevent you from turning up the thermostat).[13] Each of the calculation pages similarly leads to a tip on that aspect of life, in effect, amounting to a carbon footprint reduction list. Such exercises require a psychic operation or inner dialogue that demands attention to the quasi-fictional but practically relevant terms of carbon subjectivity as a way for individuals to appear and to governmentally regulate their carbon conduct within a larger calculus of climate change.

The cultural practices associated with these carbon footprint calculators reinforce norms in which liberal environmental tendencies of individualist consumer freedoms play major roles as solutions to ecological concerns as they track your domestic, consumer, and travel behaviours (see, for example, www.carbonfootprint.com/calculator.aspx). These calculators bear mentioning for the ways in which they co-productively generate subjects through repetition as do the lists. What Paterson and Stripple call 'carbon footprinting' or the use of carbon footprint calculators 'serves to contribute to the production of reflexive subjects, reflecting on their carbon emissions and engaging in a sort of calculative practice – combining rough and ready calculations with constant evaluation of the practices that make up the numbers' (2010, 350). While the acts that enable individuals to register as actors within climate change are not inherently bad, the sometimes competing agendas merit critical attention.

Reducing footprints = reducing costs

One of the agendas most centrally featured in the carbon footprint reduction lists is the cost-saving one. As the following example from an on-line list suggests, often the metaphoric connections yoke the notion of saving money with carbon footprints more centrally than they connect with reducing greenhouse gas emissions:

> Before moving onto the list, however, we would like to point out that *no matter what your stance is on global warming/climate change, these ideas at least stand the chance of saving you money*. Most of them don't take that much effort and at the end of the month you may notice less coming out of your bank account to pay for utilities.
>
> (Pegg 2011)

Here, even climate change sceptics are hailed by an appeal to save money, so the assumptions of a belief in anthropogenic climate change and the will to reduce one's role in this issue do not even appear central to this aspect of carbon subjectivity. Similarly, the catchy subtitle of the book How to Reduce your Carbon Footprint – '365 Simple Ways to Save Energy, Resources, and *Money*' – intimately connects financially rewarding behaviour with lowering one's carbon footprint. Carbon Footprint Ltd., a global carbon management company, also prefaces its list with the money-saving message (carbonfootprint.com nd).

In these and other lists (Bohmholdt 2010; Shimo-Barry 2008), the carbon footprint metaphor fosters attachments to often contradictory, loosely 'conservationist' behaviours in subjects through an appeal to those who respond to financial incentives. The message suggests that cost cutting and carbon-cutting are congruous acts. The tensions in the remaining appeals in these lists reveal contradictions with what may be called a conservationist approach (at least as such an approach can be traditionally tied to less consumption). There are, for example, numerous appeals to buy more efficient consumer items (Bomholdt 2010, 43; Government of BC 2008, 117). Carbonfootprint.com suggests that you 'replace your old fridge/freezer (if it is over 15 years old), with a new one with energy efficiency rating of "A."'[14] Buying energy-efficient appliances does not as the discourse suggests, in and of itself reduce one's carbon emissions. The quantitative metrics of carbon footprint analysis are highly variable and, if they entail a life-cycle analysis (LCA) of all inputs and outputs, are extremely complex. If one must buy multiple energy-efficient appliances over thirty years to replace an old one that lasted thirty years, carbon footprint accounting of GHG reductions and money saved, based reductively on energy consumed in the home, begins to feel suspect. Further, as characterized by the Jevons' Paradox (named after nineteenth-century resource economist, William Stanley Jevons' study of coal in Britain), higher-energy efficiencies obtained through technological improvements are often associated with *increased* consumption of technology energy/resources, despite widespread beliefs that efficiencies will inevitably lead to a net reduction in energy or resource use (Polimeni et al. 2008).[15] Once again, the quantitative and qualitative are enmeshed in these suggestions and while the metrics of emissions reductions are suggested in these reductive statements, a complex quantitative analysis does not (indeed cannot) play a central role in these lists. If it did, these metrics would complicate some of the suggestions on the list and the list would no longer be pithy in the ways demanded of this genre. My point here is not to insist that the metrics of the carbon footprint need be more definitive, but rather to suggest that the hint of a definitive scientific quantitative metric in this appeal to guilty carbon subjects, coupled with normative consumer-oriented practices revolving around energy efficiency, erase the metaphoricity of the carbon footprint and the political 'filling' in of the imagination in particularly contradictory ways on these lists.

While some numbers accompany carbon footprint accounts in some lists (Shimo-Barry 2008; Berners-Lee 2011), such numbers are most often mobilized as quantitatively weak appeals to saving money or financial gain. This appeal to a financial realm of intelligibility for guilty carbon subjects helps the carbon footprint metaphor to serve a variety of agendas by connecting carbon subjects to often contradictory consumer messages and behaviours. Most importantly, the affective connection between individualized appeals to lessen impacts and promises of cost-saving help to inscribe consumer-oriented and financialized responses as *the* ways for subjects to work towards climate change solutions and absolve guilt. These solutions not only urge subjects to see themselves as 'consumers over citizens' in response to environmental issues (Maniates 2001), they also buttress the norms of a liberal economic environmental order through institutionalizing a smooth transition to an offset economy of commodified carbon.

In his essay, 'Individualization: Plant a Tree, Buy a Bike, Save the World', Michael Maniates delineates how *the* (North) American contemporary response to environmental issues has been the individualization of responsibility due to the 'the core tenets of liberalism, the dynamic ability of capitalism to commodify dissent, and the relatively recent rise of global environmental threats to human prosperity' (2001, 33). Although his essay was written prior to the rise of carbon footprint lists, his critique of individualized responses – including lists like '50 Simple Things You can Do To Save the Earth' – in many ways presages the arrival of carbon footprint reduction lists, which build on and accelerate an individualized, consumer-oriented response to climate change. Maniates identifies a historical 'narrowing' of environmental imagination whereby the ability to foster multiple and contesting political responses to large-scale issues has been severely compromised under liberal mainstream environmentalism. 'Although public support for things environmental has never been greater, it is so because the public increasingly understands environmentalism as an individual, rational, cleanly apolitical process that can deliver a future ... without raising voices or mobilizing constituencies' (ibid., 41). Such a narrowing of imagination exemplified in carbon footprint reduction lists severely compromises the promising space of carbon subjectivity.

It is important to temper Maniates' critique with the insights of Paterson and Stripple who, though critical of certain aspects of this governmentality, also suggest that 'in a climate change context, it is difficult to envisage how limiting global warming to 2 degrees C (emission reductions by 50–75 percent below 1990 levels by 2050) might be achieved without such an intensive, managerial (and self-managerial) effort' (2010, 359). Nonetheless, only rarely or marginally do these carbon footprint lists engage with articulations of the complex 'relationships between individual and collective responsibilities to address climate change' (ibid., 347). For example, only on one of the last pages of her book does Joanna Yarrow suggest a range of behaviours that go beyond the individual domestic household calculus. On a page entitled 'The Bigger Picture', she suggests in five very brief bullet points, actions such as writing to an elected official and voting (2008, 122). Such a marginalization of these connections to wider systems and political institutions confirms Maniates' critique of the narrowing of the imagination of how carbon subjects can perform.

One telling exception to this lack of connection to wider political (economic) systems in these carbon footprint lists pertains to how the bodies of individual carbon subjects are affectively connected to the flows of the carbon market. What newly appears through carbon footprint reduction lists since the time of Maniates' critique of other precursors to these lists, is an explicit engagement with the *feelings* of guilt and their removal through specific financialized and marketized mechanisms enshrined through the creation of the carbon market.

Dispensing with carbon guilt

If, like many people, you find yourself feeling guilty about your oversized impact on CO_2 emissions, there is an easy way to begin to make amends, and maybe even sleep a little better at night … Using this nifty little website, you can make up for those extra cross country flights or that cozy new outdoor gas fireplace by planting trees in Africa. Or supporting Wind Energy in North Dakota. You can protect forests from development, and fund sustainable farming practices all over the world, with just a click and a credit card. And most of the offsets start at $10 to $14. You don't have to be rich in order to feel good about investing in something worthwhile.

(Bucky World website, nd)

From a section entitled 'Oversize Carbon Footprint Guilt', the website Bucky World directs carbon subjects to the organization Climatepath.org that will help you with offsets. As this appeal attests, one of the central ways that consuming carbon footprint makers can allay guilt is through the purchase of offsets within a newly established carbon market. This case above which draws into visibility the carbon sequestration work that trees planted in Africa can do for *you* to reduce your footprint to zero, is just one scheme among many that will financially neutralize the disproportionate emissions generated in *your* everyday life, through some project in a distant elsewhere. Regularizing 'extra cross-country flights' and 'outdoor gas fireplaces' as the entitlements of middle-class carbon subjects, this call to offsets ensures that with the click of a button, and a financial contribution, the guilt will go away and carbon subjects will sleep better. Hearkening to the income-generating practices of the Catholic church in Europe during the Middle Ages, carbon offsets have been likened to the selling of 'indulgences' by Catholic 'pardoners' to dispense with sins:

> Many centuries later, there are new indulgences on the market in the form of carbon offsets. The modern-day Pardoners are companies like Climate Care, the Carbon Neutral Company, Offset My Life and many others. These self-styled 'eco-capitalists' are building up what they claim are 'good climate deeds' through projects which supposedly reduce or avoid greenhouse gas emissions. These wholesale emissions reductions can then be profitably sold back at retail prices to modern-day sinners who have money, but not necessarily the time or inclination to take responsibility for their emissions, and can afford to buy the surplus 'good deeds' from the offset companies.
>
> (Smith 2007, 5)

Elaborating upon the trope of dispensation for carbon guilt through a series of metaphors – 'carbon sinners', 'good deeds', and 'pardoners', this introduction to an analysis of carbon offsets by Carbon Trade Watch reveals a key affective economy at play in this practice.

The carbon footprint metaphor is intimately yoked to these income-generating, guilt-dispensing financialized practices as this metaphor has come of age alongside carbon markets. The discursive currency of the carbon footprint metaphor peaks in 2007 to 2008 with the eruption of a global carbon market that was enshrined through the Kyoto Protocol. According to World Bank data, the carbon market increased almost sixfold, from US$11 billion to US$64 billion,[16] over the three-year period from 2005 to 2008 during which the carbon footprint metaphor obtained viral status. Entwined with the governmental politics of carbon footprint metaphors is the recognition of carbon subjects as individual investors in novel projects and initiatives of the carbon market, for the appeals in many of these metaphors involve the promise of erasing their carbon footprints and subjects' feelings of guilt through paying for offsets.

Whereas the suggestions to mobilize oneself in non-marketized community politics or electoral politics receives marginal treatment (if at all) in carbon footprint reduction lists, the notion of offsets often occupies a more prominent role at the beginning of these texts. In the introduction to her book, Yarrow offers, '[t]he idea of offsetting our carbon emissions by avoiding the release of, or removing from the atmosphere, an equivalent amount of greenhouse gas somewhere else is becoming increasingly popular' (Yarrow 2008, 9). Similarly, while Bohmholdt acknowledges that it is necessary to do all you can 'through conservation and energy efficiency' to reduce your carbon footprint, offsets can also help. 'Carbon offsets are commodities bought and sold in a voluntary market in the United States. The idea is to invest in an emissions-reduction project somewhere in the world to equivocally offset or reduce your carbon footprint' (2010, 16). The website Climatepath.org features the following endorsement for offsets as a means of reducing your carbon footprint:

> In the US, we account for 20% of man-made greenhouse gas emissions, with less than 5% of the [global] population. What if the other 95% all lived like we do? Footprint reduction through conservation and smarter consumer choices is critical, but most of us will still be far above a level that is sustainable for the planet. Without using offsets, there is no way to close this gap.[17]

This discourse hails a particular (American or equally guilty other) carbon subject, who will, through the statistics cited, understand that they are guilty of greater wealth and emissions than can be tolerated for the world at large. Although 'we' have tried our best through tinkering with our lightbulbs and buying energy efficient appliances, we still cannot do what is necessary for sustaining life on the planet, so we must buy offsets. As this passage suggests, despite the offset, 'we' are still living a lifestyle that is unsustainable for existing life on the planet, which raises the question, *what is the offset for?*

The hail from Climatepath.org contains an implicit paradoxical admission that 'we' appear in the politics of climate change as carbon subjects who can speak and act only through the very inequities that make us guilty. The implication is that if everyone were to equally become carbon subjects as 'we' are, that is guilty consuming subjects with fossil fuel intensive lifestyles, sustaining existing life on the planet would be impossible. Implicit in this appeal to buy offsets then, is an appeal to invest in preserving an asymmetrical geopolitical *status quo* that ensures that 'we' still appear as carbon subjects. The companies in the offset game to whom carbon subjects entrust their emissions dispensation and the preservation of their status, affectively attach these emissions to others through a series of hidden 'calculative technologies' (Paterson and Stripple 2010, 352). These technologies include calculations of: 'baseline emissions' that would occur without projects and relatedly, the 'additionality' of the project in the creation of novel emissions reductions; 'verification' of anticipated emissions reductions; 'systems of certification' through which the Kyoto Protocol's Clean Development Mechanism (CDM) operate; and 'legal/contractual infrastructure through which carbon units are exchanged' (ibid.). Such largely experimental calculative technologies and the struggles and failures involved in the agonizing and fraught process of what Donald MacKenzie (2009) calls 'making things the same' remain largely invisible to carbon subjects in this process. Reducing carbon footprints through offsets necessarily entails a reduced picture for carbon subjects whereby they can pick an offset project from among a few choices without engaging with the tensions involved in these projects and whether or not they 'succeed', even by their own terms, let alone as equivalents to atone for guilty behaviour of consuming carbon subjects.

Climatepath.org, for example, promises to help 'you' reduce your carbon footprint through choosing the right carbon offset project. One of the offset projects carbon subjects may fund to reduce their carbon footprint is an energy-efficient cook stove project in Cambodia.[18] This seems an important project that makes charcoal stoves more efficient, thus reducing the amount of wood and charcoal involved in the cooking process, reducing the need to cut down trees and, importantly, making cooking conditions safer for Cambodians. However, this offset project also makes it possible for carbon subjects in North America to deflect their own guilt for large carbon footprints to those remote from them. The per capita carbon 'footprint' as a measure of an average Cambodian at .84 tons CO_{2e}/year is a great deal smaller than that of an average North American at 17–19 tons CO_{2e}/year,[19] and yet, carbon subjects in North America can, through helping make Cambodians' stoves more efficient, reduce their own virtual footprint without more thoroughly examining their own emissions-producing lifestyles. Also noteworthy in this process is the way in which the carbon subject's global position is assured: 'This developing world 'low tech – clean tech' approach has significant benefits to both people and the planet.'[20] A geopolitical divide between the Global North and South[21] is preserved as the 'developing' South are the beneficiaries of 'low-tech' solutions while the developed world retains its high-tech fossil fuel-intensive lifestyle. 'As to subjectivity … this produces what might be called a 'carbon displacer' – a subject who simply displaces onto others (via a monetary exchange) the responsibility for reducing overall collective emissions' (Paterson and Stripple 2010, 352).

The affective economy of guilt and the means for allaying this guilt for carbon footprint makers dispenses carbon through a trick of the market, rather than through its actual reduction in the atmosphere or through creating sociopolitical alternatives to ecologically damaging lifestyles. Offsets ensure a sustained commodification of carbon (an analysis of this commodification will be further elaborated in Chapter 5), but they offer no guarantees in the way of emissions reductions, especially if they are pitched in this way to carbon subjects who can avoid more substantive changes. With the click of a few buttons, an 'armchair' carbon subject can comfortably rest assured that s/he has dispensed with the guilt through helping to finance a clean energy initiative that might also appear as a charitable project that will 'contribute more positively to development in the South' (Paterson and Stripple 2010, 352). The guilty feelings of carbon footprint-making subjects thus function to support an affective circuit that not only defers more substantial reductions that are beyond individual subjects and their footprints, but also serves to bolster a liberal environmentalism characterized by asymmetrical relations and often questionable results in terms of emissions reductions. As Clive Spash insists, the offset industry 'has created a powerful institutional structure which has many vested interests whose opportunities for making money rely on maintaining GHG emissions, not reducing them' (2010, 191).

While guilt may be a partly productive feeling if it moves outward to responsibility towards others (like global citizens as theorized in the following chapter), its governmental production through carbon footprint lists, and the associated mechanisms that support dispensation through offsets, generate a problematic economy of a/effects. By yoking together markets and carbon and footprints, these lists and offset opportunities generate coherence in a variety of settings for the globally dominant market regime of solutions to climate change. As Maniates argues, 'legitimating notions of consumer sovereignty and a self-balancing and autonomous market ... diverts attention from political arenas that matter. In this way, individualization is both a symptom and a source of waning citizen capacities to participate meaningfully in processes of social change' (2001, 44). Understanding an affective economy in which the carbon footprint serves to excite individual guilt, only for such guilt to serve market mechanisms that work to absolve it, prompts examination of the limits of the metaphor inasmuch as it allows carbon subjects to evade collective political action, and permits political institutions like nation states and transnational corporations to indefinitely defer more robust political responses to climate change. The sum of climate change politics is greater than its individual carbon subjects because power flows through systems and institutions that must also be considered a part of these politics. Not only have such institutions not normally been 'subject' to the hails of carbon footprint reduction lists, these institutions also often make use of these very individualized carbon footprint makers to shore up their own problematic logic of business-as-usual.

Whither the carbon subject?

The emergence of carbon subjectivity in the opening decade of the new millennium through carbon footprint reduction lists must be read as an ambivalent trace that haunts the opening of a promising space for newcomers in the cultural politics of climate change. Since 2008 to 2009 new publications of print-based book lists have dwindled, though the first ones published are still in print and widely available. At first glance, one may speculate that the reason for the decrease in this list genre is that the carbon footprint metaphor is now regularized to the point of irrelevance, that it is now history. Yet this metaphor is still proliferating in different forms such that it cannot be read as past history. Understanding this genre's historical importance suggests that perhaps what was historical was the initial hailing of a carbon subject, now a 'done-deal'. If a relative late-coming and award-winning title in this genre is any indication, the genre seems to be shifting slightly by assuming that the reader knows more about climate change and wants to do something about it, and also that the ideal reader is *already a carbon subject*. The book *How Bad are Bananas: The Carbon Footprint of Everything* (Berners- Lee 2011) does not explicitly suggest a 'you' as the carbon footprint maker, but rather inverts the formula, suggesting that activities or 'things' like bananas and text messages have carbon footprints (such a shift of footprints away from humans also carries risks that will be addressed in Chapter 5). This inversion, however, still implies a 'you' who are consuming such things and in many ways, have already become a carbon subject. The text inside the book appeals to 'you' defined at the outset as 'people who want to love their lives and for whom that now entails having some carbon awareness alongside everything else that matters to them' (Berners-Lee 2011, 3). By presenting certain data on the carbon footprint of items and activities, Berners-Lee suggests an ideal carbon subject with a range of choices that *might* inform a decision to lower their greenhouse gas emissions. The analysis is more explicitly quantitative in this book, providing a number in weight of carbon dioxide equivalents emissions generated by each activity or item; although as mentioned previously, this author launches his explanation of a carbon footprint with an acknowledgement that the footprint is a *metaphor*. Despite the differences in this more recent text in the list genre, however, what remains clear, is that the carbon subject implied, this person who wants to 'love life' is a consuming guilty subject with the freedom to choose. The affective mediations of carbon footprints in these contact zones thereby consequentially invisibilize myriad carbon connections with human and non-human others.

Notes

1   The full quotation may be more illustrative of the hybridity of the term: 'Current genre studies (which incidentally tend to concentrate on non-literary texts) probe further; without abandoning earlier conceptions of genres as "types" or "kinds" of discourse, characterized by similarities in content and form, recent analyses focus on tying these linguistic and substantive similarities to regularities in human spheres of activity. In other words, the new term "genre" has been able to connect a recognition of regularities in discourse types with a broader social and cultural understanding of language in use' (Freedman and Medway 1994, 1).

2   I am thinking of certain texts and practices in North American society as diverse as: the famous David Letterman 'Top 10' lists on a variety of different topics; Steven Covey's best-selling *Seven Habits of Highly Effective People.* Such lists expose a generalized calculative practice that is rendered in pithy digestible terms for individual subjects.

3   The Brave New Climate list from 2008 is one such example of a top-10 list that suggests offsets. Available at: http://bravenewclimate.com/2008/08/29/top-10-ways-to-reduce-your-co2-emissions-footprint/ (accessed June 7, 2017).

4   By de-centering the subject in this way, Foucault is asserting a difference between positions like: the Cartesian knowing subject that presents a unified individual through consciousness; and a Freudian or Lacanian version of 'split subjectivity'.

5   At the time of initial writing of this chapter, the term 'carbon subjectivity' did not seem to be in use as evidenced by its lack of appearance through searches in both scholarly and popular contexts. In 2014, the term 'low carbon subjectivity' seemed to be emerging on the scene in a call for papers by Johannes Stripple and Matthew Paterson, whose work on 'governmental' subjects of climate change I heavily depend on in what follows. My theorization of 'carbon subjectivity' built within carbon footprint reduction lists suggests a more ambivalent process whereby subjects are initially not always occupied with 'lowering' their carbon emissions but are responding in diverse ways to how they are connected to carbon in the cultural politics of climate change.

6   I am thinking of Judith Butler's extended and explicit engagement with the 'paradoxes' of subjectivity whereby one is subjected to forces of power through becoming subject to the forces, but one also willingly submits to the terms of subjectivity as these are also the terms by which one is guaranteed a political place as a speaking agent. *The Psychic Life of Power* (1997) presents a comprehensive engagement with these paradoxes through various theorists of subjectivity. I will not engage here with all of these theories, but I wish to flag Butler's work as exemplary of what I am calling a metaphorical struggle through theories of subjectivity. Rancière's position on the 'opening of a space for political subjectivity', though not included in Butler's account

since it arrived later, would fit within Butler's ambivalent take on subjectivity as both a precondition for, and limit to, forms of political agency.

7   As I mention below in analyzing the risks, bringing individuals into these politics offers not only promises, but the risks of de-politicizing consumer-oriented individuals as well.

8   The reference to snow on the kitchen floor in this passage revealingly gestures toward the hailing of a subject in the Global North.

9   In developing a notion of partial situated knowledges, Haraway suggests, 'We are also bound to seek perspective from those points of view, which can never be known in advance, that promise something quite extraordinary'.

10 As I indicate in Chapter 1, part of the appeal to individual carbon subjects must also be regarded as a failure of the preceding attempts to deal with climate change though structures of global and national governance.

11 I do not wish to generalize this feeling too broadly, nor to suggest that all liberal consuming subjects now feel guilt with the prospect of travelling; I simply wish to suggest that for those who most strongly feel the pull to change their practices vis-à-vis fossil fuel consumption, guilt may play a large part in examining these practices that might have been less problematic prior to climate change consciousness.

12 Food carbon accounting, for example, is notoriously complex. You are told in one list to 'buy organic' and on another, *don't* buy organic because it is more carbon intensive. Similarly, local food is pitched alternately as a hero, or as a demon. The bottom line: confusion abounds for the carbon subject.

13 www.livesmartbc.ca/homes/h_calc.html

14 www.carbonfootprint.com/minimisecfp.html

15 In *The Jevons Paradox and the Myth of Resource Efficiency Improvements* (2008), Polimeni unpacks what Jevons identified as the paradox of increased energy use in the wake of efficiency improvements (e.g. bigger cars get produced as engines get more efficient).

16 See World Bank Carbon Finance Data. Available at: http://web.worldbank.org/ WBSITE/EXTERNAL/TOPICS/ENVIRONMENT/EXTCARBONFINANCE/0,, contentMDK:22592488~pagePK:64168445~piPK:64168309~theSitePK:4125853, 00.html (accessed June 6, 2017).

17 www.climatepath.org/ June 7, 2012.

18 www.climatepath.org/projects/innovation/cambodiancookstoves

19 Figures for the year 2010. http://carbonfootprintofnations.com/content/ carbon_foot print_worldwide_1990_2010_/

20 www.climatepath.org/projects/innovation/cambodiancookstoves

21 I tentatively use the notions of Global North-Global South here and in the following chapters despite the fraughtness of the binary. Although these terms have potentially come about to disturb the teleological ring to the taxonomies of developed/developing countries, Global North/Global South can also be problematic in terms of reducing vastly different realities across and within communities deemed to be either of the Global North or the Global South. Perhaps these categories can be thought of as 'metaphors' with competing meanings as well.

References

Althusser, Louis. 1971. "Ideology and Ideological State Apparatuses (Notes towards an Investigation)." *Lenin and Philosophy and Other Essays*. Available at: www.marxists.org/reference/archive/althusser/1970/ideology.htm (accessed June 6, 2017).

Berners-Lee, Mike. 2011. *How Bad are Bananas?: The Carbon Footprint of Everything*. Vancouver: Greystone Books.

Bomholdt, Andrea. 2010. *101 Ways to Reduce your Carbon Footprint.* Chicago, IL: Silverleaf Press Books.

Bucky World: The Wisdom of Buckminster Fuller Website (nd). Available at: https://buckyworld.me/2015/02/20/oversized-carbon-footprint-guilt/ (accessed June 6, 2017).

Butler, Judith. 1997. *The Psychic Life of Power.* Stanford, CA: Stanford University Press.

Butler, Judith. 1993. *Bodies that Matter.* New York: Routledge.

Butler, Judith. 1990. *Gender Trouble.* New York, NY: Routledge.

Carbonfootprint.com. Available at: www.carbonfootprint.com (accessed March 12, 2017).

Climatepath.org. Available at: www.climatepath.org (accessed March 17, 2017).

Foucault, Michel. 1969/1989. *The Archaeology of Knowledge.* London, UK: Routledge.

Foucault, Michel. 1978/1990. Robert Hurley (Trans). *The History of Sexuality, Vol 1.* New York, NY: Vintage.

Foucault, Michel. 2008/2004. *The Birth of Biopolitics: Lectures at the College de France, 1978–79.* New York, NY: Palgrave Macmillan.

Freedman, Aviva and Peter Medway. 1994. *Genre and the New Rhetoric.* London, UK: Taylor and Francis.

Fox, Zoe 2013. "10 Actions You Can Take Today to Reduce Your Carbon Footprint." Available at: http://mashable.com/2013/10/22/reduce-carbon-footprint/#PaOARu128iq9 (accessed June 7, 2017).

Gans, Joshua S. and Vivienne Groves. 2012. "Carbon Offset Provision with Guilt-Ridden Consumers." *Journal of Economics & Management Strategy* 21, (1): 243–269.

Government of British Columbia. 2008. Appendix J: "52 ways you can reduce your carbon footprint." In: *Climate Action Plan.* Available at: www.livesmartbc.ca/attachments/appendices.pdf (accessed June 7, 2017).

Grant, Nancy. 2008. *The Pocket Idiot's Guide to Your Carbon Footprint.* Toronto: Penguin Books.

Hough, Rich. 2007. *You Can Save the Planet: A Day in the Life of Your Carbon Footprint. The Guardian,* Manchester/London, UK.

MacKenzie, Donald. 2009. "Making Things the Same: Gases, Emission Rights and the Politics of Carbon Markets." *Accounting, Organizations and Society* 34, 3–4: 440–455. doi: http://dx.doi.org/10.1016/j.aos.2008.02.004

Maniates, Michael, 2001. "Individualization: Plant a Tree, Buy a Bike, Save the World?" *Global Environmental Politics.* 1, 3: 31–52.

McLuhan, Marshall. 1964. *Understanding Media.* New York: McGraw Hill.

McFeatters, Dale. 2007. "Wallow in Guilt Over Your Carbon Footprint." *The Augusta Chronicle (1885):* Augusta, GA.

Millward, David. 2007. "Boeing Unveils the Modern Air Passenger's Dream: Less Jet Lag and Less Carbon Guilt." *Daily Telegraph,* London, UK.

Paterson Matthew and Johannes Stripple. 2010. "My Space: Governing Individuals' Carbon Emissions." *Environment and Planning D: Society and Space* 28, 2: 341–362.

Pegg, David. 2011. "25 Ways to Reduce Your Carbon Footprint." Available at: http://list25.com/25-ways-to-reduce-your-carbon-footprint/ (accessed June 7, 2017).

Rancière, Jacques. 2004. *The Politics of Aesthetics.* Gabriel Rockhill (trans.), London, UK: Continuum.

Rancière, Jacques. 2010. *Dissensus: On Politics and Aesthetics.* London, UK: Continuum.

Revelle, Roger and Hans Suess. 1957. "Carbon Dioxide Exchange between Atmosphere and Ocean and the Question of an Increase of Atmospheric CO_2 During the Past Decades." *Tellus* 9: 18–27.

Shimo-Barry, Alex. 2008. *The Environment Equation: 100 Factors that can Add or Subtract from your Total Carbon Footprint*. London, UK: Adams Media.

Smith, Kevin. 2007. *The Carbon Neutral Myth*. Carbon Trade Watch. Available at: www.carbontradewatch.org/pubs/carbon_neutral_myth.pdf (accessed June 7, 2017).

Spash, Clive L. 2010. "The Brave New World of Carbon Trading" *New Political Economy* 15, 2: 169–195. doi: 10.1080/13563460903556049. June 2014.

Weart, Spencer. 2014. *The Discovery of Global Warming* (on-line extended and up-date version of published book). Available at: www.aip.org/history/climate/index.htm (accessed June 7, 2017).

Woodward, Kathleen. 2009. *Statistical Panic: Cultural Politics and Poetics of Emotion*. Durham, NC: Duke University Press.

Yarrow, Joanna. 2008. *How to Reduce Your Carbon Footprint: 365 Simple Ways to Save Energy, Resources, and Money*. London, UK: Duncan Baird Publishers.

4 Carbon citizenship

Given the interest in the carbon footprint (CF) of products, services, companies, and investment portfolios, there have been surprisingly no consistent comparative studies to understand our collective carbon footprint on a national or global level. What consumption categories cause the CF? *How does the contribution of different activities vary across regions and stages of development?*

(Hertwich and Peters, 2009)

As the above excerpt from Hertwich and Peters' (2009) 'Carbon Footprint of Nations' report suggests, carbon footprint metaphors offer the potential to make visible complex political connections of togetherness and difference, relative responsibility, and rights across national and global scales. In order to trouble a singular reading of carbon footprint metaphors through the limited frames of carbon subjectivity, this chapter advances an analysis of carbon footprint metaphors that mobilize a political shift beyond the individual. In the above quotation, and the report from which it is extracted (described below), carbon footprint metaphors suggest the promise of evoking a form of *carbon citizenship*, drawing together people into a global collective of carbon flows, but also significantly drawing distinctions between certain nations, sectors, and 'consumption categories'.

In proposing carbon citizenship, I am drawing on contemporary notions of ecological citizenship that promote a reorientation of the concept of citizenship in the context of contemporary ecological politics (Dobson 2003). Citizenship, as influenced by the canon of political theorists from Aristotle through to Rousseau, connotes legal rights conferred upon individuals by a polity (political community, conventionally conceived as a state) and the legal responsibilities that these individuals in turn uphold as members of a polity. Thus, one might think of the rights and responsibilities of passport-carrying citizen members of nation-states as the contemporary terrain upon which citizenship unfolds. As Hartley Dean suggests, however, 'emergent ecological concerns' at a global scale require expanding the 'potential scope of citizenship' beyond these traditional conceptions (2001, 491). A growing number of scholars of environmental politics are turning to citizenship as a crucial notion for engaging with rights, responsibilities, and political community in an unevenly constituted global world of limited resources and ecological degradation where traditional boundaries of citizenship are transgressed (Dobson 2003, 2010; Latta 2007a, 2007b; Smith 2005; Dobson and Valencia Saiz 2005; Wolf et al. 2009). The debates among these scholars suggest that although the 'term ecological citizenship is not univocal' (Melo-Escriheula 2008, 114), ecological politics have reinvigorated citizenship as an important conceptual frame that centres notions of rights, and responsibilities of individuals as members of a political community, though perhaps not from a contractual or specifically nation-state centered perspective, as I elaborate below.

What I am calling 'carbon citizenship' gestures at emerging forms of political community, rights, and responsibilities in the politics of climate change that take carbon, and particularly the carbon footprint metaphor, as a central affective mediator through which membership is generated. By calling on this notion, I am borrowing from the promises of Andrew Dobson's version of ecological citizenship, a form of citizenship that explicitly recognizes global asymmetries in terms of access to resources, contributions to, and inheritances of ecological degradation (2003). The politics of connecting to fellow carbon citizens through carbon footprints may thereby catalyze climate justice initiatives that begin by acknowledging inequalities, and attempt to foster equitable sharing of carbon resources and making reparations for degradation. As Alex Latta outlines, however, the notion of 'ecological citizenship' does not, unto itself, carry forward this agenda; ecological citizenship in practice involves contestation over: how 'nature', in this case, carbon is politicized; and the citizenship regimes in which this form of citizenship unfolds (2007a). As the following analysis reveals, carbon footprint metaphors in these contact zones reveal the tensions between carbon citizenship regimes and practices that both promise to rectify inequalities and to lower emissions, and those that reinscribe pre-existing inequalities and do little, if anything, to reduce emissions. Thus, carbon citizenship, like ecological citizenship, might serve as a site from which to critically examine the 'active politicization of the human-nature and human-human relationships that coalesce in various socio-ecological orders' (Latta 2007b, 378).

Importantly, subjectivity and citizenship here are not strictly discreet political concepts, nor, crucially, are certain carbon footprint metaphors singularly indicative of one or the other; the traces of individual-oriented subjectivity and carbon guilt as theorized in the previous chapter haunt the promises of carbon citizenship here. Parsing them in this way, however, entails a politics of making visible certain human struggles involved in climate change. Whereas the first text I draw attention to above highlights a global citizenry through which a platform of global climate justice could be attempted, the latter part of the chapter highlights contact zones in which carbon footprint metaphors attach to neo-liberal citizenship regimes promoting consumption and accelerated fossil fuel development. The story of carbon citizenship as it unfolds through carbon footprint metaphors is therefore riddled with tensions. I explore the potential of carbon citizenship expressed through carbon footprint metaphors as an open-ended locus of contested membership and actions in a commonly constituted shifting world of carbon relations and processes.

Table 4.1 Per capita greenhouse gas footprint of nations

Country	Footprint (tCO₂e/p)	Domestic share (%)	Population (million)	Construction (%)	Shelter (%)	Food (%)	Clothing (%)	Manufactured products (%)	Mobility (%)	Service (%)	Trade (%)
Albania	2.5	61	3.4	9	13	35	3	6	17	10	8
Argentina	6.5	88	37.5	4	12	39	3	6	18	12	6
Australia	20.6	82	19.4	9	21	16	2	8	16	16	11
Austria	13.8	48	8.1	7	17	12	3	15	28	16	5
Bangladesh	1.1	86	132.1	7	13	55	3	4	6	11	0
Belgium	16.5	46	10.3	8	17	14	5	19	25	14	3
Botswana	5.1	54	1.6	10	8	31	1	11	11	26	2
Brazil	4.1	88	172.3	6	5	43	2	7	19	15	4
Bulgaria	6.1	81	8.1	7	32	14	1	4	10	28	7
Canada	19.6	75	31.2	8	18	8	2	9	30	18	6
Chile	4.9	73	15.4	8	11	26	6	10	27	12	5
China	3.1	94	1269.9	25	12	27	3	10	8	15	2
Colombia	3.4	89	43	5	7	45	2	5	15	16	5
Croatia	6.9	66	4.4	4	28	20	2	15	21	11	2
Cyprus	15.9	46	0.8	17	13	16	5	12	21	10	7
Czech Republic	10.8	75	10.2	2	34	15	2	11	13	22	3
Denmark	15.2	68	5.3	11	24	12	4	10	34	18	5
Estonia	12.4	78	1.4	5	49	9	1	9	15	18	1
Finland	18	67	5.2	8	24	12	2	13	18	16	9
France	13.1	64	59.5	8	19	16	3	16	19	16	4
Germany	15.1	63	82	8	22	13	4	11	22	17	5
Greece	13.7	65	10.6	14	16	19	3	10	18	15	5
Hong Kong	29	17	7.2	13	8	7	28	20	11	9	7
Hungary	9.5	76	10	6	35	14	1	9	14	19	6
India	1.8	95	1032.1	8	14	41	3	9	12	10	3
Indonesia	1.9	89	213.3	8	20	28	1	4	22	16	1
Ireland	16	56	3.8	9	15	20	3	7	23	17	8

Table 4.1 continued

Country	Footprint (tCO₂e/p)	Domestic share (%)	Population (million)	Construction (%)	Shelter (%)	Food (%)	Clothing (%)	Manufactured products (%)	Mobility (%)	Service (%)	Trade (%)
Italy	11.7	62	57.5	9	16	14	4	15	20	16	6
Japan	13.8	68	126.8	14	12	11	4	15	22	18	8
Korea	9.2	75	47.6	11	15	12	3	12	32	19	7
Latvia	6.7	58	2.4	8	23	18	2	12	21	18	7
Lithuania	5.9	59	3.7	7	21	20	2	11	19	17	9
Luxembourg	33.8	56	0.4	10	14	11	2	17	51	11	3
Madagascar	1.5	9	16	3	7	59	2	1	5	22	0
Malawi	0.7	83	11.3	1	15	26	1	8	6	41	3
Malaysia	4.2	81	23.7	9	17	12	1	13	31	25	2
Malta	13	35	0.4	2	24	12	2	17	19	21	3
Mexico	5.6	77	100.9	9	12	18	3	11	29	14	4
Morocco	1.9	73	29.2	15	12	22	1	8	12	29	2
Mozambique	1.1	86	18	6	11	46	1	2	5	28	2
Netherlands	16.7	53	16	8	18	12	3	14	21	23	7
New Zealand	11.4	69	3.8	7	15	19	3	10	21	16	14
Norway	14.9	44	4.5	6	7	15	3	14	28	21	6
Peru	2.6	83	26.1	7	7	37	4	6	20	13	6
Philippines	1.9	76	79.9	8	13	36	1	5	17	17	4
Poland	8.7	87	38.7	6	31	18	1	10	16	13	8
Portugal	10.8	60	10	18	9	20	4	12	15	19	4
Romania	5.2	84	22.3	7	33	17	1	11	17	15	2
Russian Federation	10.1	92	145.7	9	40	15	1	3	16	17	1
Singapore	24.1	36	3.3	9	11	8	2	24	28	21	11
Slovakia	8	68	5.4	11	28	18	2	12	15	19	3
Slovenia	11.9	64	2	13	15	15	2	10	26	20	4
South Africa	6	90	43.4	5	21	21	2	10	17	15	9
Spain	10.9	65	39.4	14	14	17	3	12	21	12	10

Table 4.1 continued

Country	Footprint (tCO₂e/p)	Domestic share (%)	Population (million)	Construction (%)	Shelter (%)	Food (%)	Clothing (%)	Manufactured products (%)	Mobility (%)	Service (%)	Trade (%)
Sri Lanka	1.4	67	19.4	8	12	27	3	8	20	19	4
Sweden	10.5	54	8.9	9	12	16	3	12	29	23	6
Switzerland	18.4	36	7.2	6	19	11	3	15	26	13	6
Taiwan	11.3	68	22.3	10	17	14	2	16	21	15	7
Tanzania	1.2	90	34.5	1	22	45	2	3	5	21	2
Thailand	3.2	78	62.8	11	12	21	4	8	25	17	2
Tunisia	3	68	9.7	11	15	21	4	12	21	14	4
Turkey	4.6	82	66.2	9	15	27	3	10	24	9	5
Uganda	1.1	91	22.6	4	9	61	0	1	6	16	3
United Kingdom	15.4	62	59.3	7	21	14	3	15	22	10	11
United States	28.6	82	277.5	7	25	8	3	12	21	16	8
Uruguay	6.8	77	3.4	5	3	59	3	6	12	9	3
Venezuela	8.1	88	24.7	7	10	20	3	11	32	11	7
Vietnam	1.7	80	79.5	20	15	40	1	6	8	12	1
Zambia	2.1	88	10.3	2	5	67	1	3	5	18	1
Zimbabwe	2	79	12.3	3	20	38	3	6	12	16	4

Source: Hertwich, Edgar G. and Glen P. Peters. 2009. 'Carbon Footprint of Nations: A Global, Trade-Linked Analysis.' In: *Environmental Science and Technology* Vol 43, No 16. 2009. Available at: http://pubs.acs.org/doi/full/10.1021/es803496a (accessed June 10, 2017).

Ecological-to-carbon citizenship

The 'Carbon Footprint of Nations' report (Hertwich and Peters 2009) from which the lead quote and previous figure are excerpted, implies that when carbon subjects emerge, they must be aggregated to a larger scale through comparative analyses that take into account nations, sectors, and relative stages of development in a globalized calculus of impacts. Though this particular report does not explicitly mention 'citizens', it gestures toward a complex multiscale locus of citizenship, conceived in terms of nation-states as theoretical units that operate within and against other scales and through the complex flows of carbon through trades of goods and services. This particular instance of the metaphor demands close attention as it gets taken up in influential spheres of international policy discussion in the unfolding politics of climate change. The 'Carbon Footprint of Nations' (2009) report is found on the website carbonfootprintof nations.com and also appears in the respected, peer-reviewed journal, *Environmental Science and Technology*, where it received the Top Environmental Policy Paper of the year award (2009). Notably, while the usual life span of such journal articles is somewhat limited, this article remained in the top three downloaded papers of this journal even three years after it was published, surpassing even more recent articles on significant topics such as the Fukushima nuclear disaster following the 2011 earthquake and tsunami in Japan.[1] The number of visits to their website (78,000 from 2009 to 2012 in the three years following release of the report) reveals a further audience that extends well beyond the usual limited academic dispersal.[2] The article remains, at the time of writing this book, one of the top eight downloaded articles of this journal (2017).[3] Further, the authors of this report, Edgar G. Hertwich and Glen P. Peters, and contributors to this metric as developed on the carbonfootprintofnations website rank among a veritable 'who's who' of policy-informing emerging experts on global carbon governance.[4] As such, their policy-oriented papers represent a key arena in which carbon footprint metaphors make profound impressions in the evolving politics of climate change.

Lest it appear that I am claiming that these 'experts' are singularly responsible for drawing these problematic relations and global asymmetries into visibility in this report, I contend that the authors are rather responding to the agency of many players in the global climate negotiations whose voices have loudly proclaimed the injustices built into the matter of climate change. At each round of these negotiations, voices from the small island states, represented by the Alliance of Small Island States (AOIS) have critically highlighted the need to re-direct action toward urgent emissions reductions on the part of the Global North and reparative funds for adaptation and/or relocation for these states that are most vulnerable with sea level rise (http://aosis.org/). Further, the Africa Group of Nations has 'focused on poverty eradication and environment as two intertwined issues' that are crucial but neglected in negotiations (Makina 2013, 42). Bolivia has also led, along with the Indigenous Environmental Network (IEN) in critically assessing what they call 'false solutions' of carbon markets. Such actors have highlighted the dominant market-based approaches to climate change as the problem, not the solution (as I unpack further in Chapter 5). This report then, rather than being the unique intervention of its authors, brings together a number of important actors through the attachments of the carbon footprint metaphor to highlight problematic asymmetries and wealth-linked emissions.

As Table 4.1 reveals, the main data set of this report is presented as a one-page list of carbon footprints of 80 countries. The carbon footprints on this chart have been calculated in terms of per capita tonnes of carbon dioxide equivalent emitted in this data year. On the x axis are the alphabetized names of these 80 countries and the initial three categories on the y axis are 'footprints' measured in CO_2 equivalents, followed by 'domestic share' (i.e. how much of those emissions originate domestically) and national 'population'. The following eight columns provide a breakdown of the percentage of that footprint contributed by each 'consumption category' – construction, shelter, food, clothing, manufactured products, mobility, service, and trade. The *per capita* measure of footprints thus situates national citizens bound together in a larger-scale population as members of a larger political group. This text thus introduces a novel play of possibilities through the carbon footprint metaphor; whereas this metaphor in the previously introduced list genre of texts played mostly into an individual often private and immediately marketizable agenda, the metaphor here introduces common interests that may not (immediately) be dealt with through engagement with markets. I will analyze the promises of carbon citizenship enabled by what this report makes visible, after situating the pivotal role of the carbon footprint metaphor as a connecting thread to citizenship theory and practice.

In theorizing the notion of ecological citizenship, Andrew Dobson's goal is to systematically relate ecological politics within a citizenship framework, on the grounds that 'since its contemporary re-emergence, ecological politics has been habitually associated with citizenship-sounding issues such as the reinvigoration of the public sphere, the commitment to political participation, and the sense that individuals can make a political difference' (2003, 4). Dobson asserts his view of ecological citizenship as a new form that cannot be defined through a conventional binary architecture of citizenship: the republican view of citizenship as *duty*, and the liberal expression of citizenship through *rights* (2003). Both of these expressions, he argues, generally imply a contractual and reciprocal relationship between the citizen and a polity, or organized political unit (traditionally, a nation-state). In contrast to this nation-scale and to the idea of reciprocity, Dobson's notion emphasizes a non-contractual, non-reciprocal obligation and responsibility through the concept of justice on a planetary scale. This move is necessary, he argues, because of the historical rise of global relations through an asymmetrical distribution of resources. Ecological citizenship, for Dobson, names a form of citizenship that requires understandings of limited resources and unequal global distribution and suggests moral obligation on the part of ecological debtors (the disproportionately 'developed') to creditors (the less-developed) (Dobson 2003). The relationship *between citizens* is thus highlighted rather than the relationship between a citizen and a 'constituted political authority' (74–75).

To the two dominant forms of citizenship already expressed in the literature on the topic (liberal and republican), Dobson highlights a third – cosmopolitan citizenship – found in the work of Andrew Linklater (2002). This form of citizenship accounts for the transnational character of politics in contemporary life, and posits a citizenry of 'common humanity' operating in dialogic relationships toward consensual agreement. Instead of seeing globalization through these idealistic cosmopolitan conceptions of 'interdependence' and 'interconnectedness' and transcendent principles of equality however, Dobson argues 'globalization is best regarded as a producer of this political space of asymmetrical obligation' (2003, 30). For Dobson, the notion of interdependence glosses over the very material production of injustice that instantiates global relations in the first place. The fact that cosmopolitan citizenship rests on the notion of 'common humanity', argues Dobson, erases the inequitable distribution of ecological space. Beyond this third form of citizenship, then Dobson describes a *post*cosmopolitan citizenship that attends to this resource asymmetry, and establishes the basis for elaborating ecological citizenship.

> The principle characteristics of post-cosmopolitan citizenship are the nonreciprocal nature of the obligations associated with it, the non-territorial yet material nature of its sense of political space, its recognition that this political space should include the private as well as the public realm ...
>
> (2003, 82)

One of the most pressing themes of a postcosmopolitan ecological citizenship for Dobson is the acknowledgement that material-ecological relations exceed the territoriality of nation-states and thus, membership and its relational politics cannot be thought of strictly in statist terms. Another line blurred by Dobson's version of ecological citizenship is the distinction between the public and private realm. Dobson 'takes seriously the central feminist point regarding the need to politicize the private sphere – to recognize, in other words that the private sphere is a site of the exercise of power' (2003, 53). Conventional theories of citizenship centre on masculinist notions of virtuous male actors in the public sphere with the domesticated spaces of the private sphere rendered invisible; however, feminist perspectives have troubled the dichotomy that prevents the private from being seen as a site of politics (Prokhovnik 1998). In outlining the promises of carbon citizenship, I draw out how this inclusion of both the public and the private in the terms of carbon citizenship renders visible certain key features of this citizenship further below.

In transposing *carbon* as a sub-element of 'ecological' citizenship as described above, Dobson's themes appear generative. Global carbon relations emphatically imply non-reciprocal obligations, a political space that is material but not territorially bound and one that is both public and private, as I elaborate below. The carbon footprint metaphor affectively mediates these relations in the Hertwich and Peters report. Significantly, the *ecological* footprint metaphor/metric signals the set of relations and political spaces at stake in Dobson's elaboration of ecological citizenship:

Ecological citizenship's version of the community of historical, or always-already obligation is best expressed via the earthly notion of the '*ecological footprint*'. This, in considerable contrast to the nation-state, the international community, the globe, the world, or the metaphorical table around which cosmopolitan's ideal speakers are sat, is ecological citizenship's version of political space.

(2003, 99)

Dobson highlights the *ecological footprint* as an expression of the impact through daily living of certain individuals, and groups of 'strangers near and far' (ibid., 119) since the political space evoked in ecological politics must be thought of as necessarily transnational. These strangers are the creditors to whom the ecological citizen is indebted. For Dobson, the awareness of these asymmetrical material relations through the space of the ecological footprint offers an opportunity for ecological citizens to shift from political action motivated by self-interest to action motivated by notions of justice toward their fellow citizens. Dobson's citizenship appeal is profoundly affective in that it aims to foster orientational shifts among citizens with disproportionally large footprints in order to connect them to distant fellow citizens with small ecological footprints to whom they are obliged.

No doubt influenced by their work with Mathis Wakernagel, co-founder of ecological footprint analysis, the developers of the 'Carbon Footprint of Nations' analysis mobilize the *carbon* footprint metaphor to bring into visibility the political-ecological set of relations at stake in their analysis. Although they do not explicitly suggest the carbon footprint as the political space of (carbon) citizenship, the implications are commensurate with Dobson's take on the ecological footprint as a citizenship-oriented device. I take this implicit orientation to inform my elaboration of carbon citizenship. While this association with the footprint metaphor disturbs the conventional architecture of citizenship, such disturbance is, in fact, its strength in terms of the politics it makes visible. Further, while Dobson reflectively acknowledges the imprecision that plagues the notion of footprints as quantitative metrics, he nonetheless implicitly gestures toward its metaphoric capacity to reveal how many citizens and regions 'borrow ecological space' from those in distant regions (2003, 101). 'It will be immediately apparent that difficulties of measurement dog the idea of the ecological footprint but without, in my opinion, undermining the basic idea it conveys' (Dobson 2003, 100).

Dobson implicitly returns the metaphoricity to the ecological footprint and even gestures at the wider metaphoricity of ecological citizenship as an idea (even as much of his work offers a problematic normative account of citizenship) (Latta 2007b; Latta and Garside 2005). Similarly, the carbon footprint in this instance as a site of carbon citizenship effectively disturbs norms of citizenship in complex ways.[5] It does so by simultaneously considering multiple scales and political-ecological spaces that are interwoven in cultural politics of climate change. Re-thinking (implicitly metaphorizing) political space allows new actors and processes to be admitted to the realm of politics (Magnusson 1996; Magnusson and Shaw 2003; Magnusson 2011). Why might footprints as metaphors *not* be considered a theoretical political space appropriate to ecological matters? They routinely transgress boundaries, and offer no promise of reifying somewhat fixed anthropocentric structures of governance. Footprint metaphors also potentially politicize (or recognize as already politicized) ecological spaces formerly excluded from conventions of citizenship. The idea of political space here also brings into visibility a *weighty* atmosphere laden with consequential political relations indexed through carbon footprint metaphors. Whereas, the atmosphere has not been central to the space of the *polis* in conventional theories of citizenship, in a contemporary time of anthropogenic climate change, one cannot entertain citizenship-oriented notions of rights and responsibilities without thinking of the atmosphere as a key site through which rights and responsibilities play out.

Metaphoric attachments of citizenship and carbon: Creating 'fellow feeling'

Citizenship conventionally connotes membership in a commonly ascribed 'polity' or political space/unit where individual rights and responsibilities are worked out in terms of a wider membership of citizens to foster (theoretical) equality among members (Isin and Turner 2002). Citizenship is, however, a theoretical, even metaphorical, notion that shifts in both theoretical and practical terms. 'While citizenship is certainly a legal status conferred by a state to members of its political community … citizenship [is also] a moral category and a social (as well as political) identity' (Wolf et al. 2009, 504). The ways in which I take up citizenship in this chapter more closely adhere to the notion of citizenship as a moral category and political identity or membership with an emphasis on: the role of affect and, relatedly, metaphor in generating political membership and the role of carbon and wider ecological-materiality as they shape communities of citizens.

The first key to the carbon citizenship I am conceptualizing is the role of affect. Attaching a carbon footprint to global citizens 'contribute[s] to forming particular communities of feeling or collective bodies' (Zembylas 2014, 370). Michalinos Zembylas draws attention to the 'affective means' through which citizenship unfolds in 'aligning the individual and the collective' (ibid., 380). These affective mediations can disrupt hegemonic norms of citizenship or they can serve to bolster them through, for example, nation-oriented 'sentimentality' that binds certain people together through 'commitment to particular values' that serve not only to bind community together but to set the community apart from other people (Zembylas 2014). Critically, as Sarah Ahmed insists, understanding affective community-building through what I've been calling textual contact zones entails attention not only to how bodies are affectively brought together through these contact zones, but also to how certain bodies are drawn away from other bodies in relational encounters. Affects 'involve (re)actions or relations of "towardness" or "awayness"' (Ahmed 2004, 8). In his description of 'ecological citizenship', which echoes Rancière's thoughts on citizenship inclusions/exclusions as described in Chapter 2, Alex Latta insists, '[w]hile it might seem natural to think of citizenship in terms of an inclusive practice, as that which binds together a diverse multitude, inclusion is only comprehensible in terms of it opposite: *exclusion*' (2007b, 389).

A critical exploration of carbon footprint metaphors in citizenship discourses therefore must attend to how these metaphors create communities of 'fellow-feeling' (Ahmed 2004, 8–10) whereby certain human bodies are drawn together and others apart, highlighting similarities and differences. As Ahmed explains, fellow feelings 'should not be regarded as psychological states, but as social and cultural practices' that bind communities together creating the very surfaces that shape communities and the bodies that belong (2004, 9–10). As well as insisting that feelings do not belong to psychologized individual selves, Ahmed emphasises that feelings are implicated in relations of movement or circulations of objects/ texts that are 'sticky, or saturated with affect, as sites of personal and social tension' (ibid., 11). Affect thus works through the '"sticking" of signs to bodies' (ibid., 13). As the textual analysis here reveals, carbon footprint metaphors in circulation become saturated with affects and stick to bodies to produce particular political effects; movement and attachment are key to the forms of citizenship possible and the actions enabled:

> The relationship between movements and attachment is instructive. What moves us, what makes us feel, is also that which holds us in place, or gives us a dwelling place. Hence movement does not cut the body off from the 'where' of its inhabitance, but connects bodies to other bodies: attachment takes place through movement, through being moved by the proximity of others.
>
> (Ahmed 2004, 11)

Ahmed's case studies of discourses of hate and racism reveal that what it means to be 'British' in these discourses relies on discursively connecting certain bodies together and repelling others as non-citizens. In generating attachments through affective politics, citizenship discourses and practices rely on metaphors as they circulate to generate proximity between bodies to create continuities and discontinuities 'in place'. In terms of ecological or carbon citizenship, ecological or carbon flows disturb conventional notions of citizenship as a nation-centred locus of dwelling. Carbon flows in natural-cultural circulations that are at once planetary and intra-planetary involving transnational processes; carbon citizenship attends to how these flows generate proximities among people. Sometimes these flows may be theorized in terms of national territories, but they also always exceed such boundaries as I elaborate below.

The metaphorical aspect of this carbon footprint deserves special attention in this instance of citizenship as the metaphor gestures toward a kind of pedestrian traffic of footprints across complex scales. The fact that footprints indicate *movement* is one of the strengths of these metaphors; no footprint remains neatly in place and time. Criss-crossing global footprints often overlap such that footprints are not cleanly 'of' or from one person, region, nation, sector. This is equally true of the ecological footprint and the carbon footprint; despite a very rigorous quantitative and empirical foundation to the ecological footprint based in the ecological science of carrying capacity, the *metaphor* of the footprint foundationally interrupts attempts to render ecological relations and processes stable, accurate, and definitely quantifiable. There is simply too much traffic between ecological actors for any one actor-species, to definitively account for all of the movement. While this movement might be difficult to grapple with through the conventional architecture of citizenship (Hayward 2006), it is a necessary corrective to notions of human-constructed stable architectures of citizenship at a time of rapidly shifting ecologies and climates.

The textual contact zones in which these metaphors appear reveal the tensions of 'fellow feeling' at play. The first text, cited above offers the promise of creating fellow feeling among global carbon citizens who are (in theory) deserving of an equitable share of carbon emissions. The second text that I explore later in this chapter reveals an especially emotionally charged nation-oriented case of carbon footprint metaphors in which Canadian citizens are affectively pulled toward supporting problematic resource development in Canada because 'our' nation's practices are deemed to have a lower carbon footprint and to be more ethical than those of geopolitical others. Such cases reveal 'affect as necessary for constituting collective identity and for participating in social and political actions' that have important implications for citizenship (Zembylas 2014, 370). Fellow feelings 'not only contribute to forming communities of feeling or collective bodies, but they are also mobilised for the polity to uphold firm emotional commitment to particular values such as patriotism and citizenship' (ibid., 369). Understanding how carbon footprints connect citizens in communities with/against others and the political actions that flow from such citizenship orientations demonstrates a complex politics of affect at work.

In the first text excerpted above, the carbon footprint metaphor mediates an affective connection between numbers and notions of membership in a global context where nations differ greatly in their *per capita* emissions. Although the data set is from 2001, the article was only released in 2009, after the viral emergence of the carbon footprint metaphor, as if the numbers were just waiting for this metaphor to make sense of it all. While the general tone throughout the report and on the website reflects the authors' insistence on the quantitative nature of their carbon footprint analysis, their story depends heavily on metaphoricity as a way of making sense of a complex node of entwined facts, values, politics, and ecologies. Indeed the lead paragraph of the article begins not with the data, but with a kind of popular poetics of the carbon footprint metaphor (which they notably call a 'concept'):

> The concept of a carbon footprint captures the interest of businesses, consumers, and policy makers alike. Investors watch the carbon footprint of

their portfolios as an indicator of investment risks. Purchasing managers are curious about the carbon footprint of their supply chains, and consumers are increasingly offered carbon-labeled products. Carbon footprints have become popular in spite of the term being a misnomer; it refers to the mass of cumulated CO_2 emissions, for example, through a supply chain or through the life-cycle of a product, not some sort of measure of area.

(Hertwich and Peters 2009, 6414)

Hertwich and Peters, policy analysts who are most definitely in the numbers game, insist that the footprint is a mass of emissions rather than the measure of area implied by a literal footprint. What they miss by calling this 'term' a misnomer, however, is that the very metaphoricity that captures the interest and imagination of so many is what enables the carbon footprint to serve a variety of agendas through its shifty mediations. Metaphors do not nominate a specific thing to which they directly correspond, but rather initiate what Radman calls a 'play of possibilities' (1997, 165). Further, a footprint, carbon or otherwise, whether taken literally or metaphorically, has never really been simply about a measure of an area. Contexts of footprints matter. That is not to charge these authors with the duty of understanding all of these contexts, but simply to point out that they will not be able to define in all contexts exactly what this powerful metaphor means as if it simply refers to a universal shoe size. This is one very important instance of the carbon footprint metaphor that gets taken up in international policy circles, but even here, the carbon footprint metaphor owes no singular allegiance to this interpretation. Rather, it exposes one of the sites of struggle in the politics of climate change by drawing attention to relations that may be called the concerns of carbon citizenship.

The second key feature of carbon citizenship, in addition to the role of affect, is an attention to carbon as an index of ecological materiality that must be more centrally considered in notions of citizenship. Carbon as an allotropic material and discursive element shapes citizenship in particular ways. Carbon footprint metaphors affectively mediate collective identity-building that shapes political action through notions of rights and responsibilities or obligations; these collective identities, rights, and responsibilities are elaborated in terms of *carbon* flows in a global biosphere. Here carbon indexes particular relationships of ecological materiality at a time of climate change. Following Heater (2004) who historicizes epochs of citizenship and those who recently have begun to think in environmental terms of citizenship (Smith 1998; Dobson 2003; Dean 2001; Dobson and Bell 2006; Latta 2007a, 2007b), it seems appropriate to assert the twenty-first century as an era of unfolding citizenships that more centrally and explicitly embed a polity within material ecologies and carbon flows. Given the recent and anticipated continuing rapid changes to material ecologies that are conventionally backgrounded in notions of citizenship (as land ownership, national boundaries, etc.) to a foregrounded socio-political polity, these shifting ecologies now necessarily shape conceptions of citizen rights, duties, membership, and boundaries in ways that are only now beginning to be theorized.

The promises of carbon citizenship

The 'Carbon Footprint of Nations' report troubles the notion of political space with respect to citizenship by acknowledging the category of nations as one key space, but also by recognizing that footprints move in complex ways within and across transnational spaces. An implicit form of carbon citizenship here makes visible a web of national polities, embedded within a larger planetary polity by naming nation-states as comparative categories in a global whole. Here carbon footprint metaphors reveal carbon citizenship as an elaborate entanglement of at least three entangled scales: the national, transnational, and the consuming individuals within these scales. Nation-states appear as members of a larger carbon polity, the globe itself as a biosphere of living relations and carbon flows. This global polity is conceived as a flow of trade-linked carbon footprints that in one sense properly *belong to* members, the very nation-states who demand and consume items and services that are often produced in other nations. A focus on consumer demand within nations in turn calls to presence the individual consumers as citizens whose lifestyles bear scrutiny in terms of relative footprints of fellow carbon citizens in other countries.

The overarching promise of carbon citizenship associated with the carbon footprint metaphor connects the promise of Dobson's ecological citizenship by drawing into visibility global asymmetries vis-à-vis carbon emissions and certain forms of consumer-oriented development. As the graphic data in the table lay bare, 'the average per capita footprint varies from just over 1 t per person per year (py) for several African countries and Bangladesh to 28t/py for the United States and 33 t/py for Luxemburg' (Hertwich and Peters 2009, 6415). Beginning with such asymmetries and drawing on notions of citizenship that theoretically suggest equality, reveals a 'not-yetness' in this emerging carbon citizenship. While these people are pulled together as somewhat united citizens in planetary carbon flows, the divergent size of footprints maintains a distance that is irreconcilable within the aspirational terms of citizenship.

Carbon citizenship thus begins as a problematizing gesture. In metaphorizing the political space of citizenship as it relates to carbon flows, the carbon footprint in this report draws three phenomena into visibility as I develop in the following section: First, the footprint metaphor permits *consumption* to appear and simultaneously troubles the private–public division in conventional notions of citizenship; second, and relatedly, in problematizing consumption categories in developed countries as those that generate a large 'carbon footprint', this report explicitly challenges 'normal' development patterns among global citizens of nations; and, finally, in revealing how carbon footprints (read as emissions figures) 'hop' from the consuming country of goods to the country in which they were manufactured (Petherick 2012), the metaphor challenges current dominant global climate change governance schemes that mask responsibility of developed importing nations.

Troubling private/public binary in citizenship through patterns of consumption

For Dobson's theory of ecological citizenship and for the authors of the 'Carbon Footprint of Nations' and its website, one of the strengths of the footprint metaphor is that it makes admissible as a citizenship concern that which is considered 'private' and conventionally outside of the public sphere of citizenship. 'In the Aristotelian tradition, so influential in this regard, being a citizen involves political activity in the public realm. Indeed, in this tradition politics itself is definitionally associated with the realm of the Πόλις [polis] which is contrasted with the realm of the οίκος, the household' (Dobson and Bell 2006, 7). As feminist epistemologies make clear, this stark distinction between the personal and the political has always been a false binary that consequentially removes key political questions like gendered divisions of labour from the purview of citizenship (Prokhovnik 1998). The ways in which ecological considerations trouble these boundaries is also particularly poignant; in a sense one could say that there is no private-public distinction in ecological citizenship, that these matters are material-ecological all the way down. In the comfortable developed world, for example, energy-intensive homes are not closed loops of energy and resources; rather, they belong to larger energy regimes whose sources and effects are regional and global. Indeed in their elaboration of ecological citizenship, Andrew Dobson and Derek Bell insist that decisions 'as to how we heat or cool our homes, or how and what we choose to buy to consume in them, are decisions that have public consequences in terms of the environmental impact (which may be far afield indeed) they entail. Ecological citizenship thus 'invites us to take a fresh look at a crucial piece of the architecture of citizenship' (2006, 7). Everything that carbon citizens do in their everyday spaces can be connected to a carbon calculus. While the previous critique of carbon subjectivity cautions that the spaces of climate change politics cannot be tidily reduced to the spaces of individual in their homes, this notion of carbon citizenship warns that the private spaces of domestic consumption must not be entirely removed in politics by insisting on the 'public' sphere as the solitary site of citizenship. The carbon footprint metaphor in this report yokes private and public matters as integral to these citizenship-oriented politics.

By insisting on the importance of consumption, Hertwich and Peters make clear in their 'Carbon Footprint of Nations' report that 'household environment impacts' should be brought into visibility in global climate governance even as their analysis offers a comparison between national carbon footprints across the globe. The graphic data in the 'Carbon Footprint of Nations' report significantly yokes the carbon footprint (as emissions) with consumption patterns. As far as emissions are concerned, 'on the global level, 72% are related to household consumption, 10% to government consumption ... and 18% to investments ...' (Hertwich and Peters 2009, 6417). If 72 percent of emissions are somehow connected to households, then clearly it would be a categorical mistake to ignore the private sphere in concerns of carbon citizenship. The carbon footprint yokes consumption to relative national wealth according to *per capita* expenditures on specific consumption categories. These categories are: construction, shelter, food, clothing, manufactured products, mobility, service, and trade. The analysis indicates that while the bulk of the meagre 'carbon footprint' (read as emissions) for most developing countries comes from the consumption category of food, the greatest contributors to emissions in developed countries are the categories of manufactured products and mobility (influenced largely by emissions embedded in the manufacture and use of private vehicles) (Hertwich and Peters 2009, 6417).

There may be reason for contingently preserving the two theoretical categories, private and public, regardless of seepage between them, if only to bring into visibility the mechanisms through which carbon footprint metaphors present one or the other category as the dominant arena through which to think and act upon climate change. Part of the purpose of Chapter 3, for example, is to reveal how carbon footprint metaphors in certain contact zones domesticate carbon subjects into acting primarily on an atomic private household level in a way that leaves carbon intensive systems and politics intact. Understanding the limits of carbon subjectivity, then, requires re-infusing the importance of a more public sphere, the conventional purview of citizenship. Meanwhile, understanding the limits of carbon citizenship requires tempering a conventional overemphasis on the public sphere with a sense of the importance of the private sphere. My goal here is not to burden carbon footprint metaphors with the task of accounting equally for both private and public concerns in a universalizing way in all instances, but rather to suggest that particular carbon footprint metaphors make visible particular contexts that demonstrate how publics and privates are necessarily fused in specific carbon relations. As the authors of the carbonfootprint ofnations.com suggest, it is difficult to think of a way to address climate change at a public, national, or international governance level, without also addressing consumptive lifestyles of private citizens, in both developed and developing countries (NTNU 2013).

Problematizing 'normal development'

Related to matters of consumption, the carbon footprint metaphor in this report draws into visibility the problematic ways in which footprints move not only in space, but also over time, as a function of 'normal development' in nations:

> Our main motivation for this paper was to better understand the role of *consumption* in causing climate change. We wanted to understand the importance of different consumption categories across different nations. We were surprised to see a nice pattern with a clear relationship between total consumer expenditure and the carbon footprint in different categories. There is no flattening out, no indication that the carbon footprint stabilizes at some point. This is, I'm afraid, bad news. We cannot expect that emissions are reduced as a part of normal development.
>
> (NTNY 2013, para 10)

The ways in which consumption and 'normal development' are drawn together in the space of the carbon footprint suggests that current manifestation of economic development over time inevitably leads to larger 'footprints'. The authors make it clear that what normatively constitutes development, at least in the latter part of the twentieth century and thus far in the twenty-first century, has been a sense of entitlement to consumer goods and services that depend on intensive emissions from the combustion of fossil fuels. Far from the notion of development being linked to necessary consumption categories, like food, and additional basic rights to services, such as education, a particularly dominant version of contemporary development is defined rather by lifestyle enhancements that are centrally related to the manufacture of consumer goods and private vehicles. This development orientation toward manufactured goods is also fuelled by the very processes of planned obsolescence that inevitably contribute to increasing national and global emissions.

To bring development into visibility through this frame of the carbon footprint metaphor is not to outright dismiss the trite question 'why should *they* (read "developing " not have what *we* (read developed countries) have?' but to ask why the moniker *developed* has come to mean what 'we' feel 'we' have earned or are entitled to in the Global North.[6] Developing might also, for example, gesture at a need to culture sensibilities (specifically within the largely responsible Global North, as well as more widely) about how current global relations of privilege require appropriation from lands near and far and from future generations. Indeed, Dobson advances ecological citizenship as a remedy to the lack of such sensibilities in so-called developed countries; highlighting this deficit in the Global North productively challenges the notion of 'developed' as a complete and perfect act on a progressive economic scale. The carbon footprint metaphor here in this report and through the on-going 'carbon footprint of nations' analyses, challenges consumption and wealth as these categories have come to define the 'normal' successful development of nations. 'There is a strong dependence of CO_2 emissions with wealth. With a doubling of per capita expenditure, the CO_2 emissions from fossil fuel burning and industrial processes increase by 81%' (NTNU 2013, para).

The correlation between consumption and a quantitatively higher 'carbon footprint' problematizes the notion of wealth and its related normative metrics such as gross domestic product (GDP). As Joseph Stiglitz suggests, '[t]he fact that GDP may be a poor measure of well-being, or even of market activity, has, of course, long been recognized', but nonetheless there is an on-going 'GDP fetishism' that fails to take into account heightened social and ecological changes that affect development (Stiglitz 2009, 1). 'Any good measure of how well we are doing must also take account of sustainability. Just as a firm needs to measure the depreciation of its capital, so, too, our national accounts need to reflect the depletion of natural resources and the degradation of our environment' (ibid., 2). Even as GDP has been somewhat displaced by notions like the World Bank's Human Development Index (HDI), such indices are still 'largely biased by the GDP' (Széll 2011, 548). And while radical alternatives like Bhutan's Buddhist-influenced 'Gross National

Happiness' are gaining some attention, many other alternatives to the GDP such as the 'PPP (Purchasing Power per Person) continue to regularize monetarily based indices whose ratings are bolstered by personal consumption' (ibid., 547–48).

By attaching these perceived metrics of 'success' to intensities of carbon emissions as a failure on the part of a global carbon citizenry, the carbon footprint metaphor generatively undermines these norms of success. Further, the numbers yoked to the carbon footprint tell a story of disproportionate responsibility between nations, whose footprints range from 1.1 tons of CO_2 equivalent per year in Mozambique and Bangladesh, to roughly 30 tons per year, for example, in Luxembourg and the United States (Hertwich and Peters 2009, 6416). Rather than engendering honour and feelings of pride conventionally associated with national trade and expenditures as a function of a robust and healthy economy, this report suggests rather shamefully weighty economies amongst some nations. For the authors of this report and the wider body of contributors to the website carbon-footprintofnations, the carbon footprint analysis as a life cycle calculus points directly to what is at stake in current lifestyles in the Global North, where people have been able to consume as usual and attribute emissions for consumed items to the countries in which these products are manufactured. 'The Carbon Footprint concept focuses attention on consumption and hence provides insights into the environmental repercussions of the lifestyles of the countries in question' (NTNU 2013, para 13).

Tracing 'hopping' footprints

A final intervention enabled by this contact zone is that it troubles a reading of carbon footprints as belonging in the space of the producer nation rather than the consumer nation of goods and services. Acknowledging that footprints move in political space permits understanding how they might 'hop' with consequential resonances in global governance schemes that make crucial calculative choices in how they inventory footprints as emissions. Recognizing a common pitfall in appropriate attribution of emissions, Hertwich and Peters suggest:

> The conventional inventory focuses attention on production and hence on the performance of industry. Both factors are relevant and should be taken into account. However, we want to avoid policies that shift emissions to other countries and account [sic] this as a success for the climate. To ensure that policies really reduce emissions of greenhouse gases, their effect on the carbon footprint needs to be calculated.
>
> (NTNU 2013, para 13)

This report and the carbon footprint metaphor bring into view the notion of fairness in climate policy and governance issues related to established carbon accounting practices. The carbon footprint metaphor here – as a kind of quantitative analysis – becomes charged with the task of taking into account trade-based emissions that have notoriously been displaced from the origin of demand to the supply or manufacturing side of the equation. Carbon accounting, like other forms of accounting, offers rubrics through which to displace items and bodies (and thus, responsibility) making them appear in unexpected spaces on a balance sheet, but this trade-linked carbon footprint analysis differs from the United Nations Framework Convention on Climate Change (UNFCC) emissions inventories in two ways. First, it places the responsibility for the production of items within the footprint of the consuming country, rather than the producing country and, secondly, this carbon footprint analysis also includes transportation of consumed items (ibid.). The authors, by insisting on the footprint as *belonging to* a nation, imply at least theoretically, that this metaphor entails a sense of duty related to a disproportionately large footprint brought about through consumption, even as they recognize paradoxically, that 'footprints' as emissions do not ever belong singularly to a nation as emissions inevitably travel. For Hertwich and Peters, the notion of a national body politic with a footprint names this relation of responsibility much more robustly than do UNFCC emissions data, which allow the displacement of responsibility for emissions through nebulous trading relationships. Hertwich and Peters' most complete carbon footprint analysis was conducted in the United Kingdom and 'shows that emissions embodied in imports have increased faster than emissions embodied in exports. The [carbon footprint] CF of the UK has increased substantially from 1990 to 2004, while the UK government prides itself from being on target achieving the emissions reductions committed under the Kyoto Protocol' (NTNU 2013, para 14). These authors performed similar analyses in Norway. More generally, '[t]he rise in emissions embodied in imports of OECD countries is matched by a rise in emissions embodied in exports for China', but such important trade-related emissions leakages are not accounted for in the UNFCC (ibid.).

Picking up on this issue with carbon accounting in her article evocatively entitled 'When Carbon Footprints Hop', Anne Petherick highlights the flawed method of calculating emissions based on where the fossil fuels were burned, rather than where the products were sourced (2012). While some of the transnational flows of carbon are properly accounted for within international climate change convention negotiations, 'the convention falls down when combustion occurs in the manufacture of a product before it is internationally traded' (Petherick 2012, 484). What is more, 'almost a quarter (23%) of the world's carbon dioxide output comes from goods and services that follow such a supply chain path' (ibid.). Like Hertwich and Peters, Petherick points out that the embedded emissions in China's exports far exceed the emissions embedded within their imports, so a reductive blame from the West aimed at China for its exponentially increasing emissions fails to reflect the fact that the demand for producing the emissions comes in large part from the West.

Similarly highlighting the movement of footprints, in 'Kyoto and the Carbon Footprint of Nations', Rachel Aichele and Gabriel Felbermayr point out that while many signatories to the Kyoto Protocol did appear to reduce their domestic emissions since signing on, such reductions only appear through a trick of accounting that displaces these emissions (2012). Domestic imports have risen in these countries as domestic emissions have lowered; therefore, countries are meeting their targets in part through this loophole that allows them to foist the embedded emissions from imports demanded and consumed in their countries onto the countries in which consumables were manufactured. These reports demonstrate that in a global calculus – the one that ultimately matters the most in the warming of the planet – carbon footprints (read here as greenhouse gas [GHG] emissions) have actually increased. The carbon footprint metaphor (rather than simply carbon or GHG emissions) is mobilized in each of these accounts, highlighting that the movement of the metaphor of the footprint – its ability to 'hop' – generatively troubles the ways in which carbon flows are currently conceived in global climate governance. While such attempts at climate governance through the UN Framework Convention on Climate Change have notoriously failed to generate a global consensus on equitable member-nation emissions targets, what the carbon footprint metaphor in this case and others like it demonstrates are some fundamental problems with the ways in which state's emissions are currently calculated through the United Nations framework. Indeed, Petherick notes that a novel understanding of how these carbon footprints 'hop' has led to proposed new practices within the Intergovernmental Panel on Climate Change (ibid., 485).

While I do not wish to imply that getting the numbers exactly 'right' should be the goal of carbon footprint metaphors in this report or others, the quest to quantitatively and qualitatively make visible certain flows of carbon that have 'leaked' in favour of the usual global beneficiaries provides an important corrective to existing measurements as representative. As I insist throughout this book, making the carbon footprint metaphor function singularly as a quantitative metric disregards the power of metaphor, which generatively disrupts definitive representation. The authors of the 'Carbon Footprint of Nations' report display a slight awareness of the impossibility of getting all the numbers exactly right by acknowledging the limits of their global model in providing exact 'data quality' and a sharp 'resolution' of results (Hertwich and Peters 2009, 6415). Although lacking a more profound awareness of the metaphoricity of the carbon footprint, this report still gestures toward promising forms of carbon citizenship. Hearkening to Dobson's version of ecological citizenship, the hopping of carbon footprints here reminds us that attempts to govern climate change might first begin by recognizing the asymmetries involved in the generation (and vulnerabilities) that constitute the problem.

Notably, although the report is entitled 'Carbon Footprint of *Nations*', the carbon footprint metaphor enables an analysis of at least three entangled scales: the national, transnational, and the individuals within these scales. Nation-states appear as members of a larger transnational body: the globe itself as a biosphere of living relations. This planetary body is conceived as a flow of trade-linked carbon footprints that in one sense properly *belong to* members, the very nation-states who demand and consume items and services that are often produced in other nations. A focus on consumer demand within nations in turn calls to presence the individual consumers as citizens whose lifestyles in the 'private' sphere bear scrutiny in terms of relative footprints of fellow carbon citizens in other countries. Attributing responsibility to these nations as the originators of the demand for carbon-intensive processes is thereby a key move, one which may reify the nation-state as one key site of politics. Paradoxically, however, connecting these responsibilities to certain nations requires understanding that carbon flows do not operate within the logic of human-centric political boundaries, that impacts originating from the demands of consuming nations are liberally shared beyond these borders. Carbon citizenship involves these paradoxes of individual, national, and transnational entanglements. Such is the promise of the carbon footprint (of nations) metaphor here as it allows the globe, nations, and individuals to appear in different aggregates and thereby presents a possible range of interventions across scales, particularly transnational scales.

Crucially, however, to present this instance as the defining way in which carbon footprints should be read poses limitations for participatory politics. The authorities who are analysing in this case are engineers, and energy economists – authorities whose work speaks in part through flattening nations' footprints into numbers and obscuring specificities within nations or regions. Nonetheless, the evidentiary numbers and the metaphor speak powerfully in the contexts of global governance where the UNFCC Conference of Parties (COP) continues to meet annually. This report serves to demonstrate crucial weaknesses in emissions inventories such that future attempts must necessarily include debate on how these inventories are calculated and how subjective stories on 'fairness' come with no specific pre-defined quantitative metric or mechanism, but need to be worked out. Within these contexts, the ongoing 'Carbon Footprint of Nations' analysis continues to shape a story of climate (in)justice and bring notions of *normal* development – especially in already-developed countries – into question. The sensibilities engendered through this kind of analysis would suggest that 'we' in the Global North can only leave things the way they are if we consign those countries with low carbon footprints to continue to bear the brunt for our patterns of development while insisting that they stay where they are in terms of development.

A key question that remains is: How might affectively drawing together a global citizenry in 'fellow feeling' create alternative political orientations that address these asymmetries? As Mick Smith insists, Dobson's form of ecological citizenship does not remain in a moral/ethical register of 'compassion and charity' toward others because such a register 'lacks a specific mechanism for addressing environmental harms ... Being obliged to do justice, to act in a way because it is binding rather than bonding, is for Dobson a political rather than a moral obligation. Justice is portrayed as a *binding* relationship between equals rather than the one-way revocable result of humanitarian obligations' (Smith 2005, 11). Significantly, Andrew Dobson's ecological citizenship and the carbon footprint metaphor again intersect in a particular set of proposed mechanisms that configure fellow feeling in a way that manifests a more politically binding relation.

Configuring fellow feeling: Contracting and converging footprints

> To sustain this 450 ppm greenhouse gas concentration it is proposed that all people on the planet should be allocated *an equal carbon footprint*. Currently that allocation would be about 2 tonnes per person. By 2050 that allocation would fall to about 1.5 tonnes per person due to the anticipated population increase. World carbon emissions are currently in excess of 4 tonnes per person. So, our emissions need to contract to 2 tonnes and then 1.5 tonnes by 2050, if the cap is to be met.
>
> (Climate Change Connection, nd, para 5)

In the above proposal for an *equal carbon footprint* on a public website based in Canada, the metaphor yokes concerns of carbon citizenship with Aubrey Meyer's proposed contraction and convergence (C&C) scheme in terms of an equitable distribution of rights to emit greenhouse gases (see figure at Global Commons Institute). This contact zone gives further support to the mobilization of fellow feeling in cultural politics of climate change through appealing to Meyer's scheme whereby certain underdeveloped populations would be allowed to expand their carbon emissions for a time while others, who disproportionately pollute, must contract their carbon emissions until a future time when all converge at an equitable juncture (Meyer 2001). The quotation appears on the website Climate Change Connection, which originally emerged out of Canadian responses to the Kyoto Protocol and a new national carbon consciousness.[7] Though the presence of a carbon footprint metaphor in a Canadian provincially funded site might beg the question of relevance, its manifestation here is again suggestive of an every-day appeal to citizens whereby policy-type language like 'emissions' becomes translated into the register of the carbon footprint for a public becoming carbon conscious and being shaped into communities of citizens through these affective contact zones. The carbon footprint here becomes the link between an amorphous sounding global or national pool of 'emissions' and an individual citizen whose footprint comes to count within this calculus. The explicit mission of this organization is public outreach and education and it continues to deliver globally relevant climate change news on a daily or weekly basis for publics beyond Manitoba and Canada, due to its on-line presence.[8]

Although Meyer's C&C schema is widely known to those interested in climate change politics, especially at the international policy level, an average citizen who comes to this site might not be familiar with it. The carbon footprint metaphor attaches a mode of popular sensibility to numbers that appear, but may not strongly compel a form of affective association with equitable carbon citizenship for individual citizens. The quotation above highlights the connection between 450 parts per million of carbon dioxide equivalents in the atmosphere (a number that in some climate change models is the maximum permissible to avoid catastrophic change) and a suggested appropriate amount of emissions per capita – first 2 tonnes then 1.5 tonnes by 2050 – for a global carbon citizenry with a carbon budget. The exact numbers – parts per million and per capita allowance, though highly relevant in the negotiations of international climate change governance, are not as relevant to the public because they may not make sense on their own as numerical abstractions for carbon citizens. In fact, Aubrey Meyer himself notes that these numbers need to be negotiated by global players, but that the first move is a largely qualitative one that sets up a kind of equitable citizenship regime as an aspirational goal (2001). Much of the literature on C&C uses the terms of the 'global citizen' as a figure both deserving of equal rights to emit carbon and subject to equal responsibilities around carbon's atmospheric dispersal. C&C schemes, suggest 'every global citizen is allocated an equal entitlement to the atmosphere' (Roberts and Parks 2013, 177).

'Contraction' and 'convergence' themselves are evocative metaphors that foster an ultimate coming together of global carbon citizens; indeed, elaborator of ecological citizenship, Andrew Dobson himself, proposed this model as a starting point for international climate negotiations after the failure of Copenhagen (Dobson 2014, 17–18). In beginning with divergent footprints that must converge at some point, this scheme attends to the 'not-yet ness' of this affective form of carbon citizenship in which bodies must be drawn into more proximal equivalencies. Notably, Meyer presents another ecologically meaningful metaphor, the 'global commons', upon which the principles of C&C are founded: 'The atmosphere is a global commons and everybody has an equal right to emit greenhouse gases into it. If you don't stand for that, you have to defend inequality' (Meyer 2011, 1). The carbon footprint metaphor helps to render this relationship visible. Significantly on the Climate Change connection website, this carbon footprint leads to a graphic portrayal from the award-winning climate change film, *The Age of Stupid* (Armstrong 2010) demonstrating how C&C would work (Climate Connection, nd). The graphics show a disproportionately large figure of a person representing the large quantities of present-day emissions in the United States, followed by a slightly smaller figure representing emissions of Europe, followed by figures of China, India, and Africa, whose greenhouse gas emissions are represented by respectively smaller figures. Each figure walks on a timeline and as they walk into the future, the figures of the United States, Europe and China shrink, while those of India and Africa grow for a time until about 2025 when 'each human being on the planet would have equal rights to the Earth's resources' (Climate Connection, nd). Continuing their walk on the timeline, all of the figures finally equilibrate as tiny figures with little-to-no carbon emissions by about the year 2065. The association with the footprint is made by the figures walking; their movement over time is indicative of the shrinking carbon emissions of some countries and the growth of some others with the eventual tapering off and equalization of the carbon footprints of all global citizens as the quote suggests. This image, like the 'Carbon Footprint of Nations' report troubles the notion of normal development and goes even beyond by suggesting a contraction of 'normal' emissions-intensive development.

Schemes such as Contraction and Convergence offer the promise for carbon footprint metaphors to mediate what Ahmed calls 'affective forms of reorientation'

(2004, 8–9) whereby consciousness of shared carbon flows presents possibilities of felt relationality and human connectedness that are politically manifested. Fellow feelings in these terms of carbon citizenship might imply a detaching from norms of the 'we' that are configured in the present through similar patterns of (over)consumption toward explicit affective re-attachment with a novel 'we' with whom we are already implicitly affectively attached through carbon flows. Again to remind us in Carey Wolfe's paradoxical terms of climate change, 'there is no we and yet there is nothing but we' (Wolfe 2011, personal communication). Understanding this paradox as it appears in the Hertwich and Peters report and Meyer's C&C scheme gestures toward an emerging carbon citizenship that seeks to address global inequalities that are exacerbated by climate change. I call this an emerging carbon citizenship because to those reading citizenship in conventional terms of institutionalized legal status, this form of citizenship might appear at the moment to be little more than a moral plea. After all, as some might suggest, the world is still currently organized as a system of states and citizenship in its legal sense, remains state-bound. I insist, however, with Wolf et al. (as well as all those who are working on ecological citizenships) that citizenship is also 'a moral category and a social (as well as political) identity' (2009, 504). Further, this form of citizenship, though not yet instituted in a legal sense, appears to be informing an institutional horizon in climate change governance, as the endorsements for C&C suggest. In terms of human history, an awareness of climate change by the public is a fairly recent phenomenon. The institutional bodies developing to address climate change are also novel in human history. Thinking in terms of a global political community of citizens who share an atmospheric commons represents a paradigmatic shift in how we might think of citizenship within and against our current state-centric political institutions and perhaps the 'failures' of global climate change governance thus far reveal this struggle is not an easy one. Yet this struggle is visibly emerging; a moral and political community of theoretically equal citizens may be thought of as a precursor to a legally institutionalized citizenship-to-come. These formations inform the high-stakes political arrangements that emerge in their wake. If one thinks of movements such as women's struggles for suffrage and the emancipation of slaves, for example, a moral community of theoretically equal citizens emerged as a precursor to politically instituted and legally binding arrangements. As Alex Latta suggests, ecological citizens in positions of privilege must be more attuned to the 'role of subaltern political actors in politicising the injustices of existing socio-ecological orders' (2007, 378). After the failure of the Copenhagen Accord, Dobson called attention to this tendency to ignore subaltern voices of African nations and small island nations in international climate negotiations, and insisted with the African nations and small island nations on C&C as the 'best way' forward to address the concerns of both 'developed and developing' nations:

> Justice is the key objective, since without it there will never be a sufficiently wide agreement on emissions reduction. 'Contraction and convergence' is the best way to frame future agreements, since this is fair both on 'developed'

and 'developing' countries. The sight of the world's most powerful countries putting a deal together at the last moment must not be repeated in future.

(Dobson 2010, para 2)

Although movement toward C&C may seem slow on the one hand, the gradual waves of support for this model reveal a shifting consciousness about forms of carbon citizenship and connectedness. 'C&C is now the most widely cited and arguably the most widely and diversely supported model in the UN negotiations on climate change and the debates these have given rise to' and there have been numerous endorsements for C & C including from: the heads of state of the South Asian Association for Regional Cooperation (SAARC); German Chancellor Angela Merkel; and former French President Sarkozy (Global Commons Institute 2008). The IPCC has suggested 'a formulation that takes the rights-based approach to its logical conclusion is that of contraction and convergence' (IPCC 2001). In their plea for the consideration of C&C, Meyer and Weir mobilize another evocative political metaphor: 'Averting human-caused climate change actually makes ending global apartheid necessary' (2006, 19). The reference to apartheid, an Afrikaans word that means segregation, literally 'apart – hood'[9] suggests what is at stake in this picture of carbon citizenship is a crucial redress that affectively re-composes a community through urgent ecological politics. Such a redress grants that global citizens are all equally deserving of rights and responsibilities (or 'carbon footprints') vis-à-vis carbon emissions, and consequently aims to enshrine these rights and responsibilities in emerging political agreements. C&C continues to remain a key potential contribution to policy solutions across scales. C&C models have been proposed to enact the aspirational trajectory of the Paris Accord in terms of climate justice (Santos 2017).

Ecological/carbon citizenship as metaphorical struggle

Lest it appear that carbon citizenship entails a singularly promising course of action in the cultural politics of climate change, I now more explicitly turn to carbon citizenship as it fosters problematic attachments through the carbon footprint metaphor. 'The concept of ecological citizenship can be understood in a variety of different lights, not all of them compatible' (Latta and Garside 2005, 4). As Alex Latta's case studies of ecological citizenship attest, contexts matter; these contexts animate how citizenship is articulated in crucial ways (Latta 2007a; 2007b). Rather than beginning with notions of ecological citizenship in the abstract and insisting on certain norms as does Dobson, Latta proceeds through a grounded account of a specific site of competing discursively mediated constitutions of citizenry.

Latta's case study of contesting ecological citizenships involves a hydro-electric energy development project in the Alto Bio Bio river basin of Chile where the Ralco development project required the flooding of the habitat (3500 hectares) of a traditional Mapuche community (2007b). The struggle between the local community and Endesa Chile, the privatized power provider, took place between

1990 and 2003, culminating in the relocation of the Mapuche peoples and the flooding of the habitat. This event involved a protracted struggle over identity, ideology, and interests in the post-Pinochet trauma of the country. Through a discursive analysis, Latta demonstrates how each competing articulation of citizenship was founded through different notions of citizen 'virtuosity'. In the case of the normative national discourse of citizenship, consumers within the post-Pinochet liberal regime of economic growth and energy consumption were posited as virtuous citizens through discourses on the natural hydro-electric resources available in the country that would help foster development and national self-sufficiency for Chile. On the other side of the battle, an 'insurgent ecological citizenship' was constituted through the collective articulations of the Mapuche people and their refusal 'to be normalized within the dominant regime' (Latta 2007b, 241). Although the battle in this particular location ultimately ended in the victory of the national government, Latta notes that 'insurgent ecological citizenships' are not gone, but continue to articulate in other Mapuche communities, thus he aims to recover the political possibility from plural ecological citizenship*s* that remain to animate different future outcomes against a singular neo-liberal citizenship regime (ibid., 243). Latta demonstrates that ecological citizenship can provide the ground for understanding citizenship as a tool of a polity in the construction of cohesive membership and also as an analytic discursive framework for unpacking the ways in which multiple citizenships are constructed. For Latta, 'citizenship should be understood not merely in terms of its existing (or theoretically proposed) formal basis, but also in terms of the struggles that seek to reshape it' (2007a, 389).

Latta's insights animate an analysis of how different carbon citizenships are expressed through carbon footprint metaphors. Within various instances of carbon footprint metaphors, different communities and forms of 'good' citizenship are implied. In the 'Carbon Footprint of Nations' report, the political community is developed through interweaving scales of the nation-state, and the globe as a trade and carbon linked system. Virtuosity at the transnational level of carbon citizenship, which in turn implicates private citizens of nations, entails an obligatory politics of reducing consumption, especially within the sectors identified with the highest carbon footprint (such as manufacturing and mobility); such a reduction is accompanied by a limited time increase of emissions on the part of those whose 'carbon footprint' is lower since a theoretical and eventually manifested equal entitlement to emissions is a goal for a global citizenry.

This is, however, not the only version of citizenship expressed through carbon footprint metaphors as we shall see. As Latta suggests, one must pay close attention to 'the way that citizenship and the environment become intertwined in relations of power, where the notion of citizenship is far from innocent and battles over nature are simultaneously struggles over the shape of political community' (Latta 2007b, 230). Through discursive analysis of the protracted struggle over Mapuche land in Chile, Latta elaborates two key notions that help to unpack differing expressions of ecological citizenship that also apply to emerging carbon citizenships as struggles. The first is 'political natures' and the second is 'citizenship regime'.

Political natures describe the mechanisms through which 'nature' gets taken up or is accounted for in political processes and conflicts within articulations of ecological citizenship:

> I am interested in the way that the politics of citizenship becomes ecological through its articulation with numerous different (and not all 'green') understandings of the environment. As a way of flagging this articulation, I call these understandings 'political natures.'
>
> (2007b, 231)

Importantly, Latta makes visible nature(s) here neither as a reified mute thing that can, as Latour suggests, shut down democratic processes (2004), nor as inert environment, but as a discursively and culturally mediated material relationship that varies within different citizenships. The same can be said of carbon itself and the carbon footprint metaphor that comes to take on various meanings and brings to light different associated practices of citizenship. The ways in which carbon is explicitly politicized in citizenship discourses featuring carbon footprints varies; thus, this metaphor's mediations feature a contested dynamic of the shaping of political communities.

A second pivotal notion that Latta uses is 'citizenship regime' (2007b, 236). This notion foregrounds a dominant power structure that ensures certain normative articulations of citizenship. In Latta's case of the Chilean government's neo-liberal citizenship regime, citizens were construed as marketized and economically developed energy-users for the benefit of the nation's cohesion and growth. Latta provides an elaboration of the dominant citizenship regimes as an analytic tool to uncover the ways in which a range of citizens' behaviors and actions are encoded within the norms and standards of a dominant polity and the ways in which these are challenged by 'insurgent' ecological citizenships. In his case study, the national citizenship regime was largely determined by the Pinochet administration's violent imposition of a neo-liberal agenda of economic development. This citizenship regime dictated that the 'nature' in question, the river basin and habitat of the Mapuche people, be politicized as a source of renewable energy for an economically developing nation. To oppose such a project implicated objectors as bad citizens, oppressors of the economic and social health of the emerging nation; therefore, virtuous citizenly behaviour within the national regime would dictate support for such developments of natural resources. Latta presents the notion of a citizenship regime as a kind of top-down ideological mechanism, but he also suggests that the dynamic interplay between political natures and divergent articulations of citizenship reveal myriad ecological citizenships whose presence may enable a more democratic understanding of citizenship.

Inflected in this way, the myriad articulations of carbon citizenship through carbon footprint metaphors provide a productive site of politics as contestation. Who or what counts? What does it mean to take the element of carbon as an important site of citizenships? How is 'nature' (in this case, carbon) politicized in various discourses and what does it bring into frames of visibility? In the first case featuring carbon footprint metaphors above, carbon is politicized in a particular way that brings non-reciprocal global relations into view. In the case that follows, the metaphor yokes carbon citizens to a problematic nation-oriented liberal environmental citizenship regime.

The risks of nation-oriented attachments of carbon citizenship

As those who work to push the boundaries of citizenship into ecological realms attest, notions of citizenship are subject to the overdeterminations of nation-bound discourses and practices that often reify 'current socio-cultural norms and structures' (Wolf et al. 2009, 518). Even Andrew Dobson, a strong advocate for inculcating practices of ecological citizenship, recognizes the risks of liberal democratic state-centred environmental citizenships. In such states, a widely interpreted 'sustainability' registers as one index of health and welfare of its people amongst other usually more heavily weighted indicators of economic growth and employment, such as the GDP (Dobson 2003, 150). These tensions exist in liberal democratic states, which also coincidentally happen to be those states that 'are responsible for by far the most environmental damage' (ibid., 142). Nation-oriented citizenship attachments can serve to 'repeat past associations' and this has to do with 'signs and how they work on and in relation to bodies' (Ahmed 2004, 194). The carbon footprint metaphor is not innocent in this regard; this metaphor can act as a sticky sign that produces the surfaces of nation-bound carbon citizens in opposition to global others by making these others into objects of carbon pollution and hate.

Perhaps no other carbon footprint metaphor more clearly attaches to this fraught liberal citizenship regime than the following:

> Oil sands oil actually has a smaller carbon footprint than other sources of oil, like in Nigeria where huge amounts of natural gas are simply burned off into the air as the oil is produced.
>
> (Levant 2011, 6)

From the best-selling and award-winning book, *Ethical Oil*, of well-known climate sceptic, Ezra Levant, this carbon footprint metaphor affectively mediates the shaping of a body of virtuous Canadian citizens with a smaller carbon footprint than an imagined body of citizens in Nigeria. While those responsible may not solely be citizens, but rather oil producers and the states that support them, the appeal resonates within an affective register of citizenship in Canada that draws people together in national community in part through distancing from other 'foreign' communities as Ahmed indicates. Here the carbon footprint (metaphor) is presented as a sticky sign of dirty carbon released by the burning of natural gas during the production of oil. One could question the quantitative metrics of the carbon footprint in this instance because Levant does not cite data or make reference to a report of these comparative measures; there is no life cycle analysis of carbon dioxide produced from cradle to grave in Alberta bitumen extraction versus Nigerian oil extraction processes. Notably, the more general data for *per capita* carbon emissions suggests a gaping chasm between Canada's carbon emissions of approximately 16.3 tons per year, and Nigeria's which amount to approximately 0.5 tons per year (Energy Information Administration 2012).[10] But to question such metrics may be beside the point, for the footprint here only peripherally gestures at anthropogenic climate change since Levant himself is a sceptic of anthropogenic causes of global warming. More important than the (absent) metrics here is the way in which '[t]he 'nation' becomes a shared 'object of feeling' through the 'orientation' that is taken toward it' (Ahmed 2004, 13).

The carbon footprint metaphor in the context of this book carries along the nation-centric citizenship conditions to support Levant's 'ethical oil' agenda, an emotionally charged hate-generating platform to foster the unbridled development of the bitumen sands for the economic benefit of Canadian industry and national wealth. This agenda features the profoundly important work of affect in binding bodies together in carbon citizenship; however, in this instance the mechanisms for binding bodies together in the shaping of community particularly involves sticking hate and disgust onto global others in what Ahmed calls reactions of 'awayness' (ibid., 8). The metaphor of the varying carbon footprints at the lead of Levant's book initiates a seemingly quantitative comparison between two countries' oil production techniques, which then gets yoked throughout the book to more generalized arguments about the relative virtuosity of Canada in the world; this claim of relative virtuosity is aimed at displacing the validity of critiques of oil production in Canada in re-entrenching a particularly problematic vision of a Canadian citizen.

The first of Alex Latta's key citizenship elements mentioned above – political natures – helps to unpack how carbon citizenship is affectively articulated in this discourse; the carbon footprint metaphor initiates a narrative that carries over a host of other hateful impressions of others. Carbon as allotropic material and cultural element is politicized in a way that lends to its compounding attachments to other undesirable characteristics that have no immediate relation to climate change. Attaching a larger, dirtier carbon footprint to Nigerian oil extraction is the first step in pulling together a nation of liberal environmental Canadians who might otherwise be critical of the bitumen extraction process in Canada. What is first drawn into visibility in this instance of the carbon footprint metaphor used by Levant is the image of one point in a complex chain of oil production. The image of plumes of greenhouse gas emitting billowy flames emerging at the source of production of oil in Nigeria is next yoked together with supposed corrupt and violent attributes of global others who, in Ezra Levant's thesis, are the unethical version of Canadian Oil Sands extractors, a cleaner, more civilized, and, above all, 'ethical' species of citizens. As one can see in the elaboration of Levant's ethical oil agenda, carbon gets politicized not only as an index of dirty oil production; carbon is yoked to other entities/relations as an index of a number of these other hateful attributes. By supporting our own fossil fuel industry the rhetorical 'we' of Canadian citizenry are virtuously diverting and redistributing money:

that could have helped further arm Nigeria's brutal militias, to fund Iran's hostile nuclear weapons program, to power Russia's materialistic warmongering, to prop up Venezuela's failing Marxist experiment and its suppression of citizens' rights, and to allow Saudi Arabia's princes to sponsor more terrorists and buy yet more time for their cruel and decadent regime.

(2011, 228)

Here carbon citizenship becomes saturated with the affects of a geopolitics of emotion of us/them, whereby hatred or loathing is attributed to the national bodies of Venezuela, Nigeria, and Saudi Arabia. The catalogue of Marxism, terrorism, primitivism, nuclear armament, and ('foreign'?) misogyny rampant in other countries reads as a litany of all that is at odds with the ethically purified carbon footprint of Western liberal democracy. Through this particular citizenship discourse, the nation as an object of attachment comes into effect through a process of sticking disgust and hatred to other bodies politic:

> hate creates the surfaces of bodies through the way in which bodies are aligned with and against other bodies. How we feel about others is what aligns us with a collective, which paradoxically 'takes shape' only as an effect of such alignments. It is through how others impress upon us that the skin of the collective begins to take shape.
>
> (Ahmed 2004, 54)

In order to align the intra-national dissenting bodies on the issue of Oil Sands development, the body of a Canadian national collective is evoked. The liberal democratic nation takes shape to keep out the hateful influence of global others. Says Levant: 'I don't know what God was thinking when he was handing out oil, but he gave it to all the world's bastards – Saudi Arabia, Iran, Venezuela and Nigeria. Out of the top 10 countries ranked by oil reserves, Canada is the only Western liberal democracy on the list' (Chase, 2012). 'We' Canadians have a set of values that prohibits the kinds of malevolent practices that run rampant in these other geopolitically troubled regions. 'We' do not stone our wives to death for adultery; 'we' do not kill people over oil as they do in Nigeria; 'we' do not harbour terrorists who blow up the most sacred secular institutions in the developed world as they do in Saudi Arabia and Iran (Levant 2011, 16–34). There is only one virtuous choice for oil extraction in the global reserves; selling this message to the Canadian citizenry is the first necessary step in the on-going mission of selling the crude to a global market hungry for oil, a global market that ironically, as Levant suggests, does not actually care whether the oil is ethical or not. It is as though our smaller carbon footprint helps to shed light on the manifest destiny of the keepers of Western liberal democracy and bituminous wonders to bring ethical oil to the masses of unenlightened others. To do otherwise than to support *this* Canadian ethical oil development would be, for Levant and his supporters, simply un-becoming of citizens. Such is the work of the carbon footprint metaphor presented by Levant as it politicizes the 'natural' element of carbon by yoking it with elements of what he calls 'conflict oil'. Conflict oil in Levant's discourse is that which is mixed with misogyny, government corruption, and generalized violence that characterizes global elsewheres.

A certain 'Canadian' form of carbon – bitumen, or Oil Sands oil – is also politicized by Levant in a way that naturalizes it as an indigenous element that has been part of the Canadian landscape and important First Nations cultural traditions. 'It's true there is oil seeping into the rivers north of Fort McMurray and sometimes the air smells like sulphur and the water is bitter. And that's how it's been for millennia – Aboriginals traditionally used the thick bitumen that bubbled out of the ground to waterproof their canoes' (2011, 4). Paradoxically then, this tarry sticky substance that has been referred to as one of the most difficult substances to extract and to clean when spilled as 'dilbit' or diluted bitumen (Hasemyer 2013) gets culturally refined for an imagined Canadian citizenry. This imagined community begins problematically with the very first Indigenous 'Canadians', as if the nation came into existence without the violence of a colonial past that is perpetuated in the present through large-scale extraction operations. To downplay the alarmism that Levant claims plagues the environmentalists whose opposition to the bitumen sands development relies on smeary images of the land, Levant coolly paints an affective picture of the natural and harmonious relationship that bitumen has always played in the region. Naturalizing the current extraction processes as continuous with a kind of romanticized Indigenous symbiotic co-evolution on the land does tremendous affective work for the ethical oil appeal. This appeal invisibilizes the neo-colonial extraction processes that continue to dispossess Indigenous peoples of their land and to disproportionately pollute waterways with industrial wastes. The naturalized bitumen footprint comes along with the affective stamp of Canadian virtuosity, stripped of its colonial past, present, and future.

By examining Levant's use of the carbon footprint as a lead-in to the appeal to citizenry to support 'ethical oil', I am not suggesting that Canada is 'the worst' in a comparative analysis of these countries; however, as many commentators have revealed, Canada is far from 'clean' from either an 'ethical' standpoint or an emissions-calculus standpoint (Kurek et al. 2012; McLachlan 2014; Nikiforuk 2010, 2011; Pembina 2005). Both the eruptive violence of oil production and transport (for example with the 2013 Lac Megantic Quebec train explosion that killed 47 people), as well as the more gradual violence evident at the sites of production and distribution, reveal a highly problematic set of practices within Canadian operations. One unanticipated positive effect of Levant's argument is that it initiates a broader reflection on these ethical and political arrangements within current sites of oil production and distribution.

If one takes Levant's own urge to call attention to ethics, politics of oil, and comparative emissions beyond his own argument, two important issues arise within a Canadian context. The first is the fact that Indigenous communities in Northern Alberta themselves are bearing a disproportionate burden of toxicity in relation to this bitumen extraction process, despite Levant's claim that Indigenous communities and bitumen have always been, and remain in, 'natural' harmony.

Whereas the kinds of violence evoked by Levant as present in other countries are spectacular forms that are immediately visible, there exist in Canada's oil production sites many examples of what Rob Nixon calls 'slow violence', a violence that 'occurs gradually and out of sight, a violence of delayed destruction that is dispersed across time and space, an attritional form of violence that is typically not viewed as violence at all' (Nixon 2011, 2). This long-term and cumulative kind of violence is at once social and ecological, for creating toxic loads within the air and water surrounding the site of oil production also directly impacts the human communities, predominantly Indigenous, who subsist within these ecosystems; notably, these impacts are also multi-generational (Bruner 2008). A scientific report commissioned by Environment Canada suggests, '[o]f particular concern are the atmospheric loadings and distributions of contaminants associated with oil sands surface-mining and processing activities, many of which are carcinogens and rank in the top 10 hazardous substances on the US Agency for Toxic Substances and Disease Registry' (Kurek et al. 2012, 1). These carcinogens, specifically the polycyclic aromatic hydrocarbons (PAHs), have been found to be 2.5–23 times greater than levels before the Oil Sands development in lakes as far as 90 kilometres away from the development site (ibid., 1). While this report does not go so far as to directly link increased rates of cancer among Indigenous communities in Fort McKay and Fort Chipewyan, it does suggest, against industry claims, that the scale and pace of expansion of the Oil Sands creates 'extraordinary' and undeniable impacts to these socio-ecological systems, which require further study for their longitudinal impacts (ibid., 4). Some such research has recently been undertaken through the University of Manitoba with the communities of the Mikisew Cree First Nation and the Athabasca Chipewyan First Nation that are downstream from the Oil Sands. Findings indicate 'upstream development [of the oil sands] and environmental decline are affecting cancer occurrence. Thus, cancer occurrence increased significantly with participant employment in the Oil Sands and with the increased consumption of traditional foods and locally caught fish' (McLachlan 2014, 12). Such evidence of gradual and multigenerational slow violence tempers an easy rendering of Canada's 'ethical' status.

The second issue obscured by Levant's 'ethical oil with-a-lower-carbon-footprint' narrative pertains to both the notoriously energy and water-intensive process that is involved in bitumen extraction and the unprecedented scale of development of the Oil Sands. Three to six barrels of water are extracted from the Athabasca River for each barrel of bitumen surface mined (Schindler and Donahue 2006). Summer flows in the Athabasca River have declined due to a combination of climate change and water extraction for the oil sands development and there is great concern that at the pace and scale of projected development, a lack of water security will severely threaten socio-ecological systems (ibid.). In addition to the intensive use of water, oil production at the Oil Sands site contributes a comparatively high proportion of emissions relative to other oil production sites, so the 'carbon footprint' analysis as a quantitative measure does not present Canadian production in a good light in general oil production. Even the Canadian Association of Petroleum Producers (CAPP), whose facts, if anything would be skewed to understate impacts suggests, '[o]il sands crude has similar CO_2 emissions to other heavy oils and is 9% more intensive that the U.S. crude supply' (CAPP 2014).[11] What is more, the scale of the operation of Canada's Oil Sands exceeds that of Nigeria, the one claimed to have a higher carbon footprint (with no accompanying analysis). The known quantity of oil reserves in Canadian Oil Sands far exceeds that of Nigeria, so the calculus requires a longitudinal perspective that is clearly not part of Levant's assessment (EIA 2014).

Levant's argument requires a comparative analysis that flattens time and space and tars over a potentially political-ethical space of the carbon footprint. Nonetheless, it is still an appeal to a form of carbon citizenship that suggests while 'we' are taking carbon out of the grounds (as the idealized reader knows needs to happen since we still need it for almost everything in the developed world), 'we' ought to act virtuously by supporting the values that 'we' believe in as they manifest in Canadian Oil Sands production. A similar story affectively binds Canada and the United States along the lines of 'repatriating' North American energy and avoiding the political volatility still rampant in the Middle East and Africa (TransCanada 2011). The argument short circuits many key questions including: what could be done, even through limited bitumen extraction, to enable a move away from fossil fuels; and whether the bitumen extraction operations in Canada themselves could be done more 'ethically'. As Andrew Nikiforuk notes, oil and good ethics do not generally mix, although so-called 'conflict oil' and so-called 'ethical oil' regularly do because of the masses of light crude 'conflict oil' imported as a necessary aspect of bitumen extraction process (Nikiforuk 2011). Levant's argument is entirely constructed on a false set of oppositions and choices: either *their* blood-stained carbon footprint heavy conflict oil or *our* enlightened, democratic, less-carbon intensive (by no easily defined or apparent standards) oil.

Carbon footprints metaphors in these spaces offer the initial affective mediation into a world divided along so many other lines that reify a (carbon) citizenship orientation geared inwards toward the nation. Urging Canadian citizens to make this virtuous choice is an attempt to pull together the people and groups in Canada who are internally divided on the issue of bitumen extraction. Arranging dissent against a foreign detestable 'other' diminishes dissent within the nation on this issue. Such an arrangement also amounts to continued support for bitumen development as the economic driver of health and wealth of Canadian citizens well into the future. 'Ethical' carbon footprints thus ensure citizen prospects for years to come in a liberal environmental citizenship regime.

Latta's elaboration of dominating citizenship regimes offers a key window into understanding how the possibilities for carbon citizenship are constrained by citizenship norms that exist within and across nations. In Latta's case study of the development of a hydro-electric dam on Mapuche territory, an 'energetic nationalism' was organized around the 'plenty/scarcity' discourse of energy and its relationship to development and national security, especially in light of potential dependence on natural gas from Argentina, with whom Chile has had fraught relation (2007a, 233):

The effect of drawing hydroelectric energy into the ideological space of developmentalism and national security is the self evidence of an appeal to the "common good" and hence the construction of a particular model of citizenly virtue. If sustained economic growth is the core national project – the fundamental good – then virtuosity, as a quality of citizenship, must be located in the ability to invest in productive activity.

(ibid., 233)

Although the actors are different in the case of Canadian carbon citizen's virtuous behaviour in support of 'ethical oil', the tendency is similarly geared at a common good that features developmentalism and national energy security. Given the recent recession and the plummeting prices of oil that have impacted many Canadian citizens, the discourse appealing to job creation is especially potent at both the provincial and national levels. In a concerted effort to mobilize the popular appeal of Levant's 'ethical oil' narrative in the wake of the publicity of the book release, then Prime Minister Stephen Harper stated:

The oil sands are a very important resource for our country, it's a source of economic growth and jobs across the country, not just in the West, but in Ontario and Quebec, too. It's critical to develop that resource in a way that's responsible and environmental and the reality for the United States, which is the biggest consumer of our petroleum products, is that Canada is a very ethical society and a safe source for the United States in comparison to other sources of energy.

(Chase 2011)

Here Harper not only affectively appeals to the job creation motivation for citizens, but he asserts the need for Canadians to line up behind the 'ethical oil' narrative as a connection to neighbours to the south who are 'our' biggest customers and fellow lovers of liberal democracy.

Further entrenching this oil-consuming and energy-regime supporting citizen is the emerging notion of 'energy citizens'. On the website of Canada's Energy Citizens, an initiative of CAPP, good supporters of this national energy regime are invited to 'join thousands of Canadians who are proud of the positive impacts of our energy industry. Your voice can make all the difference' (Canada's Energy Citizens 2014).

As is evident in the above instance and others like it,[12] carbon citizenship expressed through carbon footprint metaphors can easily amount to a normative reinforcement of a national political citizenship regime that fits into and bolsters a certain dominant transnational order of climate change politics. Carbon citizenships in these instances bring no promise of radical reconfiguration of global carbon relationships as a means of confronting climate change; rather, they return to a global liberal economic and environmental order. For as Levant's ethical oil thesis suggests, these intra-nation citizenship regimes interact with wider economies of scale, which feature global competition amongst nations in energy politics. In such cases of carbon citizenship, the affective mediations of carbon footprint metaphors often serve not only to bind bodies in alignment with national regimes of 'sustainable' development, but also to attempt to sever attachments to global others who are connected in complex flows of carbon.

The value of carbon citizenships mediated through carbon footprint metaphors

The carbon footprint metaphors in the instances highlighted in this chapter suggest carbon citizenship as a set of struggles that play out across a complex field of interacting scales. The promising kinds of struggles that I analyse in the first part of the chapter relate to how intersecting global, national, and cross-sectoral political communities are drawn together through the carbon footprint metaphor. The footprint suggests that, theoretically, global citizens should be both: equally deserving of rights to benefit from carbon flows as emissions; and equally responsible for lowering disproportionately large emissions legacies. When the current state of actual material relations with global others does not affirm this theoretical equality, the carbon footprint metaphor can serve to make this visible and thus, potentially alterable. While politically instituting what might seem to be a moral community of carbon footprint makers is not a simple task, nor one that is (ever will be) complete, the instances I explore reveal the metaphor as a mediator through which these crucial relations might appear and inform emerging global climate governance schemes. Citizenship, even in its non-ecological theorizations, involves a struggle over inclusionary principles, rights, and responsibilities. As Rancière notes, right from the beginning of citizenship theorizations with Aristotle, there have always been those who have been left out of the count of citizens (Rancière 2004); the value of citizenship as a theory is that it provides terms for considering participation in climate change politics. The emerging theories of ecological citizenship and their associations with carbon footprint metaphors bring new perspectives of crucial global material-ecological relations into consideration. Such relations are currently characterized by asymmetries and, as such, when these are brought into visibility through carbon footprint metaphors, certain forms of redressing asymmetry (like C&C) reach the agenda of global climate change politics. The instances cited above serve, as Latta suggests, 'to draw some of our attention away from questions of what ecological citizenship might look like as normative theory, and to redirect it toward the equally compelling possibility of using the turn toward citizenship as a springboard for advancing the democratic impulse that has long been one of the hallmarks of environmentalism' (2007a, 378). The democratic impulse at a global level of climate change politics features the contributions of many, both from developing and developed countries, who are taking a climate justice perspective. By contrast to a risky citizenship regime in which citizenship is used to reify certain conventional neo-liberal resource development projects in nations, carbon citizenship at this historical moment may be especially ripe a concept to keep open to shifting communities that are both political and ecological. Though fellow (carbon) feeling may serve to reinforce an us/them policed national boundary of citizen virtuosity as it does in the carbon footprint metaphor forwarded by Ezra Levant, in other instances the same metaphor, with different associations, may prompt contesting forms of carbon citizenship.

Taking carbon citizenship as a site that is brought into visibility through carbon footprint metaphors reveals the struggles of global world-making at a time of changing climates. Attention to the mediations of carbon footprint metaphors affords critical attention to how people are being drawn together (or apart) in political collectivities and the responses that might ensue from such politically a/effective orientations. Crucially, there is good reason to be sensitive to the limits of citizenship as it relates to historical patterns of dominance. As Bowden suggests, 'the ideal of global citizenship is inextricably linked to the West's long and tortuous history of engaging in overzealous civilising-cum-universalising missions in the non-Western world' (Bowden 2003; 350). However, as Jamie Lorimer suggests, not all particular encounters with citizenship may be reduced to this context, especially if such citizenships are enriched by the possibilities of larger-than-human sense of membership and relationality (Lorimer 2010).[13] Notably, Alex Latta's latest addition to the theories of ecological citizenship opens toward posthuman and spiritual conceptions of socio-ecological relationships (Latta 2013, 566). Perhaps, however, like practices of subjectivity, the practices of citizenship are too overwritten by anthropocentricism, so citizenship even as a metaphor may carry the burden of this weighty history. In the next chapter, I turn away from 'carbon citizenship' associations with the footprint toward the metaphor's attachments to what I call 'carbon vitality' as a means of shedding some of these anthropocentric burdens associated with the carbon footprint.

Notes

1   According to the 'most read articles' category on the website on November 23, 2012. See http://pubs.acs.org/action/showMostReadArticles?topArticlesType=recent& journalCode=esthag
2   Unique visitors represent 60,000 of these 78,000 visits. Personal communication with website administrator, Christian Solli, December 10, 2012.
3   According to the 'most read articles' category on the website on February, 2017. See http://pubs.acs.org/action/showMostReadArticles?topArticlesType=recent&journal Code=esthag
4   Edgar Hertwich is a professor of energy engineering and lead analyst in Global Energy Assessment which "defines a new global energy policy agenda" through technical and policy guidance for both the global public and the commercial sectors www.iiasa.ac.at/web/home/research/researchPrograms/Energy/Home-GEA.en.html
    Glen P. Peters is a researcher for the Centre for International Climate and Environmental Research – Oslo (CICERO) who has written numerous peer-reviewed research papers for journals such as *Climate Policy*, *Carbon Management*, and *Energy Policy*. www.cicero.uio.no/employees/homepage.aspx?person_id=1067&lang=en
    Other contributors, Tommy Wiedmann and Jan Minx, are also specialists in environmental economics and carbon accounting in the UK and Australia, and among the early definers of carbon footprint analysis.
    See Tommy Wiedmann and Jan Minx. (2008). "A Definition of 'Carbon Footprint'".

In: Carolyn C. Pertsova, *Ecological Economics Research Trends*, Chapter 1, 1–11, Nova Science Publishers, Hauppauge NY, USA.

5   Whereas the ecological footprint metaphor analysis yields a figure indicative of space (hectares of land that are appropriated, or number of 'Earths' required by given lifestyles in bioregions), the carbon footprint analysis yields a weight (tons of CO_2 equivalent). Might it then be a stretch to conceive of the carbon footprint as a political space in the way that Dobson considers the ecological footprint, which already has a geospatial measure built into the notion? Such questions that trouble what might be meant by political space and the critique of the wider intelligibility of the (ecological) footprint as it fails to definitively structure the 'where' of the polis (Hayward 2006a) lead to an understanding of the metaphorical nature of political space.

6   Again, I use the Global North–Global South categories contingently despite the troubled nature of the binary which fails to capture specificities and differences.

7   In a 2000 federal roundtable on subjects surrounding climate change, one of the outcomes suggested was the creation of hubs in each of the provinces as part of a public education and outreach initiative. This network was aimed at moving Canada toward climate change governance, which was at the time in large part guided by the principles of the Kyoto Protocol to which Canada signed on in 1998. Major focuses of the Protocol were the emissions targets of each signatory nation, so the interplay of international and national scales was brought to bear in each country who had to find their own means of moving a public and policies toward emissions reductions. In the years 2000 to 2005 under the Liberal party, a flurry of federal attention on climate change and mitigation targets enabled the development of a number of initiatives and campaigns such as the One-Tonne Challenge whose aims were to move and incentivize the Canadian public to reduce emissions. In a similar vein, with goals of outreach and education, regional hubs such as Climate Change Connection were initiated in large part through federal funding. In 2006, however, with the election of a Conservative minority in Canada, federal funding of these hubs ceased, along with any explicit agenda to deal with climate change. The Conservative government instead pursued a less contentions and less aggressive 'clean air' agenda and favoured a 'made in Canada' solution that departed from Kyoto. Despite the lack of federal funding, the Manitoba hub continued under the banner of Climate Change Connection with funding supplied by the provincial government and by the provincial energy-provider, Manitoba Hydro.

8   www.climatechangeconnection.org/default.htm

9   www.merriam-webster.com/dictionary/apartheid

10   Data are from the year 2010.

11   http://oilsandstoday.ca/topics/ghgemissions/Pages/default.aspx

12   See, for example, the UK-based website ResponsibleCitizen at www.responsiblecitizen.co.uk/the-environment-citizenship.html (accessed March 24, 2011). This frame of citizenship is one that the UK, in particular, is pushing heavily in governance discourse and educational curricula.

13   Jamie Lorimer (2010) mobilizes a combination of Latour's 'actor-network-theory' and theories of affect to analyze international conservation volunteering as an instance of global environmental citizenship that works in part through human attachments to non-humans. While such international conservation volunteering can be criticized as exemplary of neoliberal and asymmetrical geographies, Lorimer also suggests that this activity also 'brings into being a transnational more-than-human citizenry comprising multitudinous non-human forms and process' (2010, 418).

References

Aichele, Rachel and Gabriel Felbermayr. 2012. "Kyoto and the Carbon Footprint of Nations." *Journal of Environmental Economics and Management* 63, 3: 336–54.

Ahmed, Sarah. 2004. *The Cultural Politics of Emotion*. New York: Routledge.

Armstrong, Franny, Lizzie Gillett and Pete Postlethwaite. 2010. *The Age of Stupid*. Film Toronto, ON: Mongrel Media.

Bowden, Brett. 2003. "The Perils of Global Citizenship." *Citizenship Studies* 7, 3: 349–62.

Bruner, Thomas J. 2008. "Beaver Lake Battles Big Oil." *Alberta Sweetgrass* Aug. 2008, 4.

Canadian Energy Citizens website. 2014. www.energycitizens.ca/what_you_can_do

CAPP 2014. "GHG Emissions Quick Facts." Available at: www.canadasoilsands.ca/en/ explore-topics/ghg-emissions (accessed October 15, 2014).

Climate Change Connection website. (nd). "International Solutions: Contraction and Convergence." Available at: http://climatechangeconnection.org/solutions/inter national-solutions/contraction-convergence/ (accessed April 10, 2017).

Dean, Hartley. 2001. "Green Citizenship." *Social Policy and Administration* 35, 5: 490–505.

Dobson, Andrew. 2003. *Citizenship and the Environment*. Oxford; New York: Oxford University Press.

Dobson, Andrew. 2010 "Entrevista a Andrew Dobson (Interview with Andrew Dobson)" El Tiempo de Los Derechos. Government of Spain. Available at: www.tiempodelos derechos.es/es/grupos-de-apoyo/121-interview-to-andrew-dobson.html (accessed June 16, 2017).

Dobson, Andrew. 2014. "The Politics of Post Growth." Dorset, UK: Green House. Available at: www.greenhousethinktank.org/uploads/4/8/3/2/48324387/post_growth_ inside_3.pdf (accessed June 14, 2017).

Dobson, Andrew and Derek Bell. 2006. *Environmental Citizenship*. Cambridge, MA; London: MIT Press.

Dobson, Andrew and Valencia Saiz, A. (eds). 2005. *Citizenship, Environment, Economy*. New York: Routledge.

EIA. 2014. "US Energy Information Administration Oil Reserves by Country Analysis." Available at: www.eia.gov/countries/index.cfm?view=reserves (accessed October 14, 2014).

The Guardian Data Blog. 2012. "Carbon Dioxide Emissions from the Consumption of Energy" www.theguardian.com/environment/datablog/2012/jun/21/world-carbon-emissions-league-table-country (accessed June 16, 2017).

Global Commons Institute. 2008 Summary of Support. Available at: www.gci.org.uk/ Support/support.pdf (accessed May 30, 2017).

Global Commons Institute. (nd). Available at: www.gci.org.uk (accessed March 14, 2017).

Hasemyer, David 2013. "Enbridge Dilbit Spill Still Not Cleaned." *Inside Climate News*. Available at: http://insideclimatenews.org/news/20131223/enbridge-dilbit-spill-still-not-cleaned-2013-closes-irritating-epa (accessed March 14, 2017).

Hayward, Tim. 2006. "Ecological citizenship: Justice, rights and the virtue of resourceful-ness." *Environmental Politics*, 15, 3: 435–46

Heater, Derek. 2004. *A Brief History of Citizenship*. Edinburgh: Edinburgh University Press.

Hertwich, Edgar G. and Glen P. Peters. 2009. "Carbon Footprint of Nations: A Global, Trade-Linked Analysis." In: *Environmental Science and Technology* 43, 16: 2009. Available at: http://pubs.acs.org/doi/full/10.1021/es803496a (accessed June 14, 2017).

Isin, Engin F and Bryan S.Turner (eds). 2002. *Handbook of Citizenship Studies*, London: Sage.

Kurek, Joshua, Jan Kirk, Derek Muir, Ziaowa Wang, Marlene Evans and John Smol. 2012. "Legacy of a Half Century of Athabasca Oil Sands Development Recorded by Lake Ecosystems." *Proceedings of the National Academy of Science (PNAS)*.

Latour, Bruno. 2004. *Politics of Nature: How to Bring the Sciences into Democracy.* Cambridge, MA: Harvard University Press.

Latta, Alex. 2007a. "Locating democratic politics in ecological citizenship." *Environmental Politics* 16, 3: 377–93.

Latta, Alex 2007b. "Citizenship and the Politics of Nature: The Case of Chile's Alto Bío Bío." *Citizenship Studies* 11, 3: 229–46.

Latta, Alex and Garside, Nick. 2005. "Perspectives on Ecological Citizenship: An Introduction." *Environments* 33, 3: 1–8.

Levant, Ezra. 2011. *Ethical Oil: The Case for Canada's Oil Sands.* Toronto: McClelland and Stewart.

Linklater, Andrew. 1999. "Cosmopolitan Citizenship." In: *Cosmopolitan Citizenship.* New York: St Martin's Press, 35–60.

Lorimer, Jamie. 2010. "International Conservation 'volunteering' and the Geographies of Global Environmental Citizenship." *Political Geography* 29, 6: 311–22.

Magnusson, Warren. 1996. *The Search for Political Space: Globalization, social movements and the urban political experience.* Toronto: University of Toronto Press.

Magnusson, Warren. and Karena Shaw (eds). (2003). *A Political Space: Reading the Global through Clayoquot Sound.* Minneapolis, MN: University of Minnesota Press.

McLachlan, Stéphane. 2014. "Environmental and Human Health Implications of the Athabasca Oil Sands for the Mikisew Cree First Nation and Athabasca Chipewyan First Nation in Northern Alberta." Environmental Conservation Laboratory. Available at: http://onerivernews.ca/health-study-press-release-2014/ (accessed June 12, 2017).

Makina, Anesu. 2013. "Managing Climate Change: The Africa Group in Multilateral Environmental Negotiations." *Journal of International Organization Studies* 4, 1: 36–48.

Melo-Escrihuela, Carmen. 2008. "Promoting Ecological Citizenship: Rights, Duties, and Political Agency." *ACME: An International E-Journal for Critical Geographies* 7, 2: 113–34.

Meyer, Aubrey. 2001. *Contraction and Convergence: The Global Solution to Climate Change.* Totnes: Green Books.

Meyer, Aubrey. 2011. "Fiddling with Climate Change: An Interview with Aubrey Meyer." *Nature Climate Change.* Available at: www.gci.org.uk/Documents/Nature_Aubrey.pdf (accessed June 12, 2017).

Meyer, Aubrey and Kay Weir. 2006. "Support Grows for Equity-based Global Warming Plan." *Pacific Ecologist* Summer 2006/7. Available at: www.pacificecologist.org/archive/13/contraction-and-convergence.pdf (accessed June 12, 2017).

Nikiforuk, Andrew. 2010. *Tar Sands: Dirty Oil and the Future of a Continent.* Vancouver, BC: Greystone.

Nikiforuk, Andrew. 2011. "Five Falsehoods About Ethical Oil." *The Tyee.* Available at: http://thetyee.ca/Opinion/2011/09/29/Ethical-Oil-Falsehoods/ (accessed June 12, 2017).

Nixon, Rob. 2011. *Slow Violence and the Environmentalism of the Poor.* Boston, MA: Harvard University Press.

NTNU (Norwegian University of Science and Technology). 2013. "Carbon Footprint of Nations Frequently Asked Questions." Available at: http://carbonfootprintof nations. com/content/faq/ (accessed March 11, 2017).

Pembina Institute. 2005. "Oil Sands Fever: The Environmental Implications of Canada's Oil Sands Rush." Available at: www.pembina.org/reports/OilSands72.pdf (accessed October 14, 2014).

Petherick, Anne. 2012. "When Carbon Footprints Hop." *Nature Climate Change* 2: 484–5.

Prokhovnik, Raia. 1998. "Public and Private Citizenship: From Gender Invisibility to Feminist Inclusiveness" *Feminist Review* 60, Feminist Ethics and the Politics of Love, 84–104. Available at: www.jstor.org/stable/1395548 (accessed June 12, 2017).

Radman, Zdravko. 1997. *Metaphors: Figures of the Mind.* New York, NY: Springer.

Roberts, Timmons J. and Parks, Bradley C. 2007. "Fueling Injustice: Globalization, Ecologically Unequal Exchange and Climate Change." *Globalizations* 4, 2: 193–210.

Santos, Marcelo. 2017. "Global Justice and Environmental Governance: An Analysis of the Paris Agreement." *Revista Brasileira de Política Internacional* 60, 1: e008. Epub February 20, 2017. Available at: https://dx.doi.org/10.1590/0034-7329201600116 (accessed June 13, 2017).

Schindler, David. W. and William. F. Donahue. 2006. "An Impending Water Crisis in Canada's Western Prairie Provinces." *Proceedings of the National Academy of Sciences of the United States of America* 103, 19: 7210–16.

Smith, Mark J. 1998. *Ecologism: Toward Ecological Citizenship: Concepts in the Social Sciences.* Minneapolis, MN: University of Minnesota Press.

Smith, Mark J. 2005. "Obligation and Ecological Citizenship." *Environments* 33, 3: 9–23. Available at: http://search.proquest.com.ezproxy.library.uvic.ca/docview/207672365?accountid=14846 (accessed June 12, 2017).

Stiglitz, Joseph E. "GDP Fetishism." *The Economists' Voice* 6, 8: 1553–3832. doi: 10.2202/1553-3832.1651, September 2009.

Széll, György. 2011. "Beyond GDP." *Indian Journal of Industrial Relations* 46, 4: 545.

TransCanada Corporation. 2011. "Media Advisory: U.S. Department of Energy Report Supports Keystone XL Study Shows Pipeline Will Reduce Middle East Oil Dependence." Available at: www.marketwired.com/press-release/media-advisory-us-department-energy-report-supports-keystone-xl-study-shows-pipeline-tsx-trp-1389251.htm (accessed June 14, 2017).

Valencia Sáiz, Angel. 2005. "Globalisation, Cosmopolitanism and Ecological Citizenship." *Environmental Politics* 14, 2: 163–78.

Wolf, Johanna, Katrina Brown and Declan Conway. 2009. "Ecological Citizenship and Climate Change: Perceptions and Practice." *Environmental Politics* 18, 4: 503–21.

Zembylas, Michelinos. 2014. "Affect, Citizenship, Politics: Implications for Education." *Pedagogy, Culture & Society* 17, 3: 369–83.

5   Carbon vitality

On February 17, 2012, *The Tyee*, an on-line North American news publication, featured a story with a headline 'Jumbo-sized Carbon Footprint of Farmed Shrimp Tracked by Scientist'. This story and the scientist mentioned, aquaculture researcher Boone Kauffman of the University of Oregon, use the currency of the carbon footprint metaphor to present a novel calculus of the relative impacts of eating farmed shrimp:

> If you and four friends go for dinner and drinks and each have a farmed-shrimp cocktail, that releases 990 kilograms of carbon into the atmosphere. That equals burning 424 litres of gasoline. And apparently, compared with the shrimp eaters, you can drive from Vancouver to New York City in a Prius and claim the moral high ground when it comes to calculating your *carbon footprint*.
>
> (Isabella 2012, para 4)

This story appears at the time as potent news in a variety of public places because it reveals a surprisingly large impact of a farmed shrimp, an effect that comes into visibility only when one looks at a complex set of ecological relations and processes that have thus far remained under-acknowledged in the politics of climate change.

While one could read this instance of the carbon footprint metaphor as continuous with a kind of liberal environmental carbon subjectivity as described in Chapter 2, I am initially interested in the promise of this instance of the metaphor in introducing a novel larger-than-human sensibility. In order for this instance to make sense, one must follow eco-social connections that account for particular carbon flows that are at once local and transnational and that feature a highly diverse network of ecological actors across these diverse scales. These ecological actors are as ontologically diverse as: human shrimp eaters; the farming practices of the shrimp aquaculture industry; the shrimp themselves; the local peoples in mangrove ecosystems; and the mangroves (themselves multiform) within these coastal ecosystems.

In this chapter, I explore the promises and risks of tracing the carbon footprint of jumbo shrimp toward these other ecological actors who appear in this larger-than-human affective connection through what I call 'carbon vitality'. Carbon vitality promises an affective attention through carbon flows to what Jane Bennett calls a 'range of the nonhuman powers circulating around and within human bodies' (2010, ix). I am following Bennett's notion of vitality as it gestures toward the capacity of non-human actors 'not only to impede or block the will and designs of humans but also to act as quasi agents or forces with trajectories, propensities, or tendencies of their own' (ibid., viii). The problematic carbon footprint of shrimp reveals an unintended consequence of human design in a global aquaculture industry; the shrimp and other ecosystem actors connected with this footprint visibly emerge as forces with trajectories, or tendencies that trouble the partial vision of dominant human design. Understanding these force relations and shifting processes enables novel understandings of the sentience of non-humans and offers a potentially deepened sense of distributed agency as an intervention in cultural politics of climate change. I tease out this promise of the appearance of larger-than-human political forces in the first half of the chapter.

The second part of the chapter attends to the risks that might be associated with this instance of the carbon footprint. While extending the reach of this metaphor offers increased visibility of vital non-human actors and relations in specific ecologies, such an extension of the metaphor also carries over the all-too-familiar risks of rendering such actors into objects to be managed through attaching them to a human-determined carbon economy. Specific ways of capitalizing on carbon vitality in this case, turn into a risky form of 'carbon capital' in which these actors are belatedly valued as commodities and subsequently treated as instruments for human profit generation rather than as important actors with trajectories of their own interacting in larger-than-human systems. In such cases, the way that the footprint 'shifts its affections into action' (Seigworth and Gregg 2010, 2) offers no promise of emissions-reduction through distributed agency, but instead bolsters attachments to carbon markets that often have the opposite effect of increasing emissions. Tracing the carbon footprint of shrimp in this chapter thus attends both to the promises of re-configuring relations as they connect with ecological sensibilities, and to the risks involved in re-connecting these sensibilities to 'ecosystems services' approaches that monetarily evaluate – and potentially commodify – ecological relations from the perspective of the benefits that humans derive from ecosystems (Costanza et al. 1997; 2014).

This particular carbon footprint metaphor involving crustaceans merits attention for two reasons that I develop below. First, it appears later in the on-going cultural history of climate change (February, 2012), revealing that the metaphor continues to create traction in scientific and public spaces beyond its initial public emergence in 2000 to 2001 and its viral emergence in 2007 to 2008. Second, although not the only case of carbon footprints implicated in human food systems – perhaps the most iconic case to date has been the carbon footprint of Rainforest beef – this instance shifts attention to the aquatic spaces that are often forgotten for terrestrially bound dominant human societies. This shift, as the following analysis reveals, permits a novel distribution of the sensible in which previously excluded actors appear in climate change politics through the associated metaphor of 'blue carbon'.

The carbon footprint of jumbo shrimp story is especially remarkable for its purchase in a wide array of public contexts at the time of its release; this powerful purchase, I argue, relates specifically to its reinvigorated (though still implicit) metaphoricity. This story centrally features the power of metaphors to shift in time and place and even to disappear as metaphors. Perhaps this instance seems the most scientific and quantitative of all of the cases featured in this book, but again, the qualitative and poetic in this case lend potency to its promises and risks and its wide appeal beyond simply scientific circles. *The Tyee* article by Judith Isabella cited above, was just one of many sites that featured Kauffman's analysis of coastal ecosystems through this metaphorical framework. After Kauffman's presentation in Vancouver at the annual meeting of the American Association for the Advancement of Science (AAAS) in February 2012, this carbon footprint metaphor travelled widely. The AAAS, the 'world's largest general scientific society' whose mission is 'advancing science, serving society',[1] represents a key venue in which scientists share and communicate findings with other scientists, educators, and the media who further disseminate findings for other publics. The carbon footprint of jumbo-farmed shrimp soon made the headlines in many popular and specialist news sites, including: *Phys.Org*, a leading source of non-partisan science and technology news geared at scientists, researchers, and the lay-public with a readership of 1.75 million monthly;[2] Dawn.com, the on-line version of Pakistan's widely read English language newspaper;[3] Restore America's Estuaries, a national wetlands conservation not-for-profit in the United States;[4] and bon appetit.com, a daily news feed based on the popular American food magazine by the same name.[5] The headline in the latter publication reads 'Imported Shrimp Has a Carbon Footprint Ten Times Higher than Rainforest Beef'[6] and leads with an evocative animated image of a huge shrimp inside a Hummer luxury sports utility vehicle.[7] The diverse range of venues for this story attests to the power that the metaphor wields within a wide range of publics; while scientific analysis often requires translation of key concepts and frameworks, the carbon footprint metaphor itself is preserved in all of these venues, comprising a key element of the headline in most of the articles. This metaphor is indeed unique in that it often combines a scientific quantitative authority with the currency of its qualitative public appeal. In this case, the carbon footprint is used explicitly as a metric by Kauffman, whose research was extracted in multiple news stories, and the metaphor itself, a now iconic public figure, also appears in each of these multiple news stories. For a public already sensing climate change politics in and through carbon footprint metaphors, this story's traction was already largely ensured by its mobilization of the footprint metaphor.

At first glance, the scientist and originator of the carbon footprint analysis in this story, Boone Kauffman, appears prominently in all the articles. In his analysis of the carbon footprint of jumbo-farmed shrimp, Kauffman tracks the practices of a global shrimp-farming industry to specific locales in Southeast Asia where mangroves and their biodiverse coastal ecosystems have been destroyed to make room for shrimp farms. Within global science and policy circles, these mangrove ecosystems have only recently been appreciated for their role in shaping carbon cycles. The scientific accounts suggest that through complex relational processes transpiring over millennia, carbon has settled into root systems in mangrove ecosystems and away from atmospheric warming influence (Nellemann et al. 2009). The account of carbon footprints here tracks what is lost, (and what is gained in harmful carbon emissions) in the production of shrimp through the up-rooting of mangroves, whose complex carbon associations were previously not sensed within a normative, largely terrestrial and human-centric version of carbon footprint metaphors. Kauffman's calculations, based on large-scale shrimp farms that generally last only five years, suggest that 'a 100-gram shrimp cocktail repre-sents an "astonishing" 198 kilograms of carbon dioxide from the loss of the mangrove' (Stokstad 2012, para 3).

Despite beginning with the human researcher in this case, one quickly finds that the metaphor in this jumbo shrimp story, its public resonance prior to this instance, and, most importantly, its 'co-author' species, are all implicated in a way that troubles the singular human authority of a scientific analyst. This is not to suggest that the various actors all stand on equal footing vis-à-vis the power they wield in this metaphor, but to concede to what Jane Bennett (following Latour) calls a 'decisive force' of non-human actors/actants that can 'catalyze an event' or movement (2010, 9). The metaphorically mediated emergence of such actors situ-ates carbon footprint metaphors as catalyzers of novel inclusions in the politics of climate change.

The promise of defamiliarizing attachments mediated by footprints

This instance reveals the capacity of carbon footprint metaphors to affectively mediate emerging ecological sensibilities prompted by actors that have not yet been accounted for; carbon footprints are thus never too distant from their metaphorical conditioning. These metaphors are constantly re-charged to account for shifting ecological matters and carbon flows that impinge upon their contingent bearings. Now approaching the second decade since first connecting human carbon subjects to accounts of climate change, carbon foot-print metaphors in these instances reveal a power of heterogeneous larger-than-human actors to displace an accepted account of a human-domi-nated 'family of things' indexed through the footprint metaphor. In other words, these metaphors have been around long enough to achieve a kind of popular cultural recognition, but in this instance the carbon footprint metaphor defamil-iarizes previous human-specific attachments; this instance more centrally orients toward ecological actors in vital relations and processes of land and sea constituted within the footprint and within the broader cultural and material story of climate change. The re-figuring of these new actors merits public atten-tion, especially in media contexts with notoriously short attention spans that require novelty to be newsworthy. Just when the carbon footprint (metaphor) seems to become fixed and locatable within a sensible territory that might permit its (human) management, it shiftily makes another impression conditioned by the living relations and processes that animate it in new ways. The novelty of this materializing carbon footprint is what makes it powerful and what stimulates a flurry of attention in its wake.

The associative and comparative work of the carbon footprint metaphor – such that in the lead quotation, for example, the consumption of gas in a car can be compared with consumption of farmed shrimp – is central to the politics of affect it activates. By drawing on familiar associations with large emissions-generating activities, and connecting these to newly visible carbon relations, a generative shift occurs in the relational politics that follow. True to its metaphorical formation, the carbon footprint metaphor in this instance responds to a gap in knowledge that marks this historical juncture of ecological crises. The political disturbance to the status quo of carbon footprints initiated by this appearance reminds that the previous accounts written into footprints were partial (just as this one necessarily is). Since footprint metaphors move alongside shifting affective relations and accounts of carbon, their associative force similarly shifts. While the carbon footprint metaphor begins at the turn of the millennium as both an accounting tool and a qualitative account whereby human subjects historically newly register within the cultural politics of climate change, the calculus and qualities written into the carbon footprint's inscriptions necessarily shift. These metaphors begin with somewhat explicit recognition of gaps in human knowledge and language and rely on multiple associated metaphors to catalyze sense-making for new forms of social and ecological relationality within historical-ecological contexts; thus, for example, do carbon footprints lead to formulations of 'blue carbon' affectively mediating attention to aquatic flows of carbon (discussed below). To matter in new ways that the above article makes clear it should, the carbon footprint metaphor here becomes newly charged with these novel force relations. Simultaneously mobilizing a sense of familiarity, but presenting novelty that allows it to achieve wide dispersal in public contexts, the carbon footprint metaphor re-configures a vital politics of climate change.

Carbon vitality

To be sure, the carbon subjects first hailed by carbon footprint reduction lists in no way completely disappear in this instance quoted above, but the footprint metaphor here is also explicitly populated by non-human actors who appear to 'have' a footprint. That is not to suggest that these beings suddenly come into existence with the transcendental 'word' of human creation through the endowment of a metaphorical footprint to non-humans; rather, these actors come into the visible and speakable terms of climate change politics through a force of relations and processes that is affectively mediated through the metaphor. The carbon footprint metaphor remains an opening to lively forces that exceed the account thus far and thus its shifts generate a Rancièrian political act that 'repartitions the sensible ... overthrows the regime of the perceptible' such that new publics come into view (Bennett 2010, 107).

I am calling this affective force of relations and processes 'carbon vitality' because the metaphor of 'vitality' is evocative of moving relations and processes that animate carbon flows. In advocating attention to the 'vitality of matter', Jane Bennett proposes that 'the image of dead or thoroughly instrumentalized matter feeds human hubris and our earth-destroying fantasies of conquest and consumption' (2010, xi). There is a certain implicit tendency within fossil fuel culture to treat (hydro)carbons as inert, dead resources that instrumentally fuel human life. Similarly, in solutions proposed to manage carbon as an atmospheric disruption, there exists a tendency to try to isolate and neutralize this element as if carbon were not involved in lively flows that exceed human control. With Bennett, I caution '[that] [t]he figure of an intrinsically inanimate matter may be one of the impediments to the emergence of more ecological and more materially sustainable modes of production and consumption' (2010, xi). Attending carefully to the vitality of carbon flows that circulate through diversely populated larger-than-human systems marks a challenging but key intervention against relegating carbon a passive role. Relatedly, as Jane Bennett insists, the metaphor of vitality is not pre-figured with specifically human ontologies, but is open to larger-than-human entanglements (2010, xi).

Like carbon subjectivity and carbon citizenship, carbon vitality gestures toward affective attachments made through carbon footprint metaphors; however, vitality's explicit insistence on movement and larger than human force relations sets in motion attunement to a different kind of political resonance. The affects of 'carbon guilt' and 'fellow feeling' associated, in turn, with carbon subjectivity and carbon citizenship, rely heavily on affectively connecting with oneself as a *human* subject or with other *human* citizens in terms of carbon flows. Understanding diverse living relations and processes of carbon vitality requires stretching beyond human-centred affects. The affective relations of carbon vitality shift attention away from questions of how human communities are drawn together (and apart) through a politics of citizenship or subjectivity. Like Jane Bennett, I would like to 'branch out to an "affect" not specific to human bodies … to focus less on the enhancement to human relational capacities resulting from affective catalysts and more on the catalyst itself as it exists in nonhuman bodies' (Bennett 2010, xii). Understanding the catalytic force of shrimp (and other associates) in this carbon footprint metaphor entails understanding the ways in which carbon flows affectively to connect to[8] political actors conceived not solely in privileged human terms. This move away from human-centricity by no means suggests ignoring the humans in socio-ecological relations. As I suggest below, the people who co-constitute ecosystems are key. Their sensitivity to place-based relations offers a corrective to the new ocean-grabbing politics and economics that damage societies and ecosystems alike. The shift to vital carbon relations orients attention to these larger-than-human complexities.

Notably, carbon vitality is necessarily more amorphous and nebulous as a concept/metaphor than the ones I have been describing thus far because it is speculative and inherently resists what William Connolly identifies as the tendency toward 'complete explanation' (2013, 9). As Connolly suggests, such tendencies prematurely foreclose upon sensitivities to a 'variety of nonhuman force fields that impinge upon politico-economic life as it too impinges upon the force fields' (2013, 9). Given the scale and rapidly shifting pace of contemporary ecological-material entanglements, many (mostly Euro-Western)[9] theorists are coming to admit that received categories, concepts, and sensibilities of the (post)modern age are in fact incapable of explaining current predicaments, such as climate change, let alone helping us to way-find and respond to them (Bennett 2010; Connolly 2013; Morton 2013). Thus, in 'explaining' or gesturing toward an affective relation through carbon vitality, one must resist the tendency to 'completeness' and instead draw out some provisional and tentative threads that remain provisional enough to allow for the heterogeneous animating forces that displace partial human accounts (even as my own account is also inescapably partial). This is a fraught endeavour, even for seasoned scholars, like Bennett, who are self-reflexively un-doing their own previous work in order to grapple with contemporary conditions. Jane Bennett admits to the seeming contradictions of her human articulations of larger than human affects:

> I court the charge of performative self-contradiction: is it not a human subject who, after all, is articulating this theory ...? Yes and no, for I will argue that what looks like a performative contradiction may well dissipate if one considers revisions in operative notions of matter, life, self, self-interest, will and agency.
>
> (2010, ix)

Perhaps rather than contradictions, then, carbon vitality requires us to puzzle through the pressing paradoxes of climate change as a naturalcultural phenomenon in which matter, life, self-interest, and agency are, from the outset, infused with larger-than-human considerations, even as these considerations are not immediately available to us through received Euro-Western sensibilities. The carbon footprint metaphor itself, as a mediator in this contact zone, 'considers revisions in the operative notions of matter' by being pulled into novel forces of encounter that shape it, and re-direct its vital orientations. These revisions and disturbances enabled through the metaphor's mediations are crucial to its political offerings.

Jane Bennett's affective politics of vitality begin with the 'recognition of human participation in a shared, vital materiality. We *are* vital materiality and we are surrounded by it, though we do not always see it that way' (2010, 14). Rather than reifying subject/object relations that often map onto a human/nature divide, Bennett follows the vitalist principles of Spinoza and Deleuze to conceive of affective forces of 'heterogeneous assemblages' (Bennett, 23). The notion of such an assemblage re-works the term of agency whose traditional 'efficacy or effectivity ... becomes distributed across an ontologically heterogeneous field, rather than being a capacity localized in a human body or in a collective produced (only) by human efforts' (2010, 23). Bennett suggests a whole vibratory set of dynamics that works in a different register than the limited realm of human instrumentality, a world where no individual agent is singularly responsible for causal events, and where contingency or 'chanciness resides as the heart of things' (ibid., 18). The political task for Bennett then, is 'to cultivate the ability to discern nonhuman vitality, to become perceptually open to it' (14).

From this vitalist perspective, the carbon footprint metaphor in its affective mediations of shifting larger-than-human relations becomes a potential opening. As my analysis of these texts reveals, this metaphor can help to cultivate attunement to larger-than-human vitality as an intervention in cultural politics of climate change. If 'we', who tend toward attempts of complete explanation and instrumental management but who inescapably apprehend through partial vision and situated knowledges,[10] refract our gaze upon this carbon footprint of shrimp through an affective lens of carbon vitality, 'we' might cultivate a promising reorientation.

To begin to understand a complex newly revealed carbon vitality implicated in this footprint, I take two key actors in this story – the primary catalytic force of shrimp whose footprint is tracked and its associate, mangroves – and read these as cultural-material compounds. That is to say, that although each of these may surely be taken as 'ecological' (or even more reductively, 'carbon') entities that can be apprehended by science, they are also most emphatically caught up in metaphors and relations that exceed conventional scientific accounts. The footprint metaphor here mediates these cultural associations and material ecological relations in order to make new sense.

Gargantuan footprint of shrimp?

One of the ways in which this carbon footprint metaphor re-orients perception is by enacting a kind of dissonance between 'shrimp', a metaphor that figures smallness in Anglophone cultural contexts, and a seemingly impossibly large 'footprint' in terms of carbon emissions. Kauffman's findings bear repeating here: 'a 100-gram shrimp cocktail represents an "astonishing" 198 kilograms of carbon dioxide from the loss of the mangrove'. The difference in weight between the 100-grams worth of shrimp and 198 *kilograms* of CO_2 does indeed seem astonishing. Notably, there has been some critique of Kauffman's quantitative findings by the Global Aquaculture Alliance (GAA), 'an industry group underwritten by Wal-Mart, Red Lobster, and multinational seafood importers' (Carrier 2009, np) whose main concern in a press release were the 'anti-shrimp headlines' in the many articles that followed Kauffman's presentation (Aquafeed 2012). However, even if the numbers are 'off' as numbers interminably can be (conspicuously, the GAA did not immediately provide its own competing carbon footprint analysis, but belatedly commissioned a report to refute the findings based on one study of shrimp farming in one province in China),[11] the story still reveals an order of magnitude difference in weight of carbon emissions resulting from upheaval of coastal ecosystems compared with the weight of a measly 100 grams of shrimp.

Further, while the numbers in this analysis do tell a quantitatively potent story, the dispersal of this carbon footprint metaphor also suggests that numbers are not sufficient unto themselves to catalyze public attention. In fact, 'the numbers' on the socio-ecological impacts of mangrove ecosystem destruction caused by shrimp farms have been around for more than two decades, although not so prevalently within public lay contexts in the Global North. Scholarly publications and news articles in Southeast Asian press suggest that local communities within mangrove ecosystems in the Global South have long been observing and bearing the impacts of the ravages of shrimp farms along coasts (Hein 2000; Menasveta 1997; Stevenson and Burbridge 1997).This new apprehension of the relevance of this story and attention in the Global North gestures at both a quickening of consciousness that makes carbon a matter of global concern and, importantly here, the mediating effects of the figure of the carbon footprint metaphor itself that brings these relations more proximal and visible. To make sense of the gargantuan numbers implicated by tiny shrimp requires the mediation of the carbon footprint metaphor and its associated figures that animate these numbers in particular ways.

The astonishing weight of carbon emissions of tiny, yet 'jumbo' shrimp, mediated through the carbon footprint metaphor, is yoked to a variety of other analogous weights (as CO_2 emissions) of different entities in presenting this figure for a variety of publics. *The Tyee*, for example, suggests that the amount of carbon emissions/footprint from (farmed) shrimp cocktails at a group dinner is equivalent to the emissions footprint incurred from driving from Vancouver to New York City in a Prius hybrid vehicle. The *Bon Appetit* article headline, 'Imported Shrimp Has a Carbon Footprint Ten Times Higher than Rainforest Beef', similarly works through creating a connection between the notoriously sinful practices of the Rainforest beef industry, which surprisingly emerges here as less destructive than shrimp farming according to Kauffman's carbon footprint analysis. In *The Atlantic Wire*, after the headline 'Your Shrimp Cocktail is Ruining the Planet', Dashiell Bennett leads with the sentence 'A biologist has calculated that these tiny little shrimp may be the most costly animal you can eat when measured in terms of its negative impact on the environment' (Bennett 2012, np). These analogies mobilize already available associations with bigness or weightiness in terms of climate-impacting emissions and yoke them to the carbon footprint of shrimp. The Rainforest beef comparison is particularly evocative since this bovine-turned-protein figure stands as a twice-indicted climate villain in public discourse; both its legendary methane-releasing ruminant belches and the necessity to destroy carbon sequestering rainforests for its pasture have given this form of life/protein/industry the reputation as the worst of the worst (Cederberg et al. 2011; Desjardins 2012).[12] That shrimp could possibly have a carbon footprint equal to, let alone ten times the size (weight) of Rainforest beef seems to defy previously held public schema. The accompanying image of a shrimp driving a Hum-V in this article further brings 'home' to a consuming Global North the enormity of this impact, as the shrimp is connected to another particularly iconic figure of privilege and destructive impact.[13] This carbon footprint (of shrimp) metaphor therefore evocatively raises the question 'How can a little thing figure so prominently?'

The weightiness of farmed shrimp is explained in some of these articles simply, but problematically, by numbers of shrimp indicating a wealth of supply. Sam Dean, author of the *Bon Appetit* article, suggests that 'the glut of cheap South Asian shellfish is what's turned shrimp from a luxury item (remember when shrimp cocktail actually seemed fancy?) into an everyday, Taco Bell and Red Lobster kind of meat'. While Dean and others (Philpott 2012) name a 'glut' of cheap South Asian shellfish as the cause for the novel everyday quality of shrimp as food, the causes are clearly more complex than those addressed by the supply side of a supply and demand consumer equation. To weigh so heavily in climate impacts pertains to the processes necessary to produce shrimp in a farmed environment where pre-existing ecological relations are violently disturbed, as well the numbers of humans who are increasingly consuming and demanding these within complex political economies. In order to 'feed the world' through aquaculture (as is the mission of the GAA, and its affiliates, Red Lobster and Wal-Mart, among others) (Global Aquaculture Alliance 2017), new coastal territories must be appropriated and developed since the wild stock of shrimp cannot keep up to demand, especially the demand for cheap protein in a sea of industrial agriculture. This abundance of cheap shrimp identified by Dean and others must therefore be connected with multiple cultural and material contexts.

One of these cultural-material contexts is the 'Blue Revolution'. Like its metaphoric predecessor, the Green Revolution, which gestured at a promise to feed a growing human population through efficiencies gained by scaling up terrestrial forms of agricultural, the Blue Revolution evokes similar pretentions of feeding the world through scaling up industrial aquaculture. As John Volpe warns, however, the profit-orientation of this revolution trumps any seemingly altruistic attempts to feed the world and the results in blue revolution practices are '[b]ioamplified toxins in flesh, exotic escapees threatening already diminished wild stocks, and farms acting as incubators for parasites and pathogens' (Volpe 2005, 302). Inevitably, through this logic, farming ecosystems first conceived as 'closed' collapse as the human engineers and financial beneficiaries of these systems seem unwilling and/or incapable of sensing all the multiple intelligent interactions between biodiverse ecological actors within lively ecologies. Farmed shrimp are caught up in this promise of affordable protein for the world, but, as this carbon footprint reveals, their affordability is highly troubled when it comes to other ecological impacts that bear upon climate change, among other important concerns such as social justice.[14]

Just as the promises of the Green Revolution are currently fading beneath the characteristic short-sighted mechanistic approaches to industrial agriculture, the Blue Revolution is now appearing here through the carbon footprint of shrimp to be similarly susceptible to collapse leaving degradation in its wake. Kauffman tracked many shrimp farms that lasted only five to ten years and left contamination that rendered coastal spaces 'unusable for another forty years' (Bennett, 2012). A related issue identified by Volpe in this process is Jevons' Paradox (a notion I described in Chapter 3) whereby efficiencies gained and translated into cost reductions, which are passed on to the consumer, are eventually lost because of an increasing demand for the product – in this case, 'cheap' shrimp. A taste for shrimp has expanded within the Global North, on the one hand bringing a former luxury menu item for the privileged to a more affordable everyday 'Taco Bell' status.[15] This expanding fast food commodification of shrimp has not only over-turned long-standing mangrove forests, it has also created social injustices for coastal peoples in the Global South. In the wake of the Blue Revolution mono-cropping of shrimp in Bangladesh, for example, local people who formerly made a living from fishing the wild stocks of fish within mangrove ecosystems are find-ing themselves without fishing grounds, without power, and therefore, without the means to make a living. Many of these affected people have made strong appeals to consumers to stop eating shrimp from these devastating shrimp farms (Swedish Society for Nature Conservation 2011).

Revealed through the metaphor of the carbon footprint, a growing taste for shrimp in the Global North appears enabled by a particular lens that sees shrimp as small and cheap through a distancing of the vital contexts in which they are produced. The stripping bare of coastal ecosystems parallels a cultural purification that figures a clean shrimp as a healthy choice for a privileged consuming carbon subject. This carbon footprint reveals that shrimp is at once a cultural construct as a food choice, and a material-ecological entity with trajectories and forces of its own that do not always conform to human design and instrumentalism.

At first glance appearing only to specify a particular relationship between a carbon subject/consumer of shrimp and shrimp as a product, the shrimp itself carries a force in a distributive agency that disturbs the normal terrestrial-atmos-pheric and human-centric registers associated with the footprint up until this time. That aquatic creatures without literal feet could conceivably have 'footprints' suggests a revision in thinking about carbon impressions, relations, and processes that occur in cultural blind spots, especially those aquatic blind spots that are newly signalled by the metaphor 'blue'.

'Blue' carbon, social-ecological sentient mangroves

The carbon footprint of the shrimp story affectively mediates connections to coastal ecosystems in which mangroves and their larger-than-human associates interact in vital carbon relations. Despite the brief length of the news stories in which the carbon footprint of shrimp appears, many of these stories explicitly connect the footprint of these shrimp with mangroves whose upheaval are the central reason for the weightiness of the shrimp (Isabella 2012; Philpott 2012). One story notes that 'the value of intact mangroves is hard to measure' naming a vital capacity of mangroves in 'protecting the coastal ecosystems and communi-ties against storms and tsunamis' (Phys.org 2012, np). Another states, '[m]angroves, it turns out, are rich stores of biodiversity and also of carbon—and when they're cleared for farming, that carbon enters the atmosphere as climate-warming gas' (Philpott 2012, np).

Mangrove forests have always been fully implicated in these aquacultural practices and their smaller scale conventional predecessors, but these forests have remained largely hidden from view until recently in the Global North through norms that distance these supply chains and their impacts. What appears through this footprint of shrimp story is (among other things) a coastal ecosystem that pre-dates global human interventions and that is largely invisible to certain terrestrial beings[16] whose partial vision is built with neither underwater lenses nor with the multi-species sensory capabilities necessary to fully appreciate complex associa-tions and processes. In the process of creating shrimp farms, thereby making shrimp a more affordable protein for an increasing portion of the people of the planet, the coastal ecosystems in many parts of Thailand, Bangladesh and other countries have been rapidly overturned. Local peoples can apprehend this destruction in an immediate way (though, importantly, global asymmetries of power may prevent their interventions) and scientists may have instruments and data to make 'objective' sense of these impacts; however, wider publics who are implicated from afar require other affective means to re-compose a sensory field that is removed from immediate visibility. Metaphoric connections are key in this regard and this is what is at stake in this carbon footprint of jumbo shrimp; this metaphor serves as a means of creating a certain affective connection between distant consumers of shrimp and their legacies in particular coastal localities in which the farming takes place.

This carbon footprint metaphor creates a connection with 'blue carbon', an emerging metaphor signalling human understandings of crucial carbon relations embedded in coastal ecosystems. This metaphor draws into visibility a regime of carbon that had been previously largely forgotten in global circuits. Whereas a universalizing and indistinguishable 'carbon' (itself a stand-in for carbon dioxide and other greenhouse gases) formerly stood out as the key figure to be appre-hended, specifying adjectives/metaphors are now coming to define how carbon's particular relations are determined in material and cultural contexts. Pointing to the dominance of vision in the politics of human perception, colours become the specifying signifiers of these particular human-defined contexts of carbon. *Brown* carbon has come to refer to anthropogenic greenhouse gas emissions 'from energy use and industry'; *black* carbon to 'particles resulting from impure com-bustion, such as soot and dust'; *green* carbon to 'terrestrial carbon stored in plant biomass and soils in forest land, plantations, agricultural land and pasture land'; and *blue* carbon to that which appears in coastal ecosystems 'particularly mangroves, marshes and seagrasses' (Nellemann et al. 2009, 15). The late appear-ance in discourse of *blue* carbon relative to its chromatic siblings, previously all figured under a generic 'carbon', addresses a dominant tendency among certain (especially distant or non-coastal) peoples to forget the oceans, from which all life forms are thought to have emerged and in which much of the species of the world still live.[17] While oceans have been normatively and symptomatically relegated to a minor role as a conveyor of human vessels, resource for food, and a place from which to launch offshore resource extraction, the blue carbon metaphor newly situates oceans as integral and complex networks of animate actors that contribute to the carbon cycles implicated in climate change. A scientific apprehension of blue carbon suggests that ecosystems indexed through this metaphor 'are being degraded and disappear at rates 5–10 times faster than rainforests' and as emerging research is showing, their carbon storage capacities are far more profound than terrestrial systems (Nellemann et al. 2009, 15). Donato et al. (2011) similarly highlight the relative lack of attention paid to carbon rich coastal mangrove ecosystems which are being lost rapidly due to aquaculture expansion.

Although the above quantitative scientific *land management* lens offers but one reductive angle from which to view the sea as integral to carbon relations, the metaphor of blue carbon opens up to wider possibilities of revising what counts as matter, life, and agency. Water, and all of the lively interactions within and through it, are figured here as quintessentially important ecological and climatological actors. While our home planet is normatively defined as 'Earth', the planet itself and its blue ecosystems challenge the singularity of this moniker. Notably, the metaphor of the 'blue planet', based on the view of its dominant oceanic constitution as seen from space, presages the importance of water for a popular imaginary and for material ecologies in the twenty-first century. Building on this extended metaphorical vision of *blue* as it orients toward water, the blue carbon metaphor is centrally implicated in the ways in which this carbon footprint metaphor enfolds complex relationalities and processes of carbon vitality, especially in attending to relationships and processes that go on below or above the surfaces that are normally visible. Here the carbon footprint metaphor displays the movements associated with affect by being 'pulled beyond its seeming surface-boundedness by way of its relation to, indeed its composition through, the forces of encounter' (Seigworth and Gregg 2010, 3). While a carbon footprint might have, up until this point, gestured toward the surfaces of terrestrial relations that generate atmospheric effects, here coastal spaces weave in aquatic forms of carbon vitality that lead to novel perceptions.

Through the shrimp story, the carbon footprint metaphor leads to blue carbon and yet other associated metaphors described evocatively here by Steven Bouillon:

> Mangrove forests consist of a consortium of tree and shrub species adapted to cope with the saline conditions and fluctuating water levels that characterize their environment. One such adaptation is the development of different aerial root systems, such as stilt prop roots … that anchor the plants in the sediment and allow oxygen to penetrate the submerged roots. These complex root structures also slow down incoming waters during tidal inundation, causing much of the suspended material in the water column to settle onto the sediment surface. This highly efficient particle-trapping mechanism leads to the sequestration of carbon not only from the mangroves … but also from outside the ecosystem, including from rivers and adjacent seagrass meadows.
>
> (2011, 282)

Although Bouillon, a scientist in the field of soil and water management, describes a kind of mechanistic functionality of a mangrove ecosystem through the metaphor of 'sequestration', he also notably creates an opening for an affective re-composition of these same ecosystems, whereby the mangroves themselves perform a poetics of re-figuring terrestrial, aerial, and aqua-cultural relations. Mangrove forests, it appears, weave multispecies associations that have developed over millennia and constitute an integral part of complex planetary carbon flows. The extended description of mangrove forests above paints an image of distributed intelligence or *sentience* that operates in and through associations of water, land, and air as they coalesce in mangroves.

The description of lively mangroves not only figures a poetic image, making it newly sensible, but it also inadvertently dismantles the human construct of manageable boundaried ecosystems; whereas the forests are attributed with the power to store carbon from 'rivers and adjacent seagrass meadows', these are conspicuously relegated by Bouillon in the quotation above to the space 'outside the ecosystem'. If we listen to them, however, the mangroves are illustrating (in Derridean fashion[18]) *that there is no outside-ecosystem*; the sea is constitutive of land and the land, the sea. The affective mediations of the footprint metaphor help to enable such a sensibility: 'With affect, a body is as much outside as in itself – webbed in its relations – until ultimately such firm distinctions cease to matter' (Seigworth and Gregg 2010, 3). Aerial roots of mangroves bring into visibility a constitutive atmospheric relation to Earth and sea, so often taken for granted in modern histories until recent understandings of climate change. Whether we burn carbon, or up-root it, the trace of the carbon footprint through mangroves here exposes an elemental coincidence of fire – air – water – earth.

Although Bouillon's description does permit a certain ecological understanding of mangrove forests, it consequentially tends to remove the human species in its description as well. How can these understandings be both sensible to ecosystem existence prior to and in spite of human interventions, yet simultaneously figure humans as integral within contemporary ecosystems? An active reading of this carbon footprint metaphor draws out a relational ontology that reconfigures existing dominant ways of understanding coastal ecosystems being uprooted through aquaculture. No longer viewed as backgrounded environment or resource, mangrove ecosystems vitally appear in this reading as socialized and sentient spaces where mutual impressions are made. These coastal living spaces reveal particularly rich sensible and porous interactions between water, trees, soil, sea life, and peoples.

Tracing this carbon footprint of shrimp to the mangroves on the Andaman coasts of Thailand, one can sense how material and cultural matter are inextricably interwoven in conceptions of life of the Moken peoples, an Indigenous group who have, up until recently, literally lived on the seas (in boats) in these regions for over 3,500 years (McDuie-Ra 2013). The intervention of P'Noon, a Moken participant in the fieldwork of geographers Nathan Bennett and Phil Deardon (2012), brings some of these conceptions to life for those outside the community: 'If you talk about living in the community, the mangrove has a part in it … if the mangroves survive, then the community survives … the mangroves depend on us and we depend on the mangroves' (Bennett and Deardon 2012, 23). Here the mangrove is centrally figured as part of the coastal sea community; revealingly,

P'Noon's description may seem animistically reductive to those accustomed to an enlightenment epistemology of human technological re-making, whereby industrious humans engineer living conditions that often distance us from material-ecological relations. Such a distancing is a necessary feature of the Blue Revolution whose logic enables the clearing away of ecological complexities for mono-cropped shrimp as a profit-oriented approach to creating affordable protein. By contrast to such a logic, Toom, another Moken fisher on the Andaman coast constructs an image of the necessary complexity of relations and processes of healthy ecosystems, which are tellingly and metaphorically constructed as house and home:

> Without fertile mangroves, the animals would not be as numerous – shrimps, crabs, fish, birds, snakes, monkeys, squid, small shrimp. Mangroves are very important. It is a house of small trees and it is something that the villagers make use of. When people cut them, it is like you are destroying the home of small animals.
>
> (Bennett and Deardon 2012, 24)

Identifying this space as home and describing some of its inhabitants permits a localized valuation of these living spaces and, accordingly, potential orienting principals guiding their treatment. Such a valuation arrives only belatedly in the Global North with the arrival of the carbon footprint metaphor of jumbo-farmed shrimp that draws some of these complexities into view. This metaphor certainly implicates mangroves as 'carbon sinks' from a land and sea management perspective, but it also implicitly opens up the question: *What can we learn from the sentience of mangroves ecosystems that would be lost through their eradication, and how might such sensibilities contribute to the well-being of humans and non-humans alike?*

Mangrove forests can be described as a 'consortium of tree and shrub species' as Bouillon does above, but they may also appear as populated rhizomatic edifices in coastal zones that trouble the boundaries between land, water, and air. Existing only where these zones melt into indifference, mangroves assemble a plethora of vital activity by selectively trapping and releasing the vibrant matter of coastal life. While their carbon storage capacity can be instrumentalized through the logic of carbon sequestration, this is but one aspect of their sentience that may come into view through the carbon footprint metaphor. In order to follow the seemingly disproportionate carbon footprint of farmed shrimp, vital relations and processes must come into view for a portion of the human population that has yet to sense them. Living in reciprocal relations with mangroves is clearly one way of permitting a network of sentience in specific localities. The insights of P'Noon once again make this apparent:

> We are Moken, so we used to build all of our houses on stilts because they needed to be high up above the water. When I was young, there used to be mangroves in front of the community. They started to disappear when I was

in school. The new generation needed more land. I used to jump off the land and there were fish. The front bit of the community would not erode so quickly if there were mangroves. The water just keeps coming in and the sand just washes away.

(Bennett and Deardon 2012, 25)

P'Noon's description affectively recomposes mangroves as a site of childhood play, and a place that was teeming with life, but a site that has disappeared due to recent human-initiated change. Metaphorically re-figured as playful, sentient spaces, the mangrove here takes on new associations and orients toward the sensibilities of carbon vitality. The particularities of this sentient space formerly led people to construct their homes on stilts in the water, mirroring the staunch yet permeable intelligence of mangroves in their transactions with the powerful ebbs and flows of water. Their removal thus represents a greater loss than that of a single species; rather, it implies a profound perturbation in sense and sensibility for all who thrive among the material and cultural spaces of mangroves. For coastal areas particularly susceptible to tsunami and storm surges, this sentient space is particularly valuable. Following a number of particularly devastating tsunamis in the early 2000s, building companies are not only insisting that coastal mangroves be left intact where they are still in place, but also that if buildings must be constructed in these zones, they be designed to let water through on the ground floors (just as mangroves permit a flow-through of water).[19] Thus, belatedly, human engineers and designers are learning from the intelligent design of these vital relations and processes.

The return of the carbon subject, or shifts in vital kin relations?

Lest it appear that a diverse range of larger-than-human actors have obtained equal footing in the politics of these metaphors, the headlines in the stories of carbon footprints of shrimp complicate such an interpretation. What is apparent in reading most of the headlines that appear in North American contexts is that the target audiences addressed are liberal human privileged subjects who consume shrimp ('*Your* Shrimp Cocktail is Ruining the Planet'). The carbon footprint of shrimp story thus does rely on an association with a carbon subject, but carbon subjects in this instance are differently implicated in a complex relationship than when they were first hailed into climate change politics through the carbon footprint reduction lists. While these stories seem to initially hail a carbon subject, they also initiate a gradual shift away from reifying a domestic household carbon subject toward sensing a more ecologically grounded distributive agency. Whereas the early lists were often ineffective and overly extensive – they simply implicated everything superficially and therefore nothing at the same time – this carbon footprint metaphor connects to particular ecosystems and creates a more detailed image of that relationality. Because carbon is notoriously amorphous and abstract, the carbon footprint metaphor has the capacity to ground carbon in specific ways by locating it (temporarily and contingently, as footprints always suggest) within specific metaphorical spaces and bringing these specificities of carbon vitality into a political field of connection.

But why should people in the Global North care about these relationships that are seemingly so distant and how does the carbon footprint metaphor connect with this tangential path of mangroves? By following the carbon footprint (metaphor) of shrimp to mangroves in this way, two important observations can be made. First, planetary carbon connections link 'us' all, whether we see we are in the same ecosystems or not; as Jane Bennett suggests, even 'operative notions of matter, life, self, self-interest ...' shift if one concedes that relations of vitality run 'alongside and inside humans' (2010, vii-ix). Perceiving carbon vitality means 'tuning in' to these already-existing carbon flows and seeing ourselves as one part of the larger distributed agency of such vitality. Seeing ourselves in this way shifts emphasis away from subjectivity; moving away from subjectivity in turn allows for 'a better discernment of the active powers issuing from [nonhuman] nonsubjects' (Bennett 2010, ix).

The second important observation centres on the crucial role of carbon footprint metaphors to affectively mediate these connections of carbon vitality. While in some circumstances the carbon footprint metaphor functions as an imposition that overwrites pre-existing local valuations and attempts to disconnect from existing distributed carbon vitality as I discuss below, the metaphor can also foster attunement to multiscale and multispecies sentience vis-à-vis climate change. Critically reading this metaphor and understanding the significance of tracing carbon footprints of shrimp entails following the traces to mangroves, which in turn suggest social-ecological sentience, as expressed through the narratives of P'Noon and Toom above. The carbon footprint metaphor invokes novel sensibilities not only through local stories, but through the mangroves themselves whose rhizomatic structure figures carbon relations and processes that defy easy human apprehension and simultaneously disturb an either/or politics of local versus global. Repeatedly, the carbon footprint metaphor illustrates that despite certain human pretentions to quantitatively take everything into a global calculus, there always remain excesses that cannot be calculated, trapped, or sequestered by human subjects in their dominant patterns and communities.

The affective politics of carbon footprint metaphors in this instance reveal the potential for an economy of interests that extends beyond individuals and humans to an 'in-between-ness' that is open to new carbon relations. As Seigworth and Gregg suggest, '[a]ffect arises in the midst of an *in-between-ness*: in the capacities to act and be acted upon. Affect is an impingement or extrusion of a momentary or sometimes more sustained state of relation *as well as* the passage (and the duration of passage) of forces or intensities' (2010, 1). The carbon footprint metaphor here initiates an impingement on a state of relations as it defamiliarizes both the family of things that have been inscribed as having a footprint, and the dominant ways in which we have come to act upon these footprints. This suspension of familiarity opens up newly visible carbon relations and processes that permit the entrance of other fellows with whom we may share *kinship,* a crucial affective relationship in an age of climate change. Attentiveness to carbon vitality 'can inspire a greater sense of the extent to which all bodies are kin in the sense of [being] inextricably enmeshed in a dense network of relations' (Bennett 2010, 13).

Bennett's attention to kinship relations gestures at the need for an explicit recognition of carbon connections that go beyond individual subjects and the human connections of citizens; as family relations reveal, kinship needs to be composed explicitly in discourse and practices that foster connections that may be latently there (in human terms through bloodlines, social relations, etc.). The same is true for kinship in terms of carbon flows. Though 'we' may intellectually understand that we are all connected through planetary carbon cycles, practices for fostering attunement to these kinship relations are still necessary. The associative value of metaphor here is crucial; the carbon footprint metaphor affectively draws important connections that are at once cultural and material.

In many of the articles stemming from the analysis of the carbon footprint of shrimp, attention and care for mangrove ecosystems emerges as a key political action (Isabella 2012; Philpott 2012). Thus, the carbon footprint of the shrimp story suggests that mangroves are valuable not only in terms of their carbon storage function on behalf of the planet, but that they are also priceless in terms of their distributed agency of care for the larger-than-human kin communities in coastal zones: '[I]ntact mangrove forests are of value in protecting the coastal ecosystems and communities against storms and tsunamis, such as the Indian Ocean tsunami that killed some 230, 000 people' (Phys.org 2012). Although some of the mechanisms for implementing protection may be laden with implications of managerial climate change solutions (as described below), the move to bring these ecosystems into view offers an initial intervention of imagined possibilities that were previously unseen in climate change politics. To return to Rancière's meditation on the politics of aesthetics, 'it is a question of constructing an image – that is to say a certain connection between the verbal and the visual. The power of this image is that it disturbs the ordinary regime of that connection ...' (2009, 95). The image here constructed through the carbon footprint metaphor suggests that the destruction of these ecosystems may not be as easily offset by carbon subjects paying for their guilt; rather these political aesthetics, composed of larger-than-human-kin relations, demand different responses that attend to the complexities of carbon vitality.

These newly visible aesthetics suggest that no matter how we attempt to calculate and manage carbon (or other ecosystem elements for that matter) through anthropocentric systems, certain larger-than-human constituents and processes always impinge upon these systems. The carbon footprint metaphor here is revealed for its political promise as re-inscribable through a larger-than-human carbon vitality that impinges upon the 'givens'. A key epistemological intervention of the connection to mangroves through the carbon footprint metaphor is to remind again of the partiality of human vision and situated knowledges. As Toom suggests, 'sometimes, the things that we do make things that we use or eat disappear without understanding why they disappear. We cut down the mangroves to make good things without understanding what this will do' (Bennett and Deardon 2012, 24). The numbers figured through the loss of mangroves in the carbon footprint of shrimp may be somewhat surprising, thus they make an impact and are 'newsworthy' to publics; yet given Toom's insight into partial human vision and blind spots, it is somewhat unsurprising that unforeseen impacts of human management do occur. Without admitting to unforeseen impingements by actors or 'kin' with whom we are entangled in carbon flows, our large-scale anthropocentric interventions are susceptible to such failures of unilateral action by certain humans. This carbon footprint metaphor reveals that carbon connections may appear anywhere and everywhere: that we share kinship relations with shrimp and mangroves and a host of other actors, many of whom may as yet be unnamed or unaccounted for through current dominant systems. While we might attempt to turn away from such actors by attempting to define the parameters of carbon systems to manage them, these actors will appear to claim a place. Affective attunement to carbon vitality offers perceptual openings to these actors and processes.

While the carbon footprint metaphor here offers the promise of mediating these relations of carbon vitality into political responses, as affect theorists point out, the 'immanent neutrality' of affect suggests that we must also remain alert to the risks of such affective attachments. As William Connolly warns, vitality in and of itself offers no guarantees:

> For some of us, vitality is a capacity to appreciate and cultivate to the extent we can because, first, it enhances our positive sense of attachment to a cosmos that is neither predesigned for us nor that is susceptible to our control and, second, it is a gift we can draw sustenance from when new and unexpected situations arise. But ... it is an ambiguous gift if the world is not preorganized for us in either of the above two ways ... the connection between us and the world is replete with constitutive dissonances and tensions. Vitality expresses those tensions.
>
> (2013, 148)

Following up on the tensions and ambivalence of (carbon) vitality, I turn now to the risks presented through the carbon footprint of shrimp as this metaphor potentially mediates connections to marketized approaches to climate change.

The risky attachments of vital relations to carbon markets

While the entrance of larger-than-human vital relations through the carbon footprint metaphor promises a re-staging of carbon matter, it also risks the management by humans of life newly named as 'having' a carbon footprint. The shrimp, mangroves, and a network of larger-than-human actors are the animating forces that are newly identified through the footprint metaphor; the risk, however, is that almost as soon as new larger-than-human actors are affectively brought into view, they become tethered to a financialized and humanly constrained ecosystem services approach. One article suggests '[t]he catchy shrimp cocktail estimate is part of the relatively new field in science and economics called *ecosystem services*, which uses models to measure the value to human communities, in economic terms, of forests, grassland, waterways and even the air' (Phys.org 2012).[20] Despite the many possible alternative political arrangements latent within the carbon footprint of shrimp story, such considerations are foreclosed upon in the monetization of ecosystem services angle in some of the articles that pick up this story. Notably, Boone Kauffman himself initiates this association since his carbon footprint analysis ends with the implication of bringing these costs 'home' to the market: 'Based on his calculations, Kauffman says that compensating farmers for not growing shrimp would mean that each ton of carbon kept intact in mangrove soil would cost about $4.50. "That's well within the range of carbon markets," Kauffman said.' (Stokstad 2012, para 4).

The carbon markets to which Kauffman refers are those implemented by the Kyoto Protocol's Clean Development Mechanism (CDM), the global trading scheme that came into effect through what David Driesen calls a 'shotgun wedding' between the United Nations Framework Convention on Climate Change (UNFCC) along with other Kyoto Protocol signatory countries and the United States, who promised support of the Protocol on the condition that a flexible neo-liberal trading mechanism be implemented (a promise which was broken as the US did not sign on to the agreement) (Driesen 2008, 34). Here shrimp, mangroves, and their 'blue' associates appear as financialized carbon agents, reminiscent of the mechanisms through which carbon subjects have been brought into a governmental conduct of carbon conduct that ultimately legitimates carbon markets as instruments of economic growth. In this instance, the carbon footprint metaphor marks the first stage of recognition of these actors who, on the one hand, appear to be newly counted in the politics of climate change. On the other hand, however, if apprehended through a partial human vision even further reduced through a market lens, these actors offer new wealth-creation opportunities in the development of a liberal environmental order. It is not as if Boone Kauffman and his colleagues who advocate for an ecosystems services approach to blue carbon are villains who aim to profit from the internalization of these carbon agents into carbon markets; however, the ways in which the carbon footprint metaphor functions as a justification for fraught market solutions merits attention.

The affective mediation of the footprint metaphor may be seen as an initial step in the reduction of carbon vitality to a carbon calculus of species and ecosystems – a reduction that launches an ecosystem services approach to the valuation of the material and cultural element of carbon. Importantly, 'ecosystem services' itself is a contested notion/metaphor that has arisen among ecological economists to challenge the principles of *substitutability* within conventional economics. As Dempsey and Robertson suggest, 'ecological economists insist on the persistence of environmental externalities which cannot be substituted–for and must be internalized by being explicitly valued' (2012, 5). While the granting of an environmental 'outside' to market logic marks a key epistemological break-through for economics, the belated taming of these outside forces through 'internalization' to the market also risks institutionalizing a particularly reductive partial human vision as the means of solving a host of complex material-ecological crises.

It is important to recognize the myriad agendas and motivations that shape ecosystem services defined variously 'as a standard commodity or as a heuristically useful metaphor' (Dempsey and Robertson 2012, 3). Not all of the approaches signalled by this 'services' metaphor gesture at the need to commodify ecosystem actors within markets. In fact, some ecosystems services perspectives offer quite the opposite implications: that is, they suggest that exploring this metaphor/approach productively highlights how ecosystems can *never* be made into commodities in private financial institutions). 'We want to make clear that expressing the value of ecosystem services in monetary units does not mean that they should be treated as private commodities that can be traded in private markets' (Costanza et al. 2014, 157). Despite important caveats and nuances, however, what holds many of these theorizations together, are two premises: first that ecosystems are conceived as providing services *for humans;* and second, that an appropriate and necessary way of evaluating these services is to render them in terms of a universal monetary currency. These two premises guided Costanza et al. in their influential estimate of world ecosystems as providing US$33 trillion worth of ecosystem services in 1997 and in their 2014 up-date, which now estimates such ecosystem services at a value of between US$124 and 145 trillion (Costanza et al. 1997; Costanza et al. 2014). Nuances are evident in the debates about the policy and conservation structures and implications of these two premises, but many of the general tensions arise from whether 'money's use as a universal equivalent can be separated from the operation of capital to generate profit – a belief among both scientists and policy-makers' (Dempsey and Robertson 2012, 15). This belief, or what Dempsey and Robertson call 'blindness', is evident in the discussions of the sequestration power of blue carbon that lend currency to the carbon footprint metaphor in aquacultural practices as they connect to carbon markets. Following this logic, Boone Kauffman suggests that a US$4.50 compensation (according to carbon market value) to fishers for *not* growing shrimp would take care of the problem. As I describe below, however, trading in equivalencies through the commodification of carbon does not provide the easy one-size-fits-all solution that it pretends to.

In this case, the carbon footprint analysis of farmed shrimp invests in an ecosystem services approach to mangroves by apprehending their capacity to store or 'sequester' carbon. This logic then easily slips into the norms of liberal environmentalism that centre profit-orientation through the making of tradeable carbon equivalencies through reducing life to a carbon calculus. The metaphor mediates the apprehension and internalization of those actors whose carbon footprints have yet to be counted, but it does so by removing biodiverse specificities of carbon vitality. Steve Bouillon suggests that blue carbon coastal ecosystems may 'bury carbon at rates up to 50 times higher than those in tropical rainforests' (2011, 282). Through this functional lens, mangroves are valued neither for their inherent myriad relational processes and complex interactions, nor even for how they can instruct humans about how to relate to coastal marine zones (like for the Moken who build permeable temporary stilt houses inspired by the sentient structures of mangroves); rather, they are valued for their comparative ability to sequester carbon away from the atmosphere where its accumulating presence spells disaster for the human species (among others who are not equally valued). An initial apprehension of these carbon relations within an ecosystem services approach occurs through scientific instrumentation and data collecting that reveals complexities that were previously unseen and uncounted; this apprehension is also achieved through the carbon footprint metaphor that yokes together these carbon relations. Such carbon complexities, at the initial phase of metaphoric apprehension, can serve as a reminder of partial human vision and gesture toward a perennial need for human humility in composing worlds; however, when apprehended alongside an ecosystem – or more reductively – *carbon* services approach, these complexities are significantly reduced. 'In this way, carbon is individuated (separated from its local context) involving a discursive and practical cut into the world in order to name discrete chunks of reality that are deemed socially useful' (Bumpus and Liverman 2008, 136).

This initial stage of carbon reductionism institutes the conditions of possibility for carbon capital (described below), a different form of capture whose logic often defies the assumed climate change mitigation principles that serve as its foundational justification. As noted above, ecosystems services approaches already twice reduce myriad non-humans: first, by declaring them human service-providers, and then valuing these services in financial terms. Apprehending the 'carbon' services permits further reductions of myriad ecosystems – including watershed relations, microbial soil processes, and infinite other lively interactions – to one category of instrumentality indexed enigmatically as 'carbon'. When metaphorically associated with other carbon metaphors and systems, like the carbon market initiatives that watered down the Kyoto Protocol, this reduced carbon footprint metaphor risks foreclosing upon the vital sensibilities it initially promises. Through the filter of what Foucault calls 'the permanent economic tribunal for all matters of life' (2008/2004, 247), solutions to climate change are judged primarily by their ability to uphold and bolster this existing liberal environmental order.

Significantly, for carbon markets to be judged successful thus far, they do not necessarily require proof of emissions reductions at any scale. Even if they do seem to be permitting reductions at one level, such reductions are often achieved by the accounting tricks of 'hopping carbon footprints' that foist emissions from one country or region to another with no overall reductions at the global level, as I describe in Chapter 4. The 'economic tribunal' for matters of carbon life might then consequentially pivot upon how successfully carbon footprint metaphors productively foster attachments between 'species and speculative currencies' (Shukin 2009, 6).

Carbon capital

As outlined in Chapters 3 and 4, the carbon footprint metaphor has a history of becoming attached to carbon markets through the off-setting of guilt on the part of carbon subjects, or through fostering state-oriented citizenship regimes of fossil fuel development. This time, through the appearance of ecosystems associated with the carbon footprints of shrimp, new carbon actors appear ambivalently to both displace human primacy in the footprint, but also to become potentially bound within particularly encumbered human orders of ecosystem services. This appearance, through certain culturally coded carbon compounds, allows the conditions of possibility for what Nicole Shukin flags as 'animal capital', 'the paradox of an anthropocentric order of capitalism whose means and effects can be all too posthuman, that is, one that ideologically and materially invests in a world in which species boundaries can be radically crossed (as well as rein-scribed) in the genetic and aesthetic pursuit of new markets' (Shukin 2009, 11). This critique tempers an unequivocally promising story of emergence of carbon kin with whom humans share vital relations. If the metaphor of the carbon foot-print offers the potential of crossing species boundaries to disturb all-too-human accounts of carbon actors, it also certainly invests, through certain metaphoric associations, in a form of species boundary-crossing that remains anthropocentric by apprehending newly coded carbon actors and species that appear in the serv-ice of new carbon markets. The carbon footprint metaphor's ability to traffic across species lines upholds this logic of 'carbon capital',[21] an investment in the novel appearance of non-human actors as opportunities for speculative finance in carbon markets. Paradoxically, this logic grants the importance of non-humans in a carbon connected world, but it reinscribes a specific human partial vision through the 'universal' equivalent of finance capital, an equivalence that is chal-lenged not only by human societies where global asymmetries prevail, but also most certainly, by larger-than-human vitality in carbon flows.

The jumbo carbon footprint of farmed shrimp thus makes possible an affective investment in carbon capital whereby mangrove ecosystems function reductively as a standing reserve of carbon not only in their material storage capacity, but through what Michael Betancourt calls a 'semiotic exchange of immaterial assets' (2010).[22] Here the amorphous quality of metaphorical carbon distanced from its material flows functions to legitimate the generation of market value through abstraction, assimilation, and homogenization; 'once a tonne of reduced carbon becomes a credit, it is largely assumed to mean the same thing as other tonnes of reduced carbon, despite the potentially different material circumstances' (Bumpus and Liverman 2008, 137). The mediation of associated metaphors further sustains this relation. Under current regimes, putting or keeping carbon in its place – 'sequestering' it or storing it in a 'sink' – often parallels a transactional account-ing of carbon markets as emissions reductions certificates that keep in place patterns both of fossil-fuel intensive wealth generation and of unequal global wealth distribution. In many cases, it makes more sense for state and non-state actors to avoid the high costs of changing their hydrocarbon-intensive practices by investing in other countries' 'cleaner' development. 'CDM allows emission reductions to be made more cheaply by investing in other countries. In effect, capital can achieve higher rates of accumulation under carbon trading because it needs to invest less in domestic emissions' (Bumpus and Liverman 2008, 142).

Naming a mangrove forest as a carbon sink risks effacing all other complex cartographies of existence and lively social-material interactions within these sentient spaces and, relatedly, instituting neo-colonial relations. As Gavin Bridge suggests, this carbon storage logic promotes the 'enclosures and transformations necessary to produce sequestration landscapes as objects of speculation and instruments of profit' (2011, 824). While the blue revolution advancement of jumbo shrimp farms in coastal ecosystems of the Global South enacted an initial dispossession of lively spaces for local communities, the (partial) recovery of this land as carbon sinks risks initiating new forms of colonial dispossession. Building on David Harvey's critique of capital 'accumulation by dispossession', Bumpus and Liverman call this process 'accumulation by decarbonisation' (2008, 142). This process involves the creation of:

> rights to emit carbon (pollution permits) ... that become commodified and privatized, traded with transaction fees, and allocated and regulated by international and state institutions under conditions of unequal exchange between developed and developing countries, northern companies and southern communities.
>
> (Bumpus and Liverman 2008, 142)

Once the value of the carbon services of mangroves has been apprehended, abstracted, and virtualized as a commodity through the CDM, land use is regulated in a way that often amounts to the expulsion of local peoples and their traditional means of subsistence while yielding control to conservation experts from afar. The removal of local peoples 'simplifies the mangrove forests in order to make levels of carbon sequestration legible for carbon markets' (Beymer-Farris and Bassett 2011, 333). The process of recovering mangrove forests for their carbon sequestering capacities is often then accomplished through re-planting mangrove trees in coastal ecosystems that have been degraded. Mimicking the terrestrial version of carbon sink forest management, which often amounts to monocultural plantings to perform carbon sequestration for the globe, marine plantations are similarly prone to being divested of necessary biodiversity (ibid., 339). These monoculture projects planted with newly introduced non-endemic 'climate-ready' plant species often wreak havoc on local ecosystems.

Such practices risk utilizing 'climate policies to bring about a variation on the traditional means by which the global South is dominated' (Bachram 2004, 6). The 'CDM provides the economic incentive to engage in such practices as a cost effective way to generate [Certificates of Emissions Reductions] CERs' (Wilson 2011, 1012). Activists in India have called these carbon services projects 'carbon colonialism' belying their *carbon-trumps-all* logic of accumulating carbon sinks and wealth for the Global North at the expense of localized social-ecological economies (Equity Watch 2000). In apprehending ecological and carbon complexities only belatedly, if at all, such climate policies reveal the shifty metaphorical work of 'carbon' reduced to market-driven colonial practices. The paradoxically non-human, but still anthropocentric, 'carbon footprint' of shrimp may thus favour the same global beneficiaries as always.

In the carbon calculations initiated by an apprehension of the carbon footprint of farmed shrimp, the footprint metaphor may underwrite schemes that not only dispossess local populations of their land and livelihoods, by paying fishers *not to* fish, but they also leave further ecological degradation in their wake while failing to reduce global emissions and address asymmetrical relations. As Bridge suggests, '[t]he emergence in the global South of land cover regimes managed for their carbon storage or sequestration capacities is paralleled by the proliferation and consolidation of fossil fuel consumption in the global North' (2011, 826). Thus far, the results of carbon trading schemes have been antithetical to their emissions-reducing and sustainable development pretentions; on the contrary, carbon markets have perpetuated a trajectory of 'uneven development' and 'destructive ecological activities' (Bohm et al. 2012, 1632).

Although it is not my contention that all who suggest market mechanisms as potential 'solutions' to climate change are favouring profits over ecosystem health, the track record of these solutions tellingly exposes a misalignment of priorities when they are implemented. In practice, these projects of locating a carbon footprint in order to produce a carbon sink reinforce the 'compromise of liberal environmentalism' first established in the 1990s as climate change first came into public visibility (Bernstein 2000). Whereas through the Kyoto Protocol's CDM, the carbon trading market achieved immediate financial success, topping at US$64 billion in three years (World Bank 2008, 1), the emissions reductions accounts seem far less promising. In a comprehensive assessment in the *Ecology Law Quarterly*, Kylie Wilson reviews a number of CDM hydroelectric projects, forestry projects, and biomass and waste projects in developing countries (2011). Her case studies reveal that the UNFCC approves most of these projects with little oversight, tasking individual host countries with determining the length, breadth, and depth of environmental assessment and stakeholder engagement. As there are real financial incentives to fast-tracking these projects before a project developer potentially chooses to invest in a neighbouring country, and because host countries lack the capacity to do costly environmental and social assessments, 'many host countries have conceded that they are not in a position to do more than take for granted the claims made by project developers in project design documents about the expected sustainable benefits of projects' (Wilson 2011, 993). The result is a carbon trading scheme that works to enshrine carbon capital, but does not reduce overall global emissions.

Initial analysis of the unfolding Reduced Emission from Deforestation in Developing Countries (REDD) suite of solutions – the UNFCC carbon market mechanism aimed at preserving carbon stocks in terrestrial forests – suggests similarly disappointing results. A report by Coren et al. in *Climate Policy* suggests that 'forest carbon activities tend to deliver fewer credits than calculated *ex ante*' (Coren et al. 2011, 1285). The authors therefore suggest that the expectations for biophysical mitigation anticipated by this market instrument be tempered since the financial incentive is not sufficient to promote wide-scale protection of forests within international carbon markets.

In addition to failing to ensure emissions reductions, carbon capital's ability to deliver on its own profit-generating logic itself has come under scrutiny. CDM credits have earned the 'status of the world's worst performing commodity as slumping demand meets rising supply of the UN instrument traded under the Kyoto Protocol' (Wynn and Chestney 2011). The European Trading System (ETS), the EUs flagship policy for carbon trading, has been a subject of on-going critique. Whereas the price of its Emission Allowance in 2008 was €25, it remained at around €5 in the years 2013–2015 and continues to underperform in terms of profit expectations. (Brangeret al. 2015). At the time of writing, the ETS was set to enter into Phase 4 of implementation to address some of the critiques around under-performance in profit generation and emissions reductions (ICAP 2016), but it remains a failure prone system that tends to produce vastly unequal distribution effects and in its market-oriented dominance often precludes other policy instruments aimed at reducing both emissions and other socio-ecological harms (Branger et al. 2015). The supposed win-win scenario anticipated by proponents of the Kyoto Protocol's CDM – of ensuring both sustainable development for developing (non-Annex I) countries and affordable carbon emissions reductions for developed (Annex I) countries – is now looking as if it were a pipe dream. This is because it favours instituting a particular partial vision that is especially short-sighted, as David Driesen points out, cheap carbon emissions reductions will always remain at odds with attempts at 'sustainable development' in its pretenses toward the future and intergenerational equity (2008).[23]

Most crucially, in the context of mangrove reforestation, REDD risks further entrenching colonial violence through novel land-grabbing of territories newly identified as carbon sinks to perform the work of carbon capture on behalf of a planet in crisis. 'Carbon forestry initiatives are redefining socio-natural relations in ways that threaten access to, control and management of natural resources' (Beymer-Farris and Bassett 2011, 339). Many members of the Indigenous Environmental Network (IEN) have urged the UN to cancel all carbon trading and REDD schemes on the grounds that such schemes further dispossess peoples of their lands and life-sustaining practices (Goldtooth et al. 2016, np). These critiques insist that such 'false solutions' to climate change serve only to perpetuate genocide of Indigenous peoples. 'The UN's Paris Agreement on climate does not cut emissions at the source and treats Nature as capital with no real nor effective safeguard mechanisms that could guarantee the prevention of land grabs and the protection of the rights of Indigenous Peoples' (Goldtooth et al. 2016, np).

The seemingly promising notion/metaphor of 'blue carbon' attaches to these problematic norms of marketized responses. Speaking on behalf of the nation of Bolivia, Ambassador Pablo Solon has suggested:

We have seen proposals for markets for the oceans, so called 'blue carbon' we are surprised and concerned by these. The problem with the reference level for markets such as these is that it is based on assumptions that are not real. And there is the great possibility that the new market mechanisms will just create more hot air ... With parameters that are not real, countries try to get a bigger share of certificates of reductions and in that way, instead of developing new sources of finance, we will develop new sources of deterioration of our natural systems.

(Solon as cited in World People's Conference Press Release 2011, np)

Solon's caution reminds that metaphors such as blue carbon can be used to reinforce neo-colonialism and further degradation. The abstractions of metaphorical carbon itself plays to multiple agendas that require critical attention.

By offering a critique of the risks of carbon capital as they are smuggled in through the carbon footprint metaphor in this case, I am not suggesting that forms of human currency should be removed from the equation of climate change politics, nor I am insisting that non-humans are categorically separate from market considerations. As the tensions within ecosystems services reveal, what may be called non-human 'nature' is certainly imbricated within and affected by what Costanza calls the 'real economy' (2006, 749). Further, as William Connolly argues, even critics of capital must avoid the tendency to 'treat capitalism as an amazingly self-absorbent system, or reduce economic life to a "discursive system" without thinking closely about its innumerable imbrications with nondiscursive systems with impressive powers of their own' (Connolly 2013, 30). The trick is rather to 'set the stage' to attend to the complexities of 'nonhuman force fields' entangled with these systems (ibid., 31). Carbon/ecosystem services approaches in their myriad theoretical and practical manifestations present various attempts to manage these complexities, in some cases, without commodifying these services (Reid et al. 2006, 749).

Notably, prior to the United States' insistence on the addition of the Article 12 carbon trading scheme to the Kyoto Protocol, there was a strong push from the European Union and other countries to support binding targets with 'less use of trading' (Driesen 2008, 34). Meanwhile Brazil, along with the rest of the Group of 77 countries, pushed for *financial penalties* levied on Annex I parties who exceeded their permitted amount of CO_{2e} emissions (Wilson 2011, 976). Further, many countries use other regulatory mechanisms that combine targets for use of renewable energy with tax incentives and/or feed-in tariffs for renewable energy providers who contribute to the energy grid (Driesen 2008). The use of some financial mechanisms clearly addresses an important cultural-material entanglement of hydrocarbons and markets in modern human societies that must be reckoned with; however, the particularly trenchant compromise of the global carbon-trading scheme enacted by the CDM makes use of carbon's shape-shifting metaphoricity to enact carbon capital as *the* going 'false solution' (IEN)[24] to climate change. As Dempsey and Robertson warn, the use of money as a 'universal equivalent' becomes notoriously difficult to separate from money as capital and profit-generating in and of itself (2012, 15). Tracing carbon footprint metaphors' attachment to profit-generating principles exposes this particularly problematic way of managing carbon vitality.

Grasping toward carbon vitality?

The promises that I gesture toward in this chapter relate to the metaphor's openness to the relational forces of larger-than-human footprints. Whereas farmed shrimp could be viewed simply as commodities within global systems, sensing their gargantuan carbon footprint requires situating them within relations and processes that pre-existed their entrance on the scene in discourse. In this case, the mangrove forests and connected ecologies indexed belatedly through the 'blue carbon' metaphor appear as key actors with forces and trajectories that do not operate singularly in the service of human design. Carbon vitality, a novel metaphor, gestures toward this potentially powerful connection with co-present beings – be they human, shrimp, or mangroves – at this particular historical juncture of changing climates. I suggest that this is a metaphorically enabled affective relation because it permits globally dominant human populations to feel connected to ecosystems that they might not conventionally consider as their own (in the sense of bioregionally conceived, human constructs of ecosystems). The affective mediations of the carbon footprint metaphor bring these distant ecosystems into the human and political realm of visibility and speakability as a first step toward perceiving this connection. In this case, the carbon footprint of shrimp is one example of the broader capacity of this metaphor to open up perceptions to connections that might not have otherwise been sensed. As mentioned at the outset of this chapter, the 'carbon footprint' of Rainforest beef similarly connects the consumption practices of those in the Global North with a series of profit-oriented cattle-raising practices that degrade socio-ecological systems in the Global South. Whereas climate change often appears as a statistical abstraction and as something only about distant ecosystems with images of melting polar ice caps, and dying polar bears, the carbon footprint metaphor can bring into more proximal visibility the deeply entangled larger-than-human biospherical relations that climate change asks us to perceive. Provided that these relationalities and processes are not rendered in the reduced terms of carbon capital, they offer an alternative politics in which perceptions and worlds may be re(con)figured.

Notably, shifting carbon footprint metaphors influence and are influenced by wider movements that ambivalently foster attachments of all kinds, not all of them promising profound shifts away from the fraught trajectory of carbon capital; however, even in their affective attachments to carbon markets, carbon footprint metaphors may bring to light the failures of carbon capital to deliver both on its promise of steady wealth generation and real results in terms of emissions reductions. As Patrick Bond suggests, 'the limits of the market for solving climate crises via carbon trading are clearly evident, as demonstrated by the 2011 collapse of the European Emissions Trading Scheme … and the 2010 demise of

Chicago's carbon exchange' (2011, 17). Many environmental economists are now acknowledging that one of the risks of the carbon markets is the uncertainty built into the system (Branger et al. 2015; Juergens et al. 2012; Zhang and Wei 2009). They suggest 'the drivers of carbon price change, such as energy price, unexpected weather conditions, institutional information disclosure and so forth' consequentially make these markets extremely volatile (Zhang and Wei 2009, 1808).

Perhaps this story of the carbon footprint of shrimp also suggests a more foundational source of uncertainty in these markets: the larger-than-human carbon connections that emerge to register a shock or disturbance in what has been apprehended thus far in the calculus of carbon footprints. The moving footprint seems always beyond reach, suggesting that a reliable calculus of carbon markets is always elusive, that we should not be surprised that carbon markets do not do as they're told. This instability affirms the not-yetness of affective relations potentially traced through this metaphor, suggesting a different orientation. This orientation is not easy to describe in normative terms, but as William Connolly suggests, it involves 'heightened patterns of sensitivity and experimental shifts in role definition:'

> The intuition is that we must simultaneously *slow down* at key points and moments as we enhance sensitivity to the course of things outside our habitual modes of perception, expectation, and security and *speed up* a series of changes in contemporary role definitions, identities, faith, public ethos, state priorities, and economic practices.
>
> (2013, 11)

The wager here is that carbon footprint metaphors may foster *enhanced sensitivity to the course of things outside our habitual modes of perception.* Such carbon compounds in their most promising manifestations might at once be understandable in human terms, and be malleable to decisive impingements from larger-than-human relations that reveal something about the way in which worlds are organized and how they could be other-wise. The use of such compounds might risk an organized reduction of all life to carbon, presenting a kind of troubling universalism, but these compounds may also orient suspiciousness toward the effects of quantifiable universal equivalencies, interpreted as money, or as rigorous CO_2 equivalents. One of the lessons of the successes and failures of the Kyoto Protocol is that quantifiable numbers can always be manipulated (as can metaphor!). Carbon footprints here reveal the urgency of sensory attunement to the parts that have had no part in a given regime of climate change politics. As Jane Bennett suggests, following Rancière, 'a political act not only disrupts, it disrupts in such a way as to change radically what people can "see": it repartitions the sensible; it overthrows the regime of the perceptible' (2010, 107).

These metaphors, if they remain open to larger-than-human vitality, enable iterative acts of disruption and inclusion in the politics of climate change. Thus, carbon footprints are integral to what Latour calls an ongoing 'composition of the common world' (2004, 247). Notably, for those thinking of ecological politics in these troubled times of planetary ecological crisis, the world is never completely 'composed' by the human actors that attempt to politically way-find (Bennett 2010; Connolly 2013; Haraway 2004; Latour 2004; Morton 2013). The parts that have had no part in given politics emerge to temper an assumed consensus of citizens or species involved in this political world-making. The carbon footprint metaphor offers only contingent closures and thereby remains open to the traces of appearing actors and processes. Following these traces avowedly dismantles the notion that *human* carbon footprints are the singular locus of control for climate change.

In this analysis, the ecosystem revealed includes a complex interconnection that is not founded on an either/choice between human and nature. The connection enabled by the footprint reveals social and ecological actors that had no part in the original founding of practices of the problematic global aquacultural industry. The politics of aquaculture are certainly gaining public attention; where the ocean formerly provided a new frontier of harvest, certain practices – the cultural currency of the moniker of OceanWise on seafood, for example – reveal a novel (through still fraught[25]) sensibility to these ecosystems. The power of this carbon footprint metaphor involves its capacity to make visible climate change as a complex ecological matter of concern. Rather than taking climate change as an always-universalising atmospherically located matter that trumps all others, a matter to be engineered to preserve a certain lifestyle, this instance features carbon vitality as implicated in land, water, and culture in all of its diversity. Such vital relations demand different responses than those habitual practices that have come to shape the norms of liberal market environmentalism.

Notes

1 www.aaas.org/ (accessed June 10, 2017).
2 http://phys.org/news/2012-02-tiny-shrimp-giant-carbon-footprint.html (accessed March 10, 2012).
3 http://dawn.com/2012/02/19/tiny-shrimp-leave-giant-carbon-footprint-scientist/ (accessed June 10, 2017).
4 www.estuaries.org/about-us.html (accessed March 10, 2012).
5 www.bonappetit.com/blogsandforums/blogs/badaily/2012/02/imported-shrimp-has-a-carbon-f.html (accessed March 10, 2012).
6 Notably the word 'Imported' leading this headline risks a certain displacement of carbon footprints to global 'elsewheres' even as it promises to connect shrimp-eaters in the Global North to their emissions' legacies.
7 www.bonappetit.com/trends/article/imported-shrimp-has-a-carbon-footprint-ten-times-higher-than-rainforest-beef (accessed June 10, 2017).
8 And potentially *disconnect from*, as I take up later in this chapter in the section on risks.
9 I use the category of Western-European self-reflexively as one who has grown up being educated in this tradition, but whose partial Afro-Caribbean identity has alienated her from easy access to the culture of her 'home' country of Canada. It is this complex identity that has enabled a recent path toward un-learning the colonial forms of education that I have been steeped in. At the beginning stages of this un-learning

and re-learning, I see the vast socio-ecological sophistication of certain epistemologies on what Indigenous peoples call 'Turtle Island'. (Coulthard, LaDuke, Simpson, Watts) At this stage of my journey, however, I am still ambivalently using many conceptual tools that emerge from Western European traditions as they resonate with the aspirational political ecological interventions that I hope to make. I will gesture in the conclusion toward some of these other ways of knowing that offer ways of decolonizing not only political spaces on Turtle Island, but land-based political thought itself.

10   As the previous chapter insists, 'human' must still be internally differentiated, so one may think of Haraway's notion of 'situated knowledges' as they vary across intra-human lived experiences.

11   http://seafish.org/media/publications/Assessing_the_true_cost_of_farmed_seafood _D_Lee1.pdf (accessed June 10, 2017).

12   Notably, 'Rainforest beef' is a problematic culturally rendered object that removes vital specificity of non-human life independent of its protein nourishment function for humans.

13   While one could critique the fact that this image once again reinscribes a Western liberal consuming subject in its attachments, again, I would insist that this might be one of the most vital connections it makes. *If* such a subject is susceptible to what Bennett calls 'considering revisions' in what matters in terms of lives and agencies, then the connection remains promising. The Hum-V, for example, which once might have been an icon of status for a consuming privileged subject, has been shut down as a brand of vehicles for sale to the public since 2010. This instance of the carbon footprint of shrimp in 2012 makes use of the lasting impression of a Hummer as a particularly contemptible and shameful icon of wealth and ecological destruction. I will further elaborate on the 'return of the carbon subject' in a later section of this chapter.

14   I am thinking here of social justice implications of up-rooting local livelihoods. Such concerns are not necessarily indexed by the carbon footprint metaphor, but they may be associated through the ecological footprint metaphor that indexes appropriation from distant spaces (i.e. Andrew Dobson's notion of 'ecological debtors' as explained in Chapter 4 through the notion of ecological/carbon citizenship).

15   In 2011, the Taco Bell website features tells consumers to 'drop the tux' at the high-end party and come to their fast-food chain to enjoy their succulent shrimp. Available at:www.tacobell.com/Company/newsreleases/PACIFIC_SHRIMP_TACOS_2011 (accessed November 2, 2013).

16   Key nuances challenge the universalizing statement of partial 'human' vision as a species-vision as I present it here; some people who live more proximally within the ecosystems have different sensibilities from living these relations, as will be discussed.

17   "How Many Species on Earth." *Science Daily*, August 24, 2011, suggests that only 91% of marine species are known to humans. Available at: www.sciencedaily.com/ releases/2011/08/110823180459.htm (accessed June 2, 2017).

18   I am referring here to Derrida's controversial pronouncement 'il n'y a pas hors-text' (There is no outside text), which may be interpreted as a gesture toward appreciating the multiple ways in which texts can be read and understood. Also key to this enigmatic statement may be the principal that notions like 'outside' and 'inside' are actually co-constituted and not separate. In as similar vein, my point here is that ecosystems, like texts may be interpreted and delineated in myriad ways and that mangroves deconstruct the inside and outside of the human-drawn boundaries of ecosystems.

19   Says the building company REID steel on its website: 'it is not a good idea to cut down all the vegetation and produce a smooth unprotected beach. Mangrove swamps are particularly good at stopping Tsunamis … It is possible to design the walls so that they can fail at ground-to-first floor level, but the frames must be strong enough to

support the floors above without help from the walls'. Available at: www.reid steel.com/information/tsunami_resistant_building.htm#tsunamiresistant buildings (accessed June 13, 2017).

20 Available at: http://phys.org/news/2012-02-tiny-shrimp-giant-carbon-footprint.html (accessed March 1, 2013). The AFP newsfeed from which this quote is extracted found its way to a number of other websites including 'Sea Truth', the website based on the film by the same name in which overfishing is exposed as a major global disaster in the making. Available at: www.seathetruth.nl/en/2012/03/15/tiny- shrimp-leave-giant-carbon-footprint-scientist/ (accessed March 1, 2013).

21 Patrick Bond has used the term 'carbon capital' in a critique of the 'market-based false solutions' of the UNFCC (2011, 3), but I am elaborating a specific version of carbon capital as it relates to Nicole Shukin's 'animal capital'. In other words, I am using Shukin's theorizations to suggest the ways in which non-human species affectively come to register as speculative market opportunities.

22 While Betancourt's analysis is focused on the housing crisis of 2008, there are analogous claims to be made with regard to 'carbon' as a speculative derivative. Although there are profoundly material relationships and effects involved in both the 2008 housing crisis and the carbon market, these material effects are distanced semiotically through asserting fungibility of assets, whether they are housing or carbon derivatives. The allotropism of metaphorical carbon helps in this semiotic abstraction.

23 The most-cited definition of 'sustainable development' from 'Our Common Future' (also known as the Brundtland Report) suggests *Sustainable development is development that meets the needs of the present without compromising the ability of future generations to meet their own needs'* (1987, 43).

24 The IEN and Bolivia's president, Evo Morales, refer to REDD and other such carbon trading schemes as 'false solutions'. Available at: www.ienearth.org/exposing-redd-the-false-climate-solution/ (accessed June 13, 2017).

25 The OceanWise moniker emerging from the Vancouver Aquarium (and other 'green' labels of marine stewardship). Notably, it still names sea creatures as 'seafood' for human consumption for often privileged carbon subjects who can afford this premium; thus the asymmetrical politics of over-consumption may not be addressed. In addition, the politics of the OceanWise moniker are caught up in the politics 'food re-localization' which, on the one hand, productively enables novel local material understandings and ecological practices; but on the other hand, 're-localization' can also inaugurate forms of protectionism that create impacts and vulnerabilities for distant social and ecological relations based on existing dominant global regimes of agriculture and peoples.

References

Aquafeed. 2012. "Dated and Erroneous Assumptions Yield Misleading Carbon Footprint for Farmed Shrimp." Available at: www.aquafeed.com/read-article.php?id=4336 (accessed June 15, 2017).

Bachram, Heidi. 2004. "Climate Fraud and Carbon Colonialism: The New Trade in Greenhouse Gases." *Capitalism Nature Socialism* 15, 4: 1–16.

Bennett, Jane. 2010. *Vibrant Matter: A Political Ecology of Things.* Durham, NC: Duke University Press.

Bennett, Dashiell. 2012. "Your Shrimp Cocktail is Ruining the Planet" *The Atlantic Wire* February 20, 2012. Available at: http://news.yahoo.com/shrimp-cocktail-ruining-planet-120218941.html (accessed February 10, 2013).

Bennett, Nathan and Phil Deardon. (compiled by) 2012. "A Picture of Koh Phrathong: An Exploration of Change in the Environment and in Communities on the Andaman Coast of Thailand." Report prepared for Project IMPAACT, Marine Protected Areas Research Group, University of Victoria.

Bernstein, Steven. 2000. "Ideas, Social Structure and the Compromise of Liberal Environmentalism." *European Journal of International Relations* 6, 4: 464–512.

Beymer-Farris, Betsy and Thomas Bassett. 2012. "The REDD Menace: Resurgent Protectionism in Tanzania's Mangrove Forests." *Global Environmental Change* 22: 332–41.

Bohm, Steffen, Maria Misoczky and Sandra Moog. 2012. "Greening Capitalism? A Marxist Critique of Carbon Markets." *Organization Studies* 33, 11: 1917–38.

Bond, Patrick. 2011. "Carbon Capital's Trial, the Kyoto Protocol's Demise and Openings for Climate Justice." *Capitalism Nature Socialism* 22: 4, 3–17. doi: 10.1080/10455752.2011.621100

Bouillon, Steven. 2011. "Carbon Cycle: Storage beneath Mangroves" *Nature Geoscience* April 2011, 282–3. Available at: www.nature.com/ngeo/journal/v4/n5/pdf/ngeo1130.pdf (accessed June 12, 2017).

Branger, Frédéric, Oskar Lecuyer and Philippe Quirion. 2015. "The European Union Emissions Trading Scheme: Should we Throw the Flagship out with the Bathwater?" *WIREs Clim Change* 6: 9–16. doi:10.1002/wcc.326

Bridge, Gavin. 2011. "Resource Geographies 1: Making Carbon Economies, Old and New." *Progress in Human Geography* 35: 820–34.

Bumpus, Adam and Diana Liverman. 2008. "Accumulation by Decarbonization and the Governance of Carbon Offsets." *Economic Geography* 84, 2: 127–55.

Carrier, Jim. 2009. "All You Can Eat: A Journey Through a Seafood Fantasy" *Orion* March-April 2009. Available at: www.orionmagazine.org/index.php/articles/article/4395 (accessed June 12, 2017).

Cederberg, Christel, Martin Persson, Kristian Neovius, Sverker Molander and Roland Clift. 2011. "Including Carbon Emissions from Deforestation in the Carbon Footprint of Brazilian Beef." *Environmental Science & Technology* 45, 5: 1773–9. Available at: http://pubs.acs.org/doi/pdf/10.1021/es103240z (accessed June 12, 2017).

Connolly, William. 2013. *The Fragility of Things.* Durham, NC: Duke University Press.

Coren, Michael, Charlotte Streck and Erin Medeira. 2011. "Estimated Supply of REDD Credits 2011–2035." *Climate Policy* 11: 1272–88.

Costanza, Robert. 2006. "Nature: Ecosystems without Commodifying Them." *Nature* 443, 19 October, 749.

Costanza, Robert, Ralph d'Arge, Rudolf de Groot, Stephen Farber, Monica Grasso, Bruce Hannon, Karin Limburg, Shahid Naeem, Robert V. O'Neill, Jose Paruelo, Robert G. Raskin, Paul Sutton and Marjan Van Den Belt. 1997. "The Value of the World's Ecosystem Services and Natural Capital." *Nature* 387: 253–60.

Costanza, Robert, Rudolf de Groot, Paul Sutton, Sander van der Ploeg, Sharolyn Anderson, Ida Kubiszewski, Stephen Farber and Kelly R. Turner. 2014. "Changes in the Global Value of Ecosystem Services." *Global Environmental Change – Human and Policy Dimensions* 26: 152–8.

Dempsey, Jessica and Morgan Robertson. 2012. "Ecosystem Services: Tensions, Impurities, and Points of Engagement within Neoliberalism" *Progress in Human Geography* March 2012: 1–22.

Donato, Daniel C., J. Boone Kauffman, Daniel Murdiyarso, Sofyan Kurnianto, Melanie Stidham and Markku Kanninen. 2011. "Mangroves among the most Carbon-Rich Forests in the Tropics." *Nature Geoscience* 4, 5: 293–7. Available at: www.nature.com/ngeo/journal/v4/n5/full/ngeo1123.html (accessed June 15, 2016).

Driesen, David. 2008. "Sustainable Development and Market Liberalism's Shotgun Wedding: Emission Trading Under the Kyoto Protocol." *Indiana Law Review* 83, 1: 21.

Equity Watch. 2000. "Carbon Colonialism." *Equity Watch: A Climate Newsletter from the South*, October 25, 2000. Available at: www.cseindia.org/content/carbon-colonialism (accessed June 12, 2017).

Goldtooth, Tom BK, Alberto Saldamando and Juan Antonio Correa Calfin. (2016). "Carbon Offsets Cause Conflict and Colonialism." Available at: www.ienearth.org/carbon-offsets-cause-conflict-and-colonialism/ (accessed June 12, 2017).

Global Aquaculture Alliance. 2017. Available at: www.aquaculturealliance.org/about-gaa/ (accessed June 12, 2017).

Haraway, Donna. 2004. *The Haraway Reader*: New York, NY: Routledge.

Hein, Lars G. 2000. "Impact of Shrimp Farming on Mangroves along India's East Coast." *Unasylva* 51, 203. ftp://ftp.fao.org/docrep/fao/x8080e/x8080e08.pdf (accessed March 7, 2013).

ICAP. (2016). *Emissions Trading Worldwide: Status Report 2016*. Berlin: ICAP. Available at: www.ieta.org/resources/Resources/Reports/ICAP_Status_Report_2016_Online.pdf (accessed June 12, 2017).

Isabella, Jude. 2012. "Jumbo-sized carbon footprint of farmed shrimp tracked by scientist." *The Tyee* February 17, 2012. Available at: https://thetyee.ca/Blogs/TheHook/Food-Farming/2012/02/17/Jumbo-Shrimp-Carbon-Footprint/ (accessed June 12, 2017).

Juergens, Ingmar, Jesús Barreiro-Hurlé and Alexander Vasa. 2013. "Identifying Carbon Leakage Sectors in the EU ETS and Implications of Results." *Climate Policy* 13, 1: 89–109. doi:10.1080/14693062.2011.649590

Latour, Bruno. 2004. *Politics of Nature: How to Bring the Sciences into Democracy*. Cambridge, MA: Harvard University Press.

McDuie-Ra, Duncan, Daniel Robinson and Jaruwan Kaewmahanin. 2013. "Spatial Dysfunction in Post-Tsunami Baan Lion: Taking the Moken Beyond Vulnerability and Tradition." *Geoforum* 48, 0: 145–55. Available at: www.sciencedirect.com/science/article/pii/S001671851300095X (accessed June 12, 2017).

Menasveta, Piamsak. 1997. "Mangrove Destruction and Shrimp Culture Systems." *World Aquaculture* 28, 4: 36–42.

Morton, Timothy. 2013. *Hyperobjects: Philosophy and Ecology after the End of the World*. Minneapolis, MN: University of Minnesota Press.

Nellemann, Christian; Emily Corcoran, Carlos Duarte, Luis Valdes, Cassandra De Young, Luciano Fonseca and Gabriel Grimsditch. 2009. *Blue Carbon: The Role of Healthy Oceans in Binding Carbon*. UNEP Grid Arendal e-publishing house. Available at: www.grida.no/publications/rr/blue-carbon/ebook.aspx (accessed June 12, 2017).

Philpott, Tom. 2012. "Shrimp's Carbon Footprint is 10 Times Greater than Beef's." *Mother Jones*. Wednesday February 22, 2012. Available at: www.motherjones.com/tom-philpott/2012/02/all-you-can-eat-shrimp-side ecologial-ruin (accessed June 12, 2017).

Phys.org. 2012. "Tiny Shrimp Leave Giant Carbon Footprint: Scientist." *Phys Org News*. Available at: http://phys.org/news/2012-02-tiny-shrimp-giant-carbon-footprint.html (accessed June 12, 2017).

Rancière, Jacques. 2009. *The Emancipated Spectator*. London, UK: Verso.

Rancière, Jacques. 2010. *Dissensus: On Politics and Aesthetics*. London, UK: Continuum.

Seigworth, Gregory and Melissa Gregg. 2010. "An Inventory of Shimmers." In: Melissa Gregg and Gregory Seigworth. (eds). *The Affect Theory Reader*. Durham, NC: Duke University Press.

Shukin, Nicole. 2009. *Animal Capital: Rendering Life in Biopolitical Times.* Minneapolis, MN: University of Minnesota Press.

Stevenson, N. John and Burbridge, Peter R. 1997. "Abandoned Shrimp Ponds: Options for Mangrove Rehabilitation." *Intercoast Network* 1: 13–14.

Stokstad, Erik. 2012. "The Carbon Footprint of a Shrimp Cocktail." *Science NOW* February 17, 2012. Available at: www.sciencemag.org/news/2012/02/carbon-footprint-shrimp-cocktail (accessed June 12, 2017).

Swedish Society for Nature Conservation. 2011. *Murky Waters: Shrimp Farming in Bangladesh* (film). Available at: www.linktv.org/shows/earth-focus/murky-waters-shrimp-farming-in-bangladesh (accessed June 12, 2017).

Volpe, John. 2005. "Dollars Without Sense: The Bait for Big-Money Tuna Ranching Around the World." *BioScience* 55: 301–2, April 4, 2005.

Wilson, Kylie. 2011. "Access to Justice for Victims of the International Carbon Offset Industry." *Ecology Law Quarterly* 38, 4: 967–1031.

World Bank. 2008. *The State and Trends of the Carbon Market.* Washington, DC: World Bank Institute. Available at: http://siteresources.worldbank.org/NEWS/Resources/State&Trendsformatted06May10pm.pdf (accessed June 12, 2017).

World People's Conference on Climate Change and the Rights of Mother Earth. 2011. "Press Release: Bolivia Calls for Urgent High Level on Cutting Climate Pollution" https://pwccc.wordpress.com/2011/06/17/press-release-bolivia-calls-for-urgent-high-level-talks-on-cutting-climate-pollution/ (accessed June 8, 2017).

Wynn, Gerard and Nina Chestney. 2011. "Carbon Offsets near record low, worst performing commodity." *Reuters* August 8. Available at: www.reuters.com/article/2011/08/05/us-carbon-low-idUSTRE77442920110805 (accessed June 12, 2017).

Zhang, Yue-Jun and Yi-Ming Wei. 2010. "An Overview of Current Research on EU ETS: Evidence from its Operating Mechanism and Economic Effect." *Applied Energy* 87, 6: 1804–14. doi: 10.1016/j.apenergy.2009.12.019

Conclusion

Fostering critical eco-aesthetic literacies

Fostering critical eco-aesthetic literacies

> "The question is", said Alice, "whether you can make words [metaphors] mean so many different things." "The question is", said Humpty Dumpty, "which is to be the master – that's all."
>
> (Carroll 1896, 81)

Exposing the folly of language and its inherent struggle over meanings, Lewis Carroll's poetics productively up-end the world and its supposed referential mediations. Much is at stake in up-ending this word-world relation when it comes to carbon footprint metaphors and their mediating role in the cultural politics of climate change. Beyond merely making visible the struggle in which words are embroiled, as does Carroll, however, I wish to challenge the sense of (human) mastery in the last instance implicit within Humpty Dumpty's response to Alice above. My insertion of 'metaphors' in the above quotation serves as a further irritant to the notion of mastery in human language and other worldly management systems; it is this troubling force that makes metaphor politically and ecologically powerful and serves as the locus for what I elaborate as an urgent agenda of fostering critical eco-aesthetic literacies. This agenda is attentive to both deconstructive and affirmative impulses, what Paul Robbins implies through the metaphors of the 'hatchet' and the 'seed' as critical components in the field of political ecology (2012, 20). One could train a purely deconstructive lens upon the carbon footprint metaphor by using a hatchet to take down the problematic systems of mastery that it mediates, but one would then reinforce the notion that power only exists within and among certain dominant human groups. A critique using only the hatchet risks: 1) asserting its own anthropocentric forms of mastery by not attending to how those excluded come to challenge given systems; and 2) leaving a void in political imaginaries that require a response to the question *where to from here?* Environmental politics, in both theory and practice, already court the charge of too many 'no' moments and not enough 'yes' moments. The trick then is to wield the metaphorical hatchet toward asymmetrical and biospherically damaging power relations that are constructed, *and* to plant the seeds for healthy alternatives by attuning to agency among those not already accounted for within always-contingent and partial representations. Metaphors are key mediators in this regard since they are 'ontological riddles ... [that] cross and join different kinds and categories of beings' (Rueckert 2006/1982, para 1). The riddle or puzzle that metaphors present also 'initiate a deriddling process' (ibid.) as a quest of partial sense-making through yoking unlikely elements.

My extended analysis of carbon footprint metaphors has critically traced what bodies and elements get carried over as publics attempt to de-riddle and make worlds with particular carbon footprints. No definitive meaning or calculus emerges out of the affective mediations of carbon footprint metaphors; however, certain tendencies can be traced. When carbon footprint metaphors first emerged, they appear to have played a large role in hailing carbon subjects through the use of 'you' and the lists that predominated to orient certain behaviours and actions of individual human carbon subjects, they now less often call 'you' and more often gesture towards non-humans, and acts that implicate carbon relations and processes. If the move from 'your' carbon footprint to the carbon footprint of consumable 'things' (Berners-Lee 2011) indexes a subtle shift away from the centrality of individualized carbon subjects toward other-worldly carbon connections, then the stories and practices initiated by an analysis of farmed shrimp in lively mangrove ecosystems suggest yet another turn in this footprint's history. That is not to say that individual consuming carbon subjects are no longer implicated in the carbon footprint of farmed shrimp story; they most emphatically are. One could easily present this latter instance of the footprint as singularly continuous with the consumer-oriented logic of the carbon subject and carbon markets.

The critical component of eco-aesthetic literacies suggests that as crucial mediators of urgent contemporary crises, ecological metaphors may be subject to the kinds of analysis that I have initiated here for the carbon footprint. The metaphoricity of carbon footprints has largely disappeared from view as carbon footprints have become conventionalized and have achieved authority as quantifiers. The authority of such metaphors bears scrutiny as Shaw and Nerlich corroborate in their discursive attention to policy documents. 'The metaphors used to talk about climate change in high-level policy documents reflect the culture and values of modern Western societies, especially their economies' (Shaw and Nerlich 2015, 39). This reinforcement of norms depends upon the forgetting of metaphors. In what remains, however, I wish to emphasize the 'seeds' that might be planted when metaphors are reinvigorated as energetic forces that might affectively mediate different orientations and worldly politics. The limited critical studies of metaphor within climate change politics seem ironically to forget the potential power of metaphor even as they recognize that others have forgotten the power of metaphor. They do so by describing metaphors as framing devices wielded exclusively by dominant humans. 'Metaphors, in providing an alternative framing for novel and abstract phenomena, are powerful anchoring devices. As such they serve to constrain the discourse by framing a topic in such a way as to privilege particular understandings of a problem over other possible interpretations' (Shaw and Nerlich 2015, 36).

The literacy I am describing requires negotiating the paradoxes and complexities of our time, a time in which human mediations (including language and stories) are recognized for their world-creating force, yet these same human mediations are simultaneously recognized as susceptible to larger-than-human agency. A politics that senses ecologies as they connect through carbon vitality emphasizes that at this critical juncture, human language and metaphors can (and need to) be written 'back into the land [and sea]' (Abram 1997, 273). I do not mean to evoke some nostalgic return to language and human society as it was in the past; rather, I suggest that present conditions of climate change and other ecological crises call for linguistic mediators of entangled relations between 'nature' and 'culture' to be recognized for their pivotal mediating role. At their most promising, ecological metaphors outline the contours of larger-than-human perceptions, thereby challenging their prescribed roles within the norms of the cultural politics of climate change and ecological politics more broadly. The contours of this suggestive and affirmative agenda involve first asserting a pivotal role for sensing with ecological metaphor, which proceeds through a tentative, cautious engagement with anthropomorphism, then finally, elaborating how such moves can contribute to composing (carbon) confederacies through the cultural politics of climate change.

Sensing with ecological metaphor

A critical eco-aesthetic literacy does not involve 'reading' nature, but rather sensing with ecological metaphor as an explicit site of aesthetics in which worlds are composed. Literacy begins paradoxically here by situating human language as utterly imperfect, incapable of definitively representing in a manner that is faithful to some originary essence, but it proceeds through centrally figuring the most explicitly non-representational form of language: the metaphor. Such questions that have driven my analysis of carbon footprint metaphors highlight that a first principle of critical eco-aesthetic literacies begins by suspending the 'literal' authority of language and returning metaphoricity. While there may be a certain reticence involved in closing down the authority of human language,[1] the openings facilitated through such a move are deeply generative.

Highlighting the limits of formal language systems, David Abram attributes such limits to the ways in which formal phonetic alphabets have reified the 'linguistic-perceptual boundary', thereby prohibiting actors that lie beyond that boundary from informing sentient communication (1997, 256). Abram's response, however, is not to abandon language altogether; rather, he argues for a kind of re-animation of language in new ways through moments of 'magic' that lead outside of uniquely human perception. Peoples whose 'languages are more like permeable membranes binding the peoples to their particular terrains, rather than barriers,' Abram suggests, acknowledge language as 'as a margin of danger and magic, a place where the more-than-human worlds must be continually negotiated' (ibid., 256).[2] Magic, for Abram is only possible in reaching beyond a self-referential human world; it occurs through a 'spell of the sensuous' where larger-than-human passageways breathe life into reciprocal communications. The air itself is the common medium that connects reciprocal communication through respiration for Abram. Human utterances depend on the respiratory movement of air, which is itself a composition of elements (and histories of living creatures) whose present-day calibration favours (certain elements of) our species and planetary co-species. From this angle, even what seems like a circuit of human-to-human speech is exposed as utterly dependent upon an ecological materiality that transcends the human body in space and time. These utterances then may yet yield to the magic of more than human sensibilities, *if* a certain orientation is enabled. To think of language as a 'magical' place where the non-human can register seems to require a leap beyond the normative ways in which human language 'properly' refers to things it indexes through this language. Ecological metaphor, however, as a mediator of these sensibilities that challenge the authority of words as self-referential, is one specific site where this 'magic' can occur.

The energy of metaphors has long been recognized as quasi-magical in a way that resonates with Abram's description of the potential magic of porous language. Words like 'epiphany' are often used when the 'right' metaphor emerges. Epiphany itself is a metaphor (used equally in religious and scientific settings) that signals a bringing into appearance or making manifest of something that is transcendent or is gleaned from perceptual insight. In an uncharacteristically poetic moment, William Rees, who coined the metaphor of the 'ecological footprint', calls his metaphorical moment an epiphany (2008). A new 'truth' was established when the ecological footprint appeared to displace the 'regional capsule' concept/metaphor that Rees was working on as an inverted index of carrying capacity; rather than asking *how many people on a given piece of land?*, the question became *how much land (imported from distant 'elsewheres') needed for a given population?* (Rees 1992, 125). But, as mentioned in Chapter 1, the true metaphorical epiphany occurred for Rees when a new desktop computer, one with a smaller 'footprint,' was brought to his office. This 'moment' of the emergence of the metaphor might more aptly be called a magical 'quickening' of a number of moments (and actors) for Rees because he connects this moment to a moment from his childhood on his grandparents' farm, and a number of other moments that included the participation of a great deal of non-human actors.[3]

With Abram, I suggest that the magic of language comes in part from a spark of connection to a world that is beyond 'our' grasp. Metaphor exemplifies such an aspirational connection, a reach that exceeds its grasp. Ecological metaphor in particular reveals that this spark may come about through an attunement to resonances that are larger-than- human, but still recognizable to humans. One way this attunement occurs is through certain forms of human *identifying* with non-humans, even as fraught as such endeavours might be. Once again, the carbon footprint metaphor serves as a rhetorical example of such an endeavour.

Tentative anthropomorphisms of non-human actors with footprints

Footprints have always held the potential to connect to non-humans since 'we' share the attribute of feet/footprint-making appendages with many non-human animals. At first glance, the carbon footprint metaphor has, since its early days, tended to feature a bi-pedal human creature's impact, though more recent instances are shifting the focus. According the shrimp a carbon footprint, on the one hand, seems to anthropomorphically shift responsibility for carbon impacts to non-humans and, thereby, remove certain forms of human responsibility. Paradoxically, however, conceiving of shrimp with carbon footprints might also permit 'us' to see a resemblance and to sense carbon vitality with entities other than ourselves. The instances of 'carbon footprints' of non-humans problematically begin with accounts of animal-as-protein for human consumption (rainforest beef, farmed shrimp), but in doing so they begin to bring into political visibility ecosystems and practices in ways that foster consequential societal shifts.[4]

Still another fascinating case draws into visibility the 'carbon footprint of insects' – especially pine bark beetles, whose numbers and practices in recent years have dramatically shifted carbon cycles in western Canadian forests (Hunter 2010). Whereas trees in British Columbia were once regarded by human managers as 'carbon sinks' promising to hold carbon and to help achieve climate change mitigation goals, the presence of bark beetles has transformed forests into net *producers* of greenhouse gas emissions as a result of the wood decay brought on by the beetles. According to one popular source, in the year 2009, the carbon 'footprint of the beetle-killed wood in B.C. was 74 megatonnes of CO_2 equivalent. The oil sands next door generated 38 megatonnes' (Hunter 2010). The surprising carbon footprint of/caused by these beetles reveals a distributed set of force-relations at work in this carbon footprint. On the one hand, such cases of the carbon footprint metaphor seem to remain anthropocentric because they highlight *human* disruption of ecosystems. Even the case of the carbon footprint of pine bark beetles implicates humans as the agents of warming weather that prevents winter die-off of these insects such that they can increase in population and range, thereby damaging increasing numbers of trees. Arguably, however, this is what the carbon footprint metaphor is meant to do; that is to centrally figure disruptive human impacts on the climate, as certain human-centric systems are the geological forces signalled by *anthropo*genic climate change. What is more, such instances signal the paradoxes of understanding *human* force relations that cause climate change as they are necessarily entangled with larger-than-human associations and force-relations. A qualitative shift has accompanied these recent cultural cases of carbon footprints (beef, shrimp, insects) when taken from the perspective of what they bring into visibility compared with when these metaphors first appeared in the carbon-subject producing lists. Although the latest iterations still point to human responsibility for impacts, they do so by way of revealing new forms of ecological embeddedness that connect 'us' to actors other than 'ourselves' and 'our' own self-referential technologies and systems. In other words, these carbon footprint metaphors are capable of drafting maps of the visible beyond the regimes of a household economy where one can buy an electric leaf-blower instead of a gas-powered one. Such recent cases reveal a host of other actions and implicate a complex range of behaviours and systems that could not be contained within a politics of carbon offsets.

These more recent cases of carbon footprints do this work, I argue, in a way that is not anthropo*centric*, but is rather to a certain extent, anthropo*morphic* in that these instances transpose what began as a human footprint written in the carbon footprint metaphor, into an arena of larger-than-human connections. As Jane Bennett contends, anthropomorphism may not be the unequivocal enemy to ecology that it appears to be at first glance because it can function to bring into visibility a shared connection that is not normally perceived:

> In vital materialism, an anthropomorphic element in perception can uncover a whole world of resonances and resemblances – sounds and sights that echo and bounce far more than would be possible were the universe to have a hierarchical structure. We at first may see only a world in our own image, but what appears next is a swarm of "talented" and vibrant materialities (including the seeing self).
>
> (Bennett 2010, 99)

In other words, as Bennett reveals, by looking first for human likeness in non-human nature, 'we' may see beyond in ways that temper the usual hierarchies, taxonomies, and anthropocentrisms. The carbon footprint metaphor, as a moving ecological metaphor that first featured human footprints but has also shifted to include non-humans, potentially offers such openings that demand that we see carbon connections and processes that 'echo and bounce' well beyond human timelines and human economies.

As I have demonstrated in my analysis of the carbon footprint of shrimp, and as Nicole Shukin reveals in her biopolitical critique of 'animal capital' (2009), anthropomorphizing can support a variety of problematic agendas, including human profit generation. Ethologist, Frans de Waal (1997), similarly warns that not all forms of anthropomorphism are equally acceptable;[5] yet he also warns of the opposite of anthropomorphism, what he calls 'anthropodenial: a blindness to the humanlike characteristics of other animals, or the animal-like characteristics of ourselves' (ibid.). Attention to this failure (even if it is indexed somewhat awkwardly by the word 'anthropodenial') reveals that certain prohibitions against seeing likeness/connections across species risk reifying the very species divides that consequently distance 'the human' from non-human others. To proceed cautiously with what Bennett calls a 'touch' of anthropomorphism, therefore offers a potential politics of 'confederation' that explicitly connects these vibrant materialities:

> A touch of anthropomorphism, then, can catalyze a sensibility that finds a world filled not with ontologically distinct categories of beings (subjects and

objects) but with variously composed materialities that form *confederations*. In revealing similarities across categorical divides and lighting up structural parallels between material forms in "nature" and those in "culture", anthropomorphisms can reveal isomorphisms.

(Bennett 2010, 99, emphasis added)

I will pick up on Bennett's generative notion of confederacies below, but first, I will trace the potential in the movement she suggests from *anthropomorphism* to *isomorphism*. I am following Bennett's suggestion of isomorphism in a way that might draw critique from a biologist, but as biologist-metaphorician, Donna Haraway suggests, biology is *built on* metaphors (2004, 146), so I further pursue the poetic licence that Bennett takes with this term. Carbon footprint metaphors can, through the kinds of anthropomorphism hinted at above, reveal isomorphisms as converging relations of kinship. Looking for isomorphisms, or kin relations, as a political endeavour should not amount to finding or making equivalencies among all things in nature. One must be cautious to avoid the pitfalls of theorizing actors as structurally the same despite their embeddedness within different power dynamics. As Jane Bennett suggests 'to acknowledge nonhuman materialities as participants in a political ecology is not to claim that everything is always a participant, or that all participants are alike … [non human actors] have different types and degrees of power, just as different persons have different types and degrees of power'(2010, 108–109). Such a caveat is especially important in relation to carbon footprint metaphors; there are very important reasons for understanding the different characteristics of footprint makers – both in accounts of intra-human global asymmetries (as demonstrated in Chapter 4) and accounts across species lines. Thus, suggesting that all of us are on equal footing in this carbon footprint is not the goal; yet the first move to establish connection through the anthropomorphism of situating non-humans within the carbon footprint metaphor might permit accounts of connected historical and ecological trajectories that structure contingent and shared relations at the contemporary moment. 'Surely the scope of democratization can be broadened to acknowledge more nonhumans in more ways, in something like the ways in which we have come to hear the political voices of other humans formerly on the outs' (Bennett 2010, 109). If one takes seriously the present moment as the 'sixth great extinction event' (Flannery 2006, 182–183) in the life of the planet, then one can see the value of attempting to locate connections among those with whom 'we' share a common trajectory. Isomorphism here then, indicates a shared trajectory of co-species who are connected through planetary conditions, including complex carbon relations and processes, and whose fates are therefore intimately connected at a time of changing climates.

This movement from anthropomorphism to isomorphism might begin by finding human likeness in the non-human through metaphorical yoking, and then shift to thinking about how 'we' are structured (contingently, historically, and materially) by actors that are larger than human and 'our' complex interactions with them, just as these actors are reciprocally structured by 'us'. Carbon footprint metaphors, *if they are recognized as mediators of this movement*, are a key locus of this politics.

Composing (carbon) confederacies

Crucially, Bennett in the above quotation suggests 'confederations' of lively materialities. The notion of confederacies is a generative one in this elaboration as it challenges the limits of political terms and institutions that conventionally exclude ecological actors (even in Jacques Rancière's thought, which I have used extensively). I propose that carbon footprint metaphors offer the potential of bringing 'carbon confederacies' into visibility. Carbon confederacies signal a politics of relationality whose complete membership is beyond certain human apprehension. Confederacy in general terms suggests a political association between states, which entails some deliberate form of instituting loose relations. Rather than following these state and peopled notions of confederacy, I am following Jane Bennett and Donna Haraway – especially through Haraway's suggestive use of 'obligatory confederacy' as it gestures toward material-ecological and political arrangements as they may be en-coded through what she calls the 'rich field of metaphors' (2004, 146) of biology:

> Consider then, the text given us by the existence, in the hindgut of a modern Australian termite, of the creature named *Mixotricha paradoxa*, a mixed-up, paradoxical, microscopic bit of "hair" (trichos). This little filamentous creature makes a mockery of the notion of the bounded, defended, singular self out to protect its genetic investments. The problem our text presents is simple: what constitutes *M. paradoxa*? Where does the protist stop and somebody else start. ... *M. paradoxa* is a nucleated microbe with several distinct internal and external prokaryotic symbionts, including two kinds of motile spirochetes, which live in various degrees of structural and functional integration. All the associated creatures live in a kind of *obligatory confederacy*.
>
> (2004, 146, emphasis added)

The very metaphor within the name of this creature – *M. paradoxa* – reveals the limits of existing taxonomies that attempt to assert species divides despite the porous flows between lively matter. What this story and the metaphor makes visible is that we human animals, who often appear to be in charge of confederacies in certain stories, are simply not in charge. We cannot apprehend all of the obligatory confederacies that challenge our categories and taxonomies. Similarly, the boundaries of individualized 'footprints' and bodies, be they subjects, nation-states, shrimps, or mangroves are not so easily determined; we are rather *obligatory carbon confederacies*. This is not confederacy as a romanticized political foundation story of forefathers claiming to build all-inclusive nation-states out of a discursively de-populated *terra nullius*, but rather feminist-inspired confederacies as stories of belated inclusion of multiple ecological actors by dominant modern societies. Such obligatory carbon confederacies are only just recently coming into view for global society and carbon footprint metaphors are key to establishing these connections. These metaphors reveal that, on the one hand, obligatory carbon confederacies are always already there without human recognition; but on the other hand, if these confederacies are not built into dominant human political institutions and expressly recognized, they do not register in these institutions as agents with whom we can, in the words of Haraway, 'strike up conversation' (ibid., 147). The scale of geological agency on the part of some humans in the 'Anthropocene' demands that we attempt to strike up conversation and compose these confederacies more explicitly in our politics. Simply because larger-than-human actors are there, does not necessarily mean they are explicitly included in dominant political institutions whose terms conventionally exclude such actors. I suggest that on-going sensing or attunement to larger-than-human kin that speak through carbon footprint metaphors might enable a more explicit process for composing these confederacies.

For Bruno Latour, the question of 'who is speaking (for)' applies equally to human and non-human actors, so one can (and must) maintain a certain suspicious stance towards 'spokespeople' (even scientists) who often tend to shut down the 'noisy chatter' of deliberative politics in society by imposing the authority to speak on behalf of a 'mute' nature (2004, 14–15). Too often the mediations of dominant spokes*people* are removed from visibility with political consequences for both humans and non-humans alike:

> Speech is not a self-evident phenomenon that properly belongs to humans ...
> The speech of all spokespersons becomes an enigma, a gamut of positions
> running from the most complete doubt – which is called artifact or treason,
> subjectivity or betrayal – to the most total confidence – which is called accuracy or faithfulness, objectivity or unity ... That a human should speak in the
> name of several others is as great a mystery as the one in which a human
> speaks in such a way that he [sic] is no longer speaking at all; instead the
> facts are speaking for themselves through him.
>
> (2004, 70)

A tentative anthropomorphism here brought in by extending the notion of speech to the non-human, leads *not* to the recognition of the impossibility of non-human speech, but to an isomorphic recognition of the difficulty of *even* human speech as a shared enigma of articulating a common world. A fidelity to unmediated facts ascertained by a given authority is granted to no singular agent, be it human or non-human. 'Speaking' as a political act of representation is not an unmediated fact built into human species but involves struggle – 'not the speech itself but the difficulties one has in speaking and the devices one needs for the articulation of the common world' (Latour 2004, 249). As my analysis of carbon footprint metaphors reveals, such ecological metaphors can play the roles of both pointing out the difficulty of articulating the common (carbon-composed) world *and* helping to mediate and articulate these entanglements. Thus, composing carbon confederacies might begin by situating carbon footprint metaphors within this agenda of critical eco-aesthetic literacies where speech and sentience are expressly distributed.

Listening to/for larger than human actors is key, so a sketch of fostering critical eco-aesthetic literacies also relatedly suggests that a hierarchy of speaking and listening in politics must be overturned. Rancière's thought is helpful in this regard:

> Why assimilate listening to passivity, unless through the prejudice that speech is the opposite of action? These oppositions – viewing/knowing, appearance/reality, activity/passivity – are quite different from logical oppositions between clearly defined terms. They specifically define a distribution of the sensible, an *a priori* distribution of the positions and capacities and incapacities attached to these positions. They are embodied allegories of inequality.
>
> (2009, 12)

An activated sense of listening enables attention to the parts that have had no part in a politics of aesthetics. Ecological metaphor does not awaken us to a moment of human ingenuity that will move us to novel future solutions for ecological crisis – it compels us to listen to others who are simultaneously present and yet explicitly absent from politics:

> A genuinely ecological approach does not work to attain a mentally envisioned future, but strives to enter, ever more deeply, into the sensorial present. It strives to become ever more awake to the other lives, the other forms of sentience and sensibility that surround us in the open field of the present moment.
>
> (Abram, 272)

As a potentially disruptive force that cracks open the codes of human knowing through language, ecological metaphors might help us develop new forms of literacy where what Abram calls the 'earthly intelligence of our words' (1996, 273) is animated in response to the speech and rhythms evoked by larger-than-human nature.

To return the carbon footprint to its metaphoricity is to insist on the on-going and shifting struggles of human understandings in larger-than-human relationality, and the politics that are central to the subject of climate change. While relations and processes indexed through carbon footprint metaphors often appear notoriously abstract such that they could easily be sequestered to legitimate an attempt at a totalizing human off-set economy, lively carbon material relations and processes also persistently emerge through the footprint metaphor. Rather than bemoan this metaphoric openness, however, it may rather be more generative to explore these metaphoric gestures of recomposing sensibilities through the carbon footprint. By bringing into a field of vision larger-than-human kin relations, these metaphors suggest a politics of commonly constituting these relations as they emerge.

Whereas the carbon footprint has been elaborated almost exclusively as a tool/metric that might foster a politics of *mitigation* against worsening climate impacts, this metaphor also reveals itself to be a site that traces unexpected interactions in shifting ecosystems such that adaptation and mitigation need to be simultaneously thought. Attempts to get the quantifying metrics 'right' are inevitably subject to shifting carbon cycles that often frustrate quantitative mitigation efforts. Just as 'we' think the forests of British Columbia are going to perform a certain amount of carbon sequestration, the pine bark beetle 'speaks back' through the carbon footprint metaphor to suggest that all calculations are off. Following the discursive trail left from the article on the carbon footprint of insects leads to the research of Yale Ecology professor, Oliver Schmitz, who suggests, 'an unprecedented loss of trees triggered by the pine beetle outbreak in western North America has decreased the net carbon balance on a scale comparable to British Columbia's current fossil fuel emissions' (Graham Richards 2013). This carbon footprint trail thus starkly reminds of the enmeshed human and non-human agencies that trouble quantitative accounts and even future-oriented planning of reduction targets; if scenario-planning and targets are based on reductions of emissions from human-specific sources, but do not (indeed *can*not in a quantifiable sense) take into account complex ecosystem interactions and unknown variables, then such scenarios and targets cannot lead to the kinds of outcomes that they pretend to. This is not to argue for the off-loading of responsibility for unforeseen emissions onto the pine bark beetle, but to make the case that our belated apprehension of this beetle's carbon footprint (as an entangled function of human-induced warming) compels a re-orientation of a politics that anticipates as yet unknown contributions to carbon emissions. To engage the distributed power of carbon footprint metaphors is to keep these metaphors alive to these animate interactions. Sensibility to these relations suggests that instead of asking non-human agents to do the work of mitigation on our behalf as we carry on with 'business-as-usual' carbon emissions, *we might re-orient ourselves to more responsible and responsive mitigation efforts away from anthropocentric and asymmetrical growth scenarios as well as to adapt with humility, to ecosystems in flux.*

As to the potential of carbon footprint metaphors to do this work in the future, it might be worth considering whether these metaphors have a lifespan as well as a liveliness. George Orwell suggests that metaphors can potentially 'die' or at least get 'worn out' with overuse (Orwell 1946). Similarly, Paul Robbins points to this risk: 'Developing into ossified artifact[s] through repetitive habit of use, metaphors can, in a sense, die ... By forgetting their partiality and their roots in language, metaphors become mistaken for the real or total. Here, their political implications become magnified, insofar as they are accepted as true' (2013, 316). This caution resonates with the risks I have been identifying through the affective mediations of certain carbon footprint metaphors. Robbins suggests that what critical work remains for those who wish to think and act differently in terms of nature-culture is 'to jar loose the assumptions of ossified metaphors and evaluate them in urgently political terms' (2013, 317). This exploration has been an attempt to jar loose the assumptions that are mediated through an attempted literalization of *the* carbon footprint, and to trace where non-human impingements help to do this work. Whether this particular set of metaphors is up to the ongoing task remains to be determined by their mobilization well-beyond the confines of this book. My forthcoming work (2017) considers carbon itself more broadly as a 'trickster' to explore whether this carbon metaphors/story can help us compose more equitable relations in a world that is rapidly changing and uncertain.

There are many pitfalls to be avoided in composing carbon confederacies (neo-colonialism primary among them as I describe below), but composing a common world more explicitly is crucial. An absence of political institutions capable of grappling with these issues does not entail an absence of decisive political and ecological effects; business-as-usual offers only further degradation. Many will argue under the powerful banner of 'urgency' that we do not have time for the process of composing confederacies with the help of ecological metaphor; however, I contend that we need to slow down to avoid the very deadlock which now defines political (in)action on climate change.

When constituting these confederacies, the role of affect and sensory registers is paramount. I have only begun to hint at such affective economies in my analysis through notions such as carbon guilt, fellow feeling, and carbon vitality. To feel with non-human actors suggests perceptual capacities that are signalled not only through uniquely human feelings but are connected through what Abrams calls 'synaesthetic associations' as the 'intertwining of earthly place with linguistic memory' (1996, 176). As Abram suggests in learning from Australian Indigenous Dreamtime stories if one 'walk[s] through a material landscape whose every feature [is] already resonant with speech and song' (177), one's senses are open to larger than human sensibilities. The sentience of non-human actors also appears more readily in a way that troubles the division of senses and emotions that depends on a species divide.

Where confederacies already exist

Tellingly, as Abram's quote above suggests, there are limits to and political consequences from Euro-Western understandings and cosmologies that frame both climate change politics and the theories that I mobilize in this book. As Anishnaabe and Haudenosaunee scholar Vanessa Watts states, Euro-Western theories that belatedly attempt to recover larger-than-human agency do so in a hierarchical way where agency is yet limited to a 'human-centric quandary' (Watts 2013, 29). Arguably, climate change and wider ecological crises often exist in public discourses as human-centric quandaries that trouble 'us' because they foreclose upon continued dominant patterns of living for many into the future. It is only after a stage of modern (colonial) Enlightenment that was supposed to elevate humans from Earthly material concerns, that we can suggest that we need 'new' cultural-material mediators. The need for these new cultural-material mediators that we grasp for is rather the *result* of colonial processes and Modern Enlightenment as they fostered disconnecting from Earthly materiality. Watts connects past histories of colonial displacement with on-going colonial processes that continue to inflict socio-ecological harm. Crucially, she situates colonial critiques of foundational Indigenous cosmologies of Mother Earth at the heart of such perpetuating harms.

Drawing on Leanne Simpson's retelling of the Anishnaabe Creation Story, which is also shared with Haudenosaunee cosmology, Vanessa Watts tells of Sky Woman falling from another world through the clouds on a treacherous path to the waters of the Earth below. On the way down, birds help to slow her down and communicate to Turtle that Turtle should surface to catch Sky Woman. Other animals help to create the territory for Sky Woman and these relations serve as foundations for societal relations (21, 25). Watts goes on to describe that she is excerpting a story that often goes on for days with multiple species interacting as key players. She insists that the creation story is not 'lore, myth or legend' as a colonial view would have it, but a deeply embedded constitution that begins with the feminine, spiritual and larger-than-human (21).

> Habitats and ecosystems are better understood as societies from an Indigenous point of view; meaning that they have ethical structures, inter-species treaties and agreements and further the ability to interpret, understand and implement. Non-human beings are active members of society.
>
> (Watts 2013, 23)

Watts critiques a number of thinkers attempting to theorize larger-than-human agency – including Bruno Latour, Donna Haraway, and Stacy Alaimo (some of whom I draw upon) – by highlighting the ways in which these theorists preserve an 'epistemological-ontological divide' whereby non-humans are granted 'diluted formulations of agency' (28). Certainly for many theorists that I have called upon and even within my analysis of the carbon footprint metaphor, non-humans are iteratively added to the constitution *after* the human political systems have already been constituted. By contrast, Watts suggests that in 'many Indigenous origin stories the idea that humans were the last species to arrive on earth was central; it also meant that humans arrived in a state of dependence on an already-functioning society with particular values, ethics, etc.' (25). Further, for Watts, even critical theorists who are trying to dismantle oppressive systems by critiquing essentialisms risk perpetuating colonial violence by refusing the essential truth of the story of Mother Earth. A critique of Mother Earth and a rendering of Indigenous cosmologies as 'lore' evacuates key governance systems based on kin relations that derive from Mother Earth.

Watts' insights open up a host of crucial questions that are irresolvable in this book, but that animate on-going critical dialogue in cultural politics of climate change. What do her critiques mean for those of 'us' who are in colonial relations with place that is not our territory? How do we become sensitive to place-based creation stories without appropriating such stories? How do such place-based particular stories connect with larger concerns of climate justice that are featured in Chapters 4 and 5?

One important response exists in the process of un-learning and learning on the part of those of us who have been inculcated into predominantly Euro-Western systems that create the ontological-epistemological divide that Watts critiques. From there, we might temper what seem like grand statements about novelty. Timothy Morton proposes a 'nascent ecological awareness' that contemporary urgent crises, like climate change, require, which profoundly reveals that 'humans are not totally in charge of assigning significance and value to events that can be statistically measured' (2013, 16). Such a statement contributes an important critique of the hubris within certain forms of human mastery in ecological politics, but arguably, it also misses recognizing ecological awareness that has long existed outside of hegemonic and disembodied Western thought. My own theorization of the novelty of metaphors in their moments of emergence similarly risks invisibilizing such knowledge. As I build upon Jane Bennett's work to suggest a 'touch of anthropomorphism', and isomorphism as a recognition of larger-than-human kin relations, I am conscious that the W̱SÁNEĆ peoples on whose territory I live, have long seen salmon, islands, and other larger-than-human entities as people; this relationality and responsibility is built into their governing systems and practices (Claxton 2017). As I turn to Bruno Latour to offer 'listening' for non-human actors, I reflect upon Athapaskan elders Annie Ned and Kitty Smith understanding of glaciers in their territory as speaking, sentient beings that offer critical orienting guidance for negotiating through change, danger, and everyday life (Cruikshank 2006). As Watts suggests, the theoretical *terra nullius* from which emerges 'nascent emergent awareness' in Euro-Western thought has long been populated, grounded, and constituted other*wise*.

Thus, I acknowledge that the novelty of metaphors and my theorization is limited to the Anglo-American spaces that bear the legacies of Euro-Western (colonial) thought. Importantly, these are the spaces that carbon footprint metaphors predominate, as do dominant solutions proposed to climate change. Thinking differently about affective mediators in these spaces is crucial, just as is acknowledging and listening to other ways of constituting that offer transformative de-colonizing potential. One ambivalent effect of a recent (belated) widespread ecological awareness in Euro-Western thought is that these understandings are bringing with them the potential for self-reflective critique of colonial systems of thought and practice and the potential for un-settling these colonial ways of being in on-going processes (Ingold 2000; Girvan 2014; Girvan forthcoming [2017]; Nixon 2015; Turner 2007). Watts' corrective suggests we ought not impose neo-colonial critiques of essential Indigenous stories (like 'Mother Earth') that have enacted land-based laws among stewards of land. Rather, we might listen and learn from richly composed confederacies that pre-date more recent attempts to compose the world. These confederacies offer sophistication and complexity in terms of their ability to negotiate uncertainty, change, and relations in place. Further, we ought not simply instrumentalize such confederacies for the good of preserving colonial ways of living, but rather, think of distributive justice and land-based relations that must be transformed through responsibility to enduring governing systems that pre-date colonial contact and climate change conceived as a singularly human-centric quandary. Many extractivist practices and even climate change solutions, like the UN's REDD agenda for preserving forests, instrumentalize non-human kin in the service of certain human enterprises and further dispossess people of their land. Quickening crises highlight the importance of understanding *and acting* as though, firstly, trees exist in relations that are more expansive than those described by the metaphor of 'carbon sinks' and, secondly, that people who have long lived within these relations might best be knowledge-keepers, provided they are not forcibly removed from the land.[6] Resurgent Indigenous politics offer important interventions in on-going colonial systems (Coulthard 2013; Simpson 2011).

Although Watts draws a stark binary between Euro-Western and Anishnaabe cosmologies, there are places where conversations might be struck. Some Euro-Western origin stories – including geological ones and biblical ones – also situate humans as the latest to arrive in an already constituted world. Further, statements based on Muslim, Buddhist and a host of other non-Euro-Western religious origin stories are similarly emerging to disrupt harmful anthropocentric mindsets and actions (Forum on Religion and Ecology at Yale, nd). As Watts reminds, because we have belatedly and precariously arrived into a pre-existing world of relations, we might orient toward humility rather than hubris.

My forthcoming work more centrally treats colonial and de-colonial questions of carbon in the cultural politics of climate change (Girvan forthcoming [2017]), but for now, I am merely gesturing toward some places in which there might be some rapprochement between cosmologies for thinking about co-constituting with larger-than-human agency. As Dene scholar Glen Coulthard suggests, building alternative systems for Indigenous communities requires reaching out beyond localized Indigenous communities and establishing 'relations of solidarity' with many, including those who are 'struggling against imposed effects of globalized capital' and environmental degradation (2013, para 13).

Although there are significant differences between the Creation Story that Watts centres and the metaphors I am tracing, both stories and metaphors tend to be dismissed as non-material; returning the constitutional power of these entities is a key disruption to norms. While certain metaphors may be emerging from within the colonial drifts and these are not anchored in constituted space as Watts' story is, it is my hope that a critical lens on metaphor provides an opening for future de-colonial orientations. Indeed, recent proliferating metaphors build on critiques of this present moment through disrupting conventional stories of colonial, fossil-fuel based economies. These disruptive metaphors potentially foster openings for transformation.

Emerging metaphors that trouble petroculture at a time of climate change

Although three recently emerging ecological metaphors have not yet been extensively and explicitly elaborated as metaphors *per se*, these offer further extension of the power of an implicit politics of metaphorical movement. The first is 'carbon democracy' (Mitchell 2011), the second is 'energy of slaves' (Nikiforuk 2012), and the third is '*this* capitalism' (where 'this' implies fossil fuel capitalism) (Vaden 2010). I call these ecological metaphors because they, like carbon footprint metaphors, mediate the entangled relations of natureculture in ways that help to bring these relations into visibility. Whereas modern histories have tended to disregard ecological actors as central to politics and history, these metaphors write ecological actors and conditions of possibility more explicitly into history and politics in ways that map onto Bennett's description of isomorphism as a shared trajectory of mutual conditioning in natureculture.

Timothy Mitchell's *Carbon Democracy: Political Power in the Age of Oil* (2011) re-contextualizes democracy in light of its emergence alongside a material economy of fossil fuels. Whereas conventional histories of democracy have attentively traced the socio-political movements of nations and regions developing into 'mature' forms of democracy in a kind of teleological trajectory, Mitchell argues that it is impossible to tell the story of the rise of modern democracy without acknowledging its fundamental enabler: (hydro)carbons. These carbon-dependent relationships, he suggests, have not only created geopolitical vulnerabilities in the past, but are also poised to create future crises because of their treatment of hydrocarbons in modern political economies as inexhaustible givens despite their finite material availability. The carbon democracy thesis begins by revealing an isomorphism through the implicit question: *what do carbon and democracy have in common such that they can be drawn together in this metaphor?* According to Mitchell, the material element of carbon and the cultural history of democracy are inextricably linked through a history of political and material movements throughout the nineteenth and twentieth centuries. Mitchell traces the emergence of democracy alongside the move away from agrarian life based on solar, water, and wood energy on a small scale, toward larger-scale societies enabled by fossil fuels in the forms of coal and oil. These fossil fuels have led to the creation of political economies and technologies based on a seemingly inexhaustible energy regime. He argues that this shift offered opportunities for mass politics and energy on an unprecedented scale, but also created vulnerabilities: the first is 'peak oil', where the fiction of a rapid growth economy meets its limits; the second is climate change, which threatens to disturb an ecological order upon which life as we know it, and all its derivatives, including democracy, depend. Mitchell draws on hybrid historical and political-economic perspectives in order to carefully revisit and recontextualize major historical events of the twentieth century in light of carbon, which he argues has been systematically under-acknowledged as *the* fundamental enabler of the economy and geopolitics in this era. What McKay would call the 'sheer muscle' involved in connecting carbon and democracy reveals the power of metaphor to expose certain 'truths' associated with the shared structural trajectories of these seemingly unrelated entities. Although Mitchell's is an historical account, his analysis *and the metaphor itself* gesture toward future-oriented questions around the struggle over meanings of *carbon democracy*. Such struggles might foster attention to notions of citizenship, participation of non-human elements and actors, and, importantly, the creation of political institutions that are open to such complexities.

Similarly refiguring cultural-material relations involving carbon, Andrew Nikiforuk's *Energy of Slaves* (2012) connects a history of slavery dating back to ancient times, with the modern era of fossil fuel dependency as a new form of slavery. Modern societies, he argues, are still acting like slave-holders in our relentless use of cheap 'energy slaves' in the form of oil. Despite 'our' claims to moral superiority after the abolition of human slavery, Nikiforuk insists that we read our oil dependency as continuous with these forms of slavery because they analogously involve some degree of amassing a pool of cheap expendable labour/resources to do 'our' work for us. Massive casualties have always been built into the logic of slavery, whereby benefits are accrued by a few based on the degradation of a whole great many others; contemporary forms of energy slavery are no different for Nikiforuk. His elaboration of this metaphor, itself co-constituted with larger-than-human actors, brings into visibility a critical re-distribution of the sensible of energy regimes. Once again the sheer muscle involved in bringing 'slavery' and 'energy' together in this metaphor makes one ask *what do these two entities have in common?* And *how might the moral baggage that accompanies the notion of slavery come to morally charge public conversations on contemporary fossil fuel-enabled energy slave regimes?*[7]

A further example of the metaphorical work of finding parallel trajectories in 'culture' and 'nature' is Tere Vaden's re-conceptualization of 'this capitalism,' (fossil fuel-enabled capitalism) (2010). Vaden historicizes an analysis of political economies within the regime of oil in which, he argues, it must necessarily be understood. He evocatively asks: 'What if the hegemony of the West was not, after all, defined by modern natural science and technology, enlightenment and individualism but by a one-time offering of coal, gas and oil?' (2010, 1). Vaden re-connects the socio-political and ecological through the intervention of naming 'this' (fossil fuel) capitalism. For Vaden, the 'one-time' gift of fossil fuel has contributed to this specific version of capitalism, not as the end-of-history liberal democratic capitalism, which is often prescribed as the teleological maturation of political-economic forms, but as rather a very context-based and finite social-material political form of organization. *This* capitalism, metaphorically implying fossil-fuel/carbon capitalism, troubles the universalizing story of capitalism (and its critiques), by particularizing this form within its current conditions of possibility, which are far from universal and infinitely available. Again critical questions arise in this metaphoric re-distribution: *What do capitalism and fossil fuels have in common? What might come after "this capitalism"?*

'Slave energy', 'carbon democracy', 'this capitalism', 'carbon footprint' – these are all compound metaphors in which the modifying terms do the critical work of revealing the historical-material entanglements that shape contemporary conditions. An ecological-material element is compounded metaphorically with a (human) cultural element such that the cultural element is necessarily put into conversation with the material conditions of possibility that fundamentally shape it. Without their modifying terms/metaphors, the terms democracy and capitalism tend to have a teleological and authoritative 'end of history' ring to them. Without the modifying metaphor of 'slaves', energy regimes are similarly cast in positivistic terms as simply the taken-for-granted inputs that fuel trajectories of human progress *ad infinitum*. Carbon footprint metaphors walk along and through the coordinates of this consciousness of material-cultural entanglements in larger-than-human histories. Their presence always equally figures potential species absence in the precarious epoch signalled by the material-cultural metaphor of the 'Anthropocene'.

Myriad other metaphors – 'climate debt' (Bolivia 2009; Walsh 2009), 'virtuous carbon' (Paterson and Stripple 2012) – are similarly emerging to bring material-cultural entanglements into the politics of climate change. Although these metaphors require treatment that is beyond this current study, their presence gestures toward the on-going work of critical eco-aesthetic literacies in reconfiguring worlds. Against those who would read metaphor instrumentally as simply a 'tool' of communication, or something to be engineered into society, or simply a poetic frill, I insist on reading ecological metaphor as a complex network of distributed sense-making that at its greatest potential, enables larger-than human sensibilities in creative world-composing:

> Aesthetic experience has a political effect to the extent that the loss of destination it presupposes disrupts the way in which bodies fit their functions and destinations. What it produces is not the rhetorical persuasion of what must be done. Nor is it the framing of a collective body. It is a multiplication of connections and disconnections that reframe the relation between bodies, the world they live in and the way in which they are equipped to adapt to it. It is a multiplicity of folds and gaps in the fabric of common experience that change the cartography of the perceptible, the thinkable and the feasible. As such, it allows for new modes of political construction of common objects and new possibilities of collective enunciation.
>
> (Rancière 2009, 72)

As Rancière asserts, the aesthetics in which metaphors are involved disrupt the givens of the world by outlining contours that were previously unthinkable, imperceptible. Vanessa Watts reminds us not to universalize these existing maps or human-centric ways of knowing since these cartographies are not universally shared (2013). Nonetheless, these dominant cartographies need disturbing to foster ways of understanding and respecting pre-existing larger-than-human confederacies. During this epoch of quickening material-cultural movement, the need for 'the political construction of common objects and new possibilities of collective enunciation' has never been greater. To assert a role for ecological metaphors in this politics of aesthetics is to suggest that these affective mediators are involved in indeterminate processes that may generatively lead to larger than human sense-making in acts of composing worlds in flux. Against the image of the carbon footprint at the beginning that displays what Abram calls the 'ever-increasing intercourse with our own signs' (1997, 267), ecological metaphors offer to permanently defer logocentric, anthropocentric mastery to animate an on-going attunement to material relations and processes. In such a case, the answer to a re-mix of Alice's question – *can ecological metaphors mean so many things, or is one to be master?* – is kept open to disturb dominant anthropocentric, colonial norms and to foster more promising futures.

Notes

1 I am not suggesting the authority of all language be closed down simultaneously; as any text (including this one) demonstrates, a contingent authority is necessary to communicate anything at all.

2 One example of this negotiation can be found within the stories of Athapaskan elders Angela Sidney, Kitty Smith, and Annie Ned in Julie Cruikshank's *Do Glaciers Listen?* (2006) The linguistic accounts of glaciers grant that these icy formations are living, inspirited sentient beings with the power to work with and against the people in their proximity.

3 The way that Rees tells the story of this epiphany through his talk 'Epiphany, Serendipity and the Genesis of Ecological Footprint Analysis' (2008) suggests a magical connection that began with a childhood moment in which he felt profoundly connected to the land. Sitting down to eat at his family's farm, he realized that he had participated in the growing of everything on his plate and felt rooted and ecologically grounded through this – an insight that could only have been gained through the participation of non-humans in this experience.

4 Beef consumption in the US is at an all-time low in the past 50 years, available at: http://grist.org/list/2012-01-12-american-beef-consumption-is-at-a-50-year-low/ (accessed June 13, 2017). Food commentator, Mark Bittman credits campaigns and social movements like 'meatless Monday' and 'flexitarianism' for such reductions, available at: http://opinionator.blogs.nytimes.com/2012/01/10/were-eating-less-meat-why/?_r=0 (accessed June 13, 2017).

   According to recent statistics, shrimp consumption is also down and consumers and retailers are demanding supply chains adhere to 'sustainability' demands. Available at: www.intrafish.com/free_news/article1378688.ece (accessed June 13, 2017).

5 De Waal describes an oil company advertisement 'that claimed its propane saved the environment'. In the advertisement, 'a grizzly bear enjoying a pristine landscape had his arm around his mate's shoulders. In fact, bears are nearsighted and do not form pair-bonds, so the image says more about our own behavior than theirs'. Such uses of anthropomorphism, he argues, 'can provide insight only into human affairs and not into the affairs of animals' (1997).

6 I do not mean to reinforce here a stereotype that all Indigenous people are anti-developmental and act singularly in what colonial culture deems as 'ecological' ways. Tripathy and Mohapatra (2014) offer an important critique of how vastly different Indigenous people are often reduced to 'Avatars' (from the James Cameron film). Rather, I am following Vanessa Watts on understanding how Anishnaabe and in her words, Indigenous place-based cosmologies as they are practised in place, offer sophisticated ways of constituting governance systems.

7   Notably, the morally charged language on energy regimes is used not only by climate change 'believers' who want to change energy regimes; such language is also used by climate change sceptic, Ezra Levant in his 'ethical oil' thesis as I mentioned in Chapter 4.

References

Abram, David. 1997. *The Spell of the Sensuous: Perception and Language in a More-Than-Human World*. Toronto: Vintage.

Bennett, Jane. 2010. *Vibrant Matter: A Political Ecology of Things*. Durham, NC: Duke University Press.

Berners-Lee, Mike. 2011. *How Bad are Bananas? The Carbon Footprint of Everything*. Vancouver: Greystone Books.

Bolivia, 2009. Commitments for Annex I parties under paragraph 1(b)(i) of the Bali Action Plan: evaluating developed countries' historical climate debt to developing countries, 25 April. Bonn: UNFCCC, 44–51.

Carroll, Lewis. 1896. *Alice Through the Looking Glass*. Available at: https://birrell.org/andrew/alice/lGlass.pdf (accessed June 13, 2017).

Claxton, Nick. 2017. "Land, Language and Knowledge: Indigenous Resurgence and Education in WSÁNEĆ" (Public Talk) Indigenous Resurgence in an Age of Reconciliation Symposium. March 17, 2017. First Peoples House, University of Victoria, Victoria BC.

Coulthard, Glen. 2013. "For our Nations to Live, Capitalism Must Die." *Unsettling America – Decolonization in Theory and Practice*. Available at: https://unsettlingamerica.wordpress.com/2013/11/05/for-our-nations-to-live-capitalism-must-die/ (accessed June 13, 2017).

Cruikshank, Julie. 2006. *Do Glaciers Listen? Local Knowledge, Colonial Encounters, Social Imagination*. Vancouver, BC, Canada: UBC Press.

De Waal, Frans. 1997. "Are We in Anthropodenial?" *Discover*. July 1997. Available at: http://discovermagazine.com/1997/jul/areweinanthropod1180 (accessed June 13, 2017).

Flannery, Tim. 2006. *The Weather Makers*. Toronto: Harper Collins.

Forum on Religion and Ecology at Yale. (nd). "Climate Change Statements from World Religions." Available at: http://fore.yale.edu/climate-change/statements-from-world-religions/ (accessed June 15, 2017).

Girvan, Anita. 2014. "Cultivating Longitudinal Knowledge: Alternative Stories for an Alternative Chronopolitics of Climate Change" In: Mario Trono and Robert Boschman (eds) *Found in Alberta: Environmental Themes for the Anthropocene*. Waterloo, ON: Wilfred Laurier University Press, 347–69.

Girvan, Anita. Forthcoming (2017). "Trickster Carbon." *Journal of Political Ecology*. TBC.

Graham Richards, Michael. 2013. "Pine Beetle Impact on Carbon Balance as Important as British Columbia Fossil Fuel Use." *Tree Hugger* October 16, 2013. Available at: www.treehugger.com/climate-change/pine-beetle-impact-carbon-balance-important-british-columbia-fossil-fuel-use.html (accessed June 16, 2017).

Haraway, Donna. 2004. *The Haraway Reader*: New York, NY: Routledge.

Hunter, Justine 2010. "Pine Beetles Transform BC Forests into Greenhouse Enemy." *The Globe and Mail*. Available at: www.theglobeandmail.com/news/british-columbia/pine-beetles-transform-bc-forests-into-greenhouse-enemy/article4187388/ (accessed June 13, 2017).

Ingold, Timothy. 2000. *The Perception of the Environment: Essays in livelihood, dwelling and skill.* New York: Routledge.

Latour, Bruno. 2004. *Politics of Nature: How to Bring the Sciences into Democracy.* Cambridge, MA: Harvard University Press.

Mitchell, Timothy. 2011. *Carbon Democracy: Political Power in the Age of Oil.* London, UK: Verso.

Morton, Timothy. 2013. *Hyperobjects: Philosophy and Ecology after the End of the World.* Minneapolis, MN: University of Minnesota Press.

Nikiforuk, Andrew. 2012. *The Energy of Slaves: Oil and the New Servitude.* Vancouver, BC: Greystone.

Nixon, Rob. 2015. "Environmentalism and Postcolonialism." In: Ken Hintner (ed.) *Ecocriticism: The Essential Reader.* New York, NY: Routledge, 196–210.

Orwell, George. 1946. "Politics and the English Language." Available at: www.orwell.ru/library/essays/politics/english/e_polit/ (accessed March 25, 2017).

Paterson, Matthew and Johannes Stripple. 2012. "Virtuous Carbon." *Environmental Politics* 21, 4: 563–82.

Rancière, Jacques. 2004. *The Politics of Aesthetics.* Gabriel Rockhill (trans.), London, UK: Continuum.

Rancière, Jacques. 2009. *The Emancipated Spectator.* London, UK: Verso.

Rees, William E. 1992. "Ecological Footprints and Appropriated Carrying Capacity: What Urban Economics Leaves Out." *Environment and Urbanization* 4 2: 120–130.

Rees, William E. 2008. "Epiphany, Serendipity, and the Genesis of the Ecological Footprint analysis." Public Lecture. February 10, 2008, Environmental Professional Series: YMCA: Vancouver BC.

Robbins, Paul. 2012. *Political Ecology: A Critical Introduction.* 2nd ed. Chichester, UK: J. Wiley & Sons.

Robbins, P. 2013. "Choosing Metaphors for the Anthropocene: Cultural and Political Ecologies." In: Nuala C. Johnson, Richard H. Schein and Jamie Winders. (eds). *Cultural Geography.* Malden, MA; John Wiley & Sons Ltd, 305–19.

Rueckert, William H. 2006/1982. "Metaphor and Reality: A Meditation on Man, Nature and Words." *KB Journal* 2 (2).

Shaw, Christopher and Brigitte Nerlich. 2015. "Metaphor as a Mechanism of Global Climate Change Governance: A Study of International Policies, 1992–2012." *Ecological Economics* 109: 34–40.

Simpson, Leanne. 2011. *Dancing on our Turtle's Back: Stories of Nishnaabeg Re-creation, Resurgence, and a new Emergence.* Winnipeg: Arbeiter Ring Pub.

Tripathy, Jyotirmaya and Dharmabrata Mohapatra. 2014. "Environmental discourse and third world difference: Perspectives from India." *Journal of Third World Studies* 31, 1: 51–68.

Turner, Nancy. 2007. *The Earth's Blanket: Traditional Teachings for Sustainable Living.* Vancouver: Douglas & McIntyre.

Vaden, Tere. 2010 "Oil and the Regime of Capitalism" *CTheory.* Available at: www.ctheory.net/articles.aspx?id=658 (accessed June 14, 2017).

Walsh, Bryan. 2009. "Do Rich Nations Owe Poor Ones a Climate Debt?" *Time*, 10 December.

Watts, Vanessa. 2013. "Indigenous Place-thought and Agency Amongst Humans and Non-humans (First Woman and Sky Woman go on a European World Tour!)." *Decolonization: Indigeneity, Education & Society* 2, 1: 201–34.

Index